NUMBER SIXTEEN:
Kenneth E. Montague Series in Oil and Business History
Joseph A. Pratt, General Editor

Labor, Civil Rights, and the Hughes Tool Company

MICHAEL R. BOTSON JR.

TEXAS A&M UNIVERSITY PRESS • COLLEGE STATION

M/L

The paper used in this book meets the minimum requirements
of the American National Standard for Permanence
of Paper for Printed Library Materials, Z39.48–1984.
Binding materials have been chosen for durability.
∞

Library of Congress Cataloging-in-Publication Data

Botson, Michael R., 1951–

    Labor, civil rights, and the Hughes Tool Company / Michael R. Botson, Jr. — 1st ed.

      p.   cm. — (Kenneth E. Montague series in oil and business history ; no. 16)

    Includes bibliographical references and index.

    ISBN 1-58544-438-3 (cloth : alk. paper)

    1. Labor unions—Texas—History—20th century.   2. Labor movement—Texas—History—20th century.   3. African Americans—Employment.   4. African Americans—Civil Rights.   5. Hughes Tool Company.   I. Title.   II. Series.

    HD6517.T4B67   2005

    331.88′1223382′09764—dc22

                        2005000862

Dedicated to Judith Stevenson Botson
and to Ivory Davis
and the memory of C. Columbus Henry

CONTENTS

TABLES

ACKNOWLEDGMENTS

THE ORIGINS OF THIS BOOK go back to the spring of 1993 when
I was a graduate student at the University of Houston trying to find
a topic for my master's thesis. My original intention was to write the
labor history of the Armco Steel Corporation's Houston mill that was
opened on the eve of the Second World War. I gravitated toward that
topic and company because I had been a steelworker for nine years, a
union man, and now was one of the forgotten, faceless multitude of
American blue-collar workers who had been downsized out of a job
during the country's deindustrialization of the 1980s. Writing about
the historical experiences of a group of blue-collar workers that I knew
something about, and whose livelihoods were and continue to be under siege, was the only topic I was willing to devote myself to in order
to complete my thesis. I also came to regard the project as a catharsis
in helping me bring closure to the latent rage still lurking in my psyche
eleven years after being cast out of industrial employment. I have written a history but it is not about Armco Steel.

In the course of my initial research I discovered only a scant paper
trail on the labor history of Armco's Houston mill. Panic began to set
in until my investigations uncovered a large and promising paper trail,
the twenty-pound sledgehammer in the historian's toolbox, tracing the
labor history of another and much better known Houston firm, the
Hughes Tool Company. Indeed, over time it became clear that the documentation of Hughes Tool's contentious labor history was enormous
and I had found my topic. Even more importantly, the documentation
chronicled the struggles of black employees to eliminate job discrimination and Jim Crow segregation. The two topics of most historical
interest to me and the only two in my mind that would justify putting

up with the indignities of graduate school any longer—labor and civil rights—were there at the Hughes Tool Company just waiting for me to write about. More than eleven years later that paper trail has helped produce my master's thesis, doctoral dissertation, and now this book. In the course of that journey I have incurred the debt of numerous people who have helped me along the way. Bringing it to publication reminds me how much this has been a collective effort and how reminiscent it is of the working-class spirit of solidarity.

Several scholars have read the manuscript or parts of it and given generously of their time, expertise, and knowledge in helping me complete this book. Joe Pratt and George Green allowed me to tap into their immense knowledge of Texas business, labor, and political history, and their unwavering support and enthusiasm for my book has sustained me when my energies waned and I was on the verge of just giving up. They along with Virginia Bernhard energized my interest in Texas history and inspired my scholarly forays into the Lone Star State's past. I am grateful to them for encouraging me to challenge popular myths that pass as Texas history. My gratitude extends to Robert Buzzanco, Truman Clark, Charles Robinson, Jack Sheridan, and Amilcar Shabazz, who read all or segments of the manuscript, and to Emilio Zamora, my thesis adviser. Chris Drake, East Texas Renaissance man, Texas liberal in the best tradition of John Henry Faulk, colleague, and friend offered invaluable insights into tightening up the introduction and conclusion.

I could not have completed this project without the enthusiastic support I received from former employees of the Hughes Tool Company who graciously consented to be interviewed and tell me their stories: Allison Alton, Harry Callender, Ivory Davis, Wayne Dearman, Maurice Easterwood, Chuck Hamilton, C. Columbus Henry, Arthur Hensley, John Gray, Halbert Mabry, George McMahon, Lonnie Rhone, Bill Stewart, and C. D. Wilson. Jack Golden, former director of United Steelworkers of America District 37, opened up the union hall for a group of us to meet and then afterward treated us to lunch. I owe a special thanks to the members of the Hughes Tool Company Over the Hill Gang, an association of retired employees. They welcomed me to their meetings, made me feel right at home, and let me talk to them about this project. The late Chris Dixie, prominent Houston labor lawyer; former NAACP labor secretary Herbert Hill; and Robert Kuldell generously allowed me to interview them. All these folks are simply amazing because they represent a typical group of Americans who characterize what I believe is the lifeblood and strength of our country, workaday people doing extraordinary things in the face of adversity. It has been my distinct privilege and honor to know them.

The staffs of numerous libraries and archives have helped me locate materials for this study. Staff at the National Archives in Washington, D. C., College Park, Maryland, and the southwest region in Fort Worth, Texas, and at the Library of Congress, photo archivists Charles Hamilton and Joel Draut plus the staff in the Texas Room of the Houston Metropolitan Research Center of the Houston Public Library have been especially helpful, as have staff members at the Texas Labor Archives at the University of Texas at Arlington, the United Steelworkers of America Archives at the Pennsylvania State University Library at College Park, Pennsylvania, and Special Collections at the University of Houston M. D. Anderson Library.

I am grateful for having received a Cullen Research Fellowship in the summer of 1998 that allowed me to travel and complete my research at the National Archives, College Park, Maryland, and in Washington, D. C. Many thanks go to the librarians at Houston Community College who helped in securing materials through interlibrary loan. The late Joe Washburn located any documents I requested regardless of their obscurity, and he is sorely missed. Librarians Hortensia Rodriguez and Mary Beth Ducote ably assisted Joe by making sure the materials I requested were delivered. Norma Jean Brand, our computer wizard at Houston Community College, Northwest College, has my eternal gratitude for the countless hours she spent correcting my misuses of Microsoft Word when I typed this manuscript. This project simply could not have been finished without her expert and cheerful help.

My colleagues in office suite AD2 at Houston Community College, Town and Country Center, Anthony Pearson, Donna Rhea, Chris Drake, Dale Foster, Ali Faegh, Ann Bragdon, and honorary member Ira Black deserve special mention and kudos for their patience in putting up with my idiosyncrasies and mood swings when the pressures of teaching and writing a book overwhelmed me. They never failed to offer me a kind word of support to pick up my spirits. Iconoclasts and freethinkers all, they enrich my life far more than they will ever know.

I recognize my colleagues in the history department at Houston Community College, Northwest College, Gisela Ables, Bryant Evans, Patience Evans, J. Kent McGaughy, Madeline Merriman, James Thomas, and Mary Alice Wills for their interest in my topic.

The last paragraph is reserved for my best buddy and forever friend, Judith Stevenson Botson. The usual spousal clichés cannot begin to describe her contribution in bringing our book to publication. Through the entire process, and for more than thirty years, she has been the source of my inspiration, hope, and happiness. During the lean years she toiled long hours in her beloved nursing profession to keep a roof over our heads, food on the table, and provide a home for the numerous stray cats and dogs that became our nuclear family. During the alternating frenzies and woes of research and writing, she never failed in her patience and inspiration. I am most fortunate to be spending my life with *ma belle femme sans pareil.*

LABOR, CIVIL RIGHTS, AND THE HUGHES TOOL COMPANY

ON JULY 1, 1964, the National Labor Relations Board (NLRB) de-certified the racially segregated Independent Metal Workers (IMW) Union as the collective bargaining agent at Houston's Hughes Tool Company. The ruling ended nearly fifty years of Jim Crow unionism at Hughes Tool, one of Houston's premier manufacturing plants. But much more importantly, for the first time in the Labor Board's history it ruled that racial discrimination by a union violated the National Labor Relations Act (NLRA) and therefore was illegal.[1] In a unanimous decision, the five-member board revoked the certification of the IMW because the union had failed to fairly represent African Americans at the company by systematically discriminating against them.

In 1962 Ivory Davis, a black material handler, longtime employee at Hughes Tool, and union member, filed charges against the company and union with the Labor Board that eventually led to the decision. Davis's action against the union stemmed from the white leadership's refusal to file a grievance on his behalf after management denied him an apprenticeship because of his race. The union's labor agreement with Hughes Tool reserved apprenticeships for whites only. In 1962 Davis and the black union leaders decided to challenge the validity of the race-based labor contract between Hughes Tool and the IMW. They did so by taking the unusual step of seeking to decertify their union as the collective bargaining agent for the company's employees. Their action was the beginning of a two-year struggle that combined the efforts of the federal government, the National Association for the Advancement of Colored People (NAACP), and African American unionists at Hughes Tool to break Jim Crow's grip over the company's workforce.

Ivory Davis's struggle for shop floor racial equality at Hughes Tool has a deeper meaning when placed within the context of the early 1960s civil rights movement and the growing militancy of black workers nationwide who demanded justice and equality in industrial America. Black workers capitalized on the country's growing commitment to civil rights and desegregation to launch an assault against institutionalized racism in organized labor. They received help from new federal policies such as President Kennedy's Executive Order 10925 issued in March 1961, which called for an end to racial discrimination by federal contractors such as Hughes Tool; from the NAACP's increased attacks on racism in organized labor; and from the willingness of individual black workers, such as Ivory Davis, to fight racism within their unions.

The Hughes Tool decision sharply defined the role unions would play in protecting black workers' civil rights. The NLRB now demanded that unions enjoying its protection must take responsibility for eliminating racial segregation and discrimination along with their traditional missions of improving wages and working conditions, and protecting seniority rights. For black unionists the NLRB's ruling at Hughes Tool reverberated with the same promise of equality generated by the U.S. Supreme Court's *Brown v. Board of Education* decision, which had struck down segregation in public schools ten years earlier.

The justices of the Court unanimously concluded in 1954 that Jim Crow segregation had no place in American schools because "[s]eparate educational facilities [for blacks] are inherently unequal" and deny them equal opportunity guaranteed by the Fourteenth Amendment. The *Brown* ruling overturned fifty-eight years of racial segregation in public education that the Supreme Court had legalized in 1896 with its decision in *Plessy v Ferguson*. The NLRB's Hughes Tool decision overturned twenty-nine years of legalized racial segregation in unions that the NLRA, the nation's primary labor law, had codified in 1935. Using the legal argument formulated by the Court in *Brown*, the NLRB overturned its previous decisions that defended Jim Crow unions by declaring that segregated unions are inherently unequal and deny African American unionists equal protection and opportunity under the law. The Hughes Tool case laid the foundation for ending Jim Crow unionism, just as *Brown* paved the way for ending public school segregation. The NLRB's decision earned the company a prominent place in the national struggle for civil rights within the labor movement.[2]

Historians have devoted a great deal of energy to studying the desegregation of public places such as schools and racism within organized labor. But as the historian Alan Draper has pointed out, few studies focus strictly on the intersection of civil rights and labor. In those that are available, historians disagree over the labor movement's record on civil rights. Draper's work focused on the political alliances forged between the two movements in the struggle for voting rights. He applauds leaders like the NAACP's Lenny Wilkins and the AFL-CIO's George Meany for recognizing the intractable dilemma of trying to integrate southern unions and eliminate job discrimination and not letting those issues deflect them "from what each considered the more important task at hand: black enfranchisement in the South." Draper found that the AFL-CIO played a role in fighting for voting rights, but his research also compelled him to conclude that organized labor's record on shop floor civil rights, meaning abolishing job discrimination and Jim Crow unionism, "is not a pretty one."[3]

Meany, labor's supreme chieftain, and southern subordinates such as Claude Ramsey, who headed Mississippi's AFL-CIO, faced the unenviable task of balancing calls for civil rights and recognizing that black equality "threatened the class privileges southern whites enjoyed at work and the caste privileges they enjoyed outside of it. . . . [T]here was nothing delusory or insignificant to white workers about the benefits they enjoyed over blacks in the Jim Crow South." Southern labor leaders like Ramsey feared alienating a white rank and file that included "its share of racists whose membership was essential for the vitality of southern unions." A dramatic example of this is seen in Birmingham, Alabama, where members of the United Steelworkers of America (USWA) warned union leaders that "[i]f we have to choose between staying in the union or see our segregated way of life being destroyed, we will pull out."[4]

Herbert Hill, who served as the NAACP's labor secretary in the 1960s and was one of the few whites to serve on the staff of the national NAACP, is an outspoken critic of labor's record on civil rights and of historians who in his view misrepresent its dismal record on civil rights. Hill accuses historians of "[c]elebrating the episodic occurrences of interracial solidarity [in unions] while ignoring the overall historical pattern [of racism]." He stridently criticizes them for finding it "necessary to minimize or deny racism in the labor movement because its existence conflicts with the usable past that they are constructing as labor history." Hill ignited a firestorm of criticism from labor historians in 1988 with his critique of the late Herbert Gutman's 1968 essay "The Negro and the United Mine Workers." He criticized

Gutman for mythologizing interracial unionism in the United Mine Workers of America that obscured the union's dismal record on race. Hill charged Gutman with romanticizing the working class, creating "examples of class consciousness among workers that transcended race, even if that meant ignoring data which conflicted with cherished ideological assumptions."[5] More recent skirmishes over labor's record on civil rights have pitted Hill against such prominent labor historians as Nelson Lichtenstein and Judith Stein.[6]

Daniel Letwin, Brian Kelly, Joe William Trotter, and others responded to Hill's critique by focusing on where and how labor and African American history intersect. Letwin authored a well-received study of interracial solidarity of Alabama's coal miners that challenged Hill's position, asserting that the scholarship on race, labor, and interracial solidarity is "far more nuanced than the Hill critique suggests." Letwin discovered transitory interracial solidarity in Birmingham that ultimately foundered on the shoals of white supremacy and Jim Crow segregation. Nonetheless, Letwin asserted that "the corrosive effects of racism upon the relations of black and white workers do not negate the significance of interracial organization where it materialized." Based on his findings among Alabama coal miners, Letwin cautions against conceptualizing "relations between black and white workers as either [only] harmonious or antagonistic, glossing over gradations between these two poles."[7]

Bruce Nelson has also pondered whether unions have been successful advocates for racial equality or merely another obstacle in pursuit of that goal. Though less critical of labor historians than Herbert Hill, Nelson acknowledges that there is "a widespread and largely unconscious tendency to portray the working class as white (and usually male)—either to minimize the importance of race in writing the history of American workers or to assign it a distinctly secondary role as [an] explanatory factor." Much like Alan Draper, Nelson also makes a distinction between a predominantly racist rank and file and progressive-minded union leaders. He found that a "great majority of white workers were unwilling to unite with African Americans around a program that would have challenged deeply-rooted patterns of racial inequality in factory, mine, and mill as well as in the larger society."[8]

In his important study of black workers at the Atlanta Steel Company, Nelson found that the USWA failed to break down the barriers of job discrimination and, in fact, battled to keep them in place. The union refused to confront "the burning issue of racial discrimination in the steel industry . . . [and] for the most part the discriminatory structure stayed in place." A similar situation can be seen when the USWA launched an organizing drive at Hughes Tool in 1963–64. One day when Ivory Davis and a group of black employees were reporting for work, Eddie Ball, a USWA organizer in Houston and future treasurer of the International Union, tried to enlist them by promising that the union would fight racial discrimination at Hughes Tool. When Davis challenged Ball to walk one block down the street and make the same promise to a group of white employees, "Ball refused and changed his tune real quick."[9]

The events at Atlanta Steel are all the more significant because in 1962 black workers at the company with the NAACP's help brought a case similar to Ivory Davis's to the Labor Board against the USWA, a powerful AFL-CIO affiliate, and lost. Concurrently the NAACP had also been working up the case against the Independent Metal Workers Union because it was a weak independent union and its discrimination "constituted a clear and unambiguous example of unfair representation [so] the NAACP decided to concentrate its resources on Hughes Tool."[10] My findings on the intersection of labor and race at Hughes Tool generally support the views of Hill and Nelson: labor's leadership lacked the will to decisively challenge white rank-and-file racism and failed to eliminate racial discrimination within their unions.

Only when forced by civil rights activists, NLRB decisions, and federal legislation did union leaders push to eliminate workplace bigotry. After 1964 those union leaders who committed themselves to civil rights found themselves increasingly under attack from a white rank and file who now "identified their own unions as part of a liberal establishment that promised preferential hiring and affirmative action that further narrowed already bleak employment prospects for them and their families [by the 1970s and 1980s]."[11] My conclusions are also influenced by a working-class upbringing, nine years of industrial work experience between 1973 and 1982 as a journeyman millwright, and successive membership in the United Steelworkers, United Autoworkers, and International Association of Machinists. Hill's and Nelson's interpretations bear a greater relevance to the shop floor racism I witnessed and the segregated Westside neighborhood in Cleveland, Ohio, where I grew up. My reading of the historical literature, Hill's and Nelson's interpretations and analyses, and personal experiences have influenced this study of race and labor at Houston's Hughes Tool Company.

Overall, little is known about the role that Houston's working class played in struggles for labor and civil rights. During the twentieth century Houston emerged as the South's preeminent city and became what city boosters liked to call the "golden buckle of the Sunbelt." The discovery of oil at Spindletop in 1901 ushered in a new era of unprecedented growth, transforming Houston into a major manufacturing center. By 1940, of all southern cities, only Birmingham, Alabama, surpassed Houston in manufacturing capacity. Eastern capital flowed into Texas and financed the transformation. Investors and bankers from Pittsburgh, New York, and Chicago contributed substantial sums to Houston's oil refining and oil-related industries. Oil and Houston became linked, like Pittsburgh and steel, Detroit and automobiles. Houston's population eventually surpassed all other southern cities and along with that milestone came the dubious distinction of becoming the South's largest Jim Crow city. Booming business and the oil industry joined segregation and racial discrimination to define the city's character.[12]

Houston's labor unions unblinkingly segregated their memberships. Black unionists suffered prejudice in the workplace, but detailed accounts of their subordination are noticeably lacking. A book-length study of labor history in Houston is also lacking. A case study of the Hughes Tool Company sheds light on both issues. How did African Americans respond to organized labor's racism? Did they see unions as symbols of "white only" privilege and spurn them, or did they regard unions as merely the means to secure economic advancement dismissing any civil rights potential? Where did black community leaders line up in the debate over minority membership? In addition to the race issue, a case study of Hughes Tool Company tells us about the nature of Houston's working class and whether it supported collectivist unions to protect its interests. It identifies the city's business elites who opposed organized labor and the measures taken by them to keep unions out of their plants.

Thirty-two years ago F. Ray Marshall, a pioneer in the study of race and organized labor in the South wrote, "There unfortunately is no current systematic history of the Texas labor movement."[13] Only marginal progress has been made over the years to fill this void. George Green, Texas' leading labor authority, has contributed an important study of the United Autoworkers' effort to organize Ford Motor Company's Dallas assembly plant in the 1930s; Marilyn Rhinehart's study of coal miners in Thurber, Texas, stands as a singularly useful work.

Rick Halpern produced a fine study of race and labor focused on Fort Worth's meatpackers, and Ernest Obadele-Starks gathered a collection of Texas labor history vignettes. But for the most part historians have passed over this virgin territory.[14]

My look at the Hughes Tool Company and its workers is the first book-length study of the intersection between Houston's organized labor and the civil rights movement. It is a response to Marshall's three-decades-old call for more information about the labor and racial struggles in Texas. My work seeks to illuminate an obscure aspect of Houston's history: a proud heritage of union activism by a determined working class.

Chapter 1 sets the stage for an examination of Hughes Tool thru a narrative of Houston's labor movement back to the 1830s. It traces a spirit of conservatism that characterized the city's labor movement from the nineteenth century through most of the twentieth century. The conservatism of Houston's working class can be attributed to at least two things. First, before World War I the city did not have large, mass-production industries that required tens of thousands of un-skilled immigrant workers from eastern and southern Europe. The addition might have exerted a militant and radical influence, as it did in northern industrial cities. Second, Houston's white working class was steeped in southern Jim Crow racial tradition. Consequently, as Houston emerged as a southern manufacturing center in the twenti-eth century, its working class lacked a radical tradition and unques-tioningly embraced traditional white supremacy.

The second chapter examines Howard Hughes Sr.'s early twentieth-century foray into the Texas oil boom and the formation of his tool company. It discusses Hughes's acquisition of a revolutionary rotary drilling bit that revolutionized oil exploration. Demand for the Hughes drilling bit transformed the small company with its handful of em-ployees into an immense impersonal manufacturing plant. By the early 1920s, Hughes Tool emerged as Houston's first vertically integrated manufacturer, aping Henry Ford's assembly line methods and labor policies. Hughes Sr. mixed paternalism, relatively high wages, anti-unionism, and racial bigotry to control his workforce. Like Ford, he hired blacks as common laborers to do menial, hot, heavy, and dirty tasks. This chapter includes a look at the post–World War I strife that plagued Hughes Tool, Houston, and the nation.

Chapters 3 and 4 focus on the Great Depression and the New Deal, 1929–40. It describes the growing anger among employees over austerity measures implemented by management to weather the depression, which included laying off half the workforce, reducing hours for those remaining on the payroll, speedups, stretchouts, and the cancellation of Hughes Tool's employees' welfare program. With the election of Franklin Roosevelt in 1933 and the passage of the National Industrial Recovery Act and later the National Labor Relations Act (NLRA), union activism at Hughes Tool experienced a renaissance. The open shop era of the 1920s was giving way at last.

The NLRA created an environment that spawned the birth of the Congress of Industrial Organizations (CIO). The CIO transformed the labor movement when it organized powerful industrial unions enlisting all workers, regardless of job classification, skill, or skin color.[15] However, industrial and interracial unionism provoked a powerful reaction from industrialists and the American Federation of Labor (AFL). Undaunted by the ferocious antiunionism of Houston's employers and the AFL's red-baiting, the CIO sent organizers to Houston and focused on Hughes Tool. The CIO believed that if it could successfully organize Hughes Tool, one of Houston's largest and most strident antiunion plants, then workers in the city's other shops would rally to the union's banner.[16]

Chapters 5 and 6 deal with the critically important theme of race, Jim Crow unionism, and the CIO between 1940 and 1946. The CIO experienced firsthand the difficulty of trying to organize an interracial union in a Jim Crow city. Its promise of racial equality undermined its effectiveness among whites. On the other hand, while the CIO attracted black employees, African American support was not monolithic. A number of black employees challenged the CIO's claims of racial egalitarianism, resulting in a bitter fight between them, their supporters in Houston's black community, and African Americans loyal to the CIO.

The racial dispute contributed to the escalating labor turbulence between 1943 and 1946 when the CIO faced determined opposition from management and the Independent Metal Workers Union. The progeny of Hughes Tool's company unions from the 1920s and 1930s, the IMW represented only workers at Hughes Tool, was unabashedly racist, and was an uncompromising foe of the CIO. It prided itself on its independence from what IMW officials called the big-shot labor bosses who controlled the CIO. The IMW enjoyed a close relationship with management and shared management's staunchly conservative racial views. Its leadership viciously criticized the federal government's role in labor relations, routinely castigated the NLRA, the Labor Board, and the National War Labor Board, and regarded them as CIO patsies. Often times, it was impossible to distinguish the IMW's anti-union rhetoric from management's. Chapters 7 and 8 are devoted to the IMW era spanning the years from 1946, when it race-baited the collective bargaining rights from the CIO at Hughes Tool, through 1964 when the Labor Board decertified the union.

This study of Hughes Tool cannot and does not presume to tell the complete story of Houston's working-class experience in the twentieth century, the desegregation of the industrial workplace, or the role of organized labor in the civil rights movement. However, following the decertification of the IMW, black workers across the country finally had a legal remedy to fight union racism. So a case study of Hughes Tool, placed within the national context, offers a better understanding of the troubled relationship between labor and race that so undermined America's working-class solidarity. I hope this case study also contributes to a better understanding of the critically important role played by the federal government in the labor and civil rights movements, and makes a useful addition to the story of unionism in Texas history. The narrative that follows captures a moment in time when, after enduring decades of discrimination on the factory floor, a segment of Houston's working class seized the moment and won economic and racial justice for themselves and their brothers and sisters.

CHAPTER ONE

Houston's Working Class and the Origins of Organized Labor in the Bayou City

FOUNDED IN 1836 by the brothers Augustus and John Allen, Houston was a town built on speculative growth and dedicated to the spirit of unfettered capitalism. Located on the desolate Texas coastal plain about fifty miles north of Galveston, the city they envisioned along the banks of White Oak and Buffalo Bayous eventually became the leading financial, commercial, and industrial center in the Southwest. Between the 1830s and the 1890s it slowly transformed itself from a frontier society into a growing economic center. Cotton, timber, and railroads fueled Houston's economic growth in the nineteenth century. The three interacted together, as cotton and timber harvested in the outlaying regions encouraged railroad construction. By the end of the nineteenth century Houston had established itself as the region's second most important commercial center behind Galveston. It served as the hub for an increasing number of railroads and was home to the East Texas cotton and lumber industry.[1] As the twentieth century dawned two events propelled Houston past Galveston as Texas' leading financial center.

On September 8, 1900, a hurricane destroyed Galveston and left more than six thousand people dead in its wake. Afterward, prominent Galveston merchants and bankers transferred their operations inland to Houston in order to protect their economic interests from the destructiveness of Gulf hurricanes. The second happened on January 10, 1901, with the discovery of oil at Spindletop near Beaumont. Within several years after the first oil strike, other important oil discoveries were made near Houston and the city became the logical location for the newly emerging Texas oil industry. Due to its previous experience in serving the financial, administrative, and transportation needs of the timber and cotton industries, Houston quickly became home to dozens of industrial and commercial enterprises associated with the oil industry. The oil and oil-related industries grew and flourished in Houston in the first two decades of the twentieth century. Established in 1908 the Hughes Tool Company manufactured patented rotary drilling bits for the petroleum industry.[2]

When the Spindletop oil gusher blew in at the beginning of the twentieth century Houston was a bustling city of approximately forty-four thousand people. A sizable working class called Houston home in 1901, and many of its members labored in the construction and repair shops of the Southern Pacific and the twelve other railroads that had maintenance facilities in the city. In addition to these industrial employers, there were numerous car and wheel shops and foundries that served the railroads' needs. All these concerns employed skilled tradesmen such as machinists, boilermakers, blacksmiths, and patternmakers, as well as unskilled labor. The skills and experience of these workers were readily transferable to the new oil tool companies such as Hughes Tool. An important but overlooked aspect of Houston history is that it was home to a substantial working class with a tradition of union-mindedness, labor activism, and racism.

The first vestiges of Houston's labor movement can be traced back to the late 1830s, and the city can lay claim to being the home of Texas' first two bona fide labor unions. In April 1838 journeyman printers in Houston organized the Texas Typographical Association to promote the interests of their trade within the Texas Republic. At its first meeting the printers proposed a standardized wage scale, elected officers, adopted a constitution and bylaws, and invited all Texas printers to join. During its first year the Typographical Association was very active. Monthly meetings were held, and several new members were "elected and qualified." In October 1838 the union went out on strike in Houston over wages and won a 25 percent wage increase. Houston carpenters organized in 1839 in order to establish uniform wages and to exact what their "services justly deserve." The record is sketchy about whether the carpenters succeeded in their quest for uniform wages, and the carpenters and printers unions faded into obscurity. No evidence exists of any labor union activity in Houston between 1839 and 1866.[3] Several factors retarded the growth of organized labor in the antebellum period.

The small number of workers and the lack of industrial development in Texas at this time were major contributing factors. Texas' geographic isolation likewise played a role, and Texas workers appeared to have little contact with or knowledge of labor in other areas. The extent of outside contact was limited to the individual workers who moved to Texas with some prior contact with organized labor. No outside union, national or local, gave any aid to organizational efforts in Texas before 1870. Texas workers did know of other labor unions, but distance and poor transportation and communication placed them beyond the influence of labor activism in other sections of the country. The frontier nature of Texas society, with its emphasis on individualism, most assuredly played an important role. Group identity, collective action, and class identification were weak in antebellum Houston.[4] Despite these obstacles the seeds of worker activism were sown in antebellum Houston, and following the Civil War the city's labor movement would reemerge with new vitality.

Between 1865 and 1914 Houston's workers established numerous unions that were active in promoting working-class issues such as wages, hours, and access to political power. From 1865 to 1889 a number of small trade unions, such as the Houston Typographical Union Number 87, with a charter membership of about twenty printers, organized. Between 1889 and 1914 other unions, such as the Workmen's Club, Lone Star Division of the Brotherhood of Locomotive Engineers Number 139, the Machinists and Blacksmith's Union, and a Workingmen's Benevolent Association, were established.[5]

By the 1880s the Knights of Labor had become Houston's most prominent labor union, with seven locals totaling approximately 740 members. The Knights continued as a force in the city's labor movement until the mid 1890s when its power waned and it was replaced by the Houston Labor Council.[6] An important characteristic that tainted Houston's labor movement and showed its ties to southern traditions was an unyielding commitment to racism, white supremacy, and Jim Crow segregation. Race prejudice segregated Houston's workers occupationally, socially, and economically and established a racial caste system that defined the city's labor movement. The racism that infected Houston's working class was rooted in antebellum slavery and the Jim Crow social structure established in the city during the 1870s.

Many of Houston's early white settlers brought slaves with them. The first recorded accounts of African Americans in Houston place them in the city in the summer of 1836 when they and Mexican prisoners captured in the war of Texas independence were put to work clearing land for the original town site. As justification for using black and brown labor for the backbreaking job, a popular myth was cultivated by Anglos that said nonwhite labor was essential to clearing the swampy area because no white could have endured the insect and snake bites, malaria, impure water, and other hardships associated with the task. Other slaves in Houston worked as house servants or worked on farms and plantations on the edge of town. Some were employed as cooks and waiters in hotels, as teamsters, or as laborers on the docks and warehouses along Buffalo Bayou. Slave labor helped build roads and railroads over which agricultural produce entered the city, and they helped construct the city's commercial buildings. Although most slaves performed unskilled labor, some skilled black craftsmen in the city alarmed white workers, who felt threatened by them. One objective of the early Houston labor movement during the antebellum period was to limit the employment opportunities of skilled black tradesmen and protect white jobs.[7]

Following the Civil War jobs became the most important need for former slaves. Before the Civil War slave labor had been critical to Houston's economy and emancipation did not diminish the city's need for black labor. Former skilled slaves who had been hired out for wages operated blacksmith shops and worked as shoemakers. Although these black craftsmen were small in number, white craftsmen feared this black encroachment into white employment areas. The relatively successful black craftsmen were the exception, and most freedmen ended up as low-paid, unskilled workers.[8] The abolition of slavery did not significantly alter the relationship between blacks and whites in postbellum Houston.

White Houstonians regarded blacks as inferior beings that needed to be kept in their place. In the wake of the Civil War hundreds of former slaves flooded into the city and caused great unease among the city's white population. By 1870 blacks numbered 3,691 and comprised nearly 40 percent of the city's population. Fearing the rising number of blacks living within their midst, in the 1870s white Houstonians enacted local ordinances to segregate the races and subordinate African Americans to whites, a situation that Reconstruction had temporarily suspended.[9] Jim Crow segregation enveloped every aspect of life for Houston's black population, and the city's schools, churches, social functions, and civic clubs were nearly totally segregated by 1875. White privilege and overriding prejudice among Anglo workers limited the number of jobs open to blacks and dictated that the city's unions be racially segregated.[10]

Houston's major industries during the later nineteenth and early twentieth century included sawmilling, blacksmithing, carpentry, printing, flour- and gristmilling, railroad repair shops, foundries, and car and wheel shops. Houston's industries clearly had a significant demand for unskilled workers, and African Americans filled most of those positions. For example, in the 1880s blacks comprised 39 percent of the city's population and made up 79 percent of the unskilled workforce; whites monopolized all the semiskilled and skilled positions. African Americans who did possess skills were for the most part barbers or other personal service workers, though there were a few black carpenters and blacksmiths. Since African Americans were generally shut out of the skilled and semiskilled work, their wages were considerably lower and the work they performed was generally more physically demanding than that performed by whites.[11] Spurned by Houston's white unions, which were instrumental in creating the occupational plight in which blacks found themselves, African Americans recognized that they would have to organize themselves in order to safeguard their economic interests. The first instance of black workers organizing in Houston can be traced to the National Labor Union in 1871.[12]

The National Labor Union represented the first attempt by the American working class to organize on a national scale and protect itself from the growing power of America's industrial tycoons. Industrialists embraced the economic doctrines of laissez faire and regarded labor as a commodity to be bought as cheaply as possible with little or no regard for workers' humanity. Consequently workers challenged their reduction to a commodity in the new industrial order by organizing on a national level and attempting to create national unity within the ranks of labor. Though the National Labor Union regarded southern and northern workers as potential allies in its battle against large industrial combinations, its white leadership roundly condemned racial mixing and ultimately insisted on segregated locals.[13] This was clearly borne out in Houston.

Black Houstonians established a branch of the National Labor Union for Colored in 1871, and it became the first union in the city's history affiliated with a national labor organization. Despite the union's commitment to racial segregation, Houston's black workers proved willing to establish a local as a means to promote their issues. At this time they had nowhere else to turn to for organization, since the few white unions in Houston excluded them. Organizing a colored local of the National Labor Union was the one option open to them, and they seized it.[14] At this early stage in the city's labor history African Americans proved much more willing than whites to affiliate with a national labor union, even when the union segregated them by race. This suggests the importance that Houston's black working class placed on organizing unions to protect their class interests. Houston's black unionists endured a much harder struggle than their white counterparts because they faced not only employer opposition to unions but racism from white unionists and employers. Despite its promise, this early effort at black unionization in Houston turned out to be short lived. The National Labor Union began to decline following the death of its charismatic president William Sylvis in 1869, and by 1872 the national organization passed into oblivion. This contributed to the demise of Houston's colored local, but what ultimately killed it was vicious white condemnation of organizing blacks.

Local newspapers railed against the National Labor Union and warned that "in the great struggle between capital and labor, labor must find some skillful strategy, or the battle will go against it." Including blacks should not be part of the strategy. Houston's white working class regarded the National Labor Union as a threat because they believed, unjustifiably so, it would be a race leveler and that its call for collective worker action would disrupt their happy land where "thrift and industry will raise any laborer . . . to any position that he may choose to assume within the compass of his intellectual powers."[15] In contrast Houston's African American working class willingly joined national labor unions in their struggle for economic justice and solidarity. During the 1880s the Knights of Labor emerged as the city's most prominent union and was popular among whites and blacks. But the union bowed to Houston's racial segregation and organized separate assemblies for whites and blacks.

The Knights of Labor became the quintessential expression of the American labor movement in the last three decades of the nineteenth century and the first successful mass organization of the American working class. Launched as a secret fraternal society among Philadelphia tailors in the late 1860s, the Knights grew in the 1870s and 1880s by actively recruiting skilled, semiskilled, and unskilled workers in the railroad, steel, and mining industries. By the late 1880s membership reached three-quarters of a million and became the country's first true national labor union. The Knights introduced the radical concept of industrial unionism that nurtured working-class solidarity by organizing workers by industry rather than by narrowly defined craft lines that often excluded semiskilled and unskilled workers in an entire industry. Besides the usual working-class issues such as higher wages and better working conditions, the organization concentrated on the moral and political uplift of the working class.[16]

Only if workers could come together in a great brotherhood pledged to mutual aid and cooperation could they understand that "an injury to one is the concern of all."[17] The Knights sought to reform industrial capitalism so workers could fully enjoy the wealth they helped create and to help laborers "develop their intellectual, moral, and social faculties, [enjoy] all the benefits of recreation, and share in the gains and honors of advancing civilization." At its peak the Knights helped sustain a national debate over the social implications of industrial capitalism.[18] Although the Knights of Labor welcomed all workers regardless of race, the union segregated its black and white membership into separate locals.

By 1885 Houston's workers had established five white and two black assemblies of the Knights of Labor and boasted a membership of approximately 740. The five white locals mixed skilled, semiskilled, and unskilled workers in the same assemblies and drew their members from among the industries most common in Houston at the time; blacksmithing, bootmaking, carpentry, railroad repair shops, sawmilling, and tinsmithing. The Knights' joining of skilled, semiskilled, and unskilled workers in the same assemblies had an unanticipated negative effect. The practice undermined its effectiveness as a collective bargaining agent by making it difficult for the Houston lodges to address members' concerns in a specific trade or industry. The Houston Knights also embraced a conservative philosophy concerning the battle between capital and labor. Its membership spurned "[making] war on capital or capitalists" and simply demanded "justice [and] a fair day[']s work for a fair day[']s pay." The Houston lodges promoted their aims through political action, through social activities, and in some cases strikes. The Knights also published a local paper, the *Houston Labor Echo.* The paper served as the official news organ of the union and enjoyed a large circulation not only among the membership but also in all the city's railroad repair shops and among skilled tradesmen.[19] In all these instances the racial barrier was rigidly enforced. The white assemblies simply ignored blacks and refused to accept them in a wide range of activities such as picnics, festivals, sporting events, excursions, Labor Day celebrations, and strikes.[20]

The Knights of Labor reached its zenith in Houston in 1886 and afterward began a slow decline that culminated in oblivion by 1900. In 1886 the Knights of Labor suffered a crushing defeat in the Great Southwest Strike when it struck the Southwest Railroad System controlled by Jay Gould, a powerful, astute, and unscrupulous financier.[21] Houston, unlike most Texas cities, escaped the strike but the union's defeat and intense labor repression nationally following the Haymarket Square bombing in Chicago devastated the Knights and marked the beginning of its end. After 1886 Houston's skilled workers abandoned the industrial unionism and idealistic social vision called for by the Knights and focused on organizing themselves into craft unions. By 1900 only four Houston assemblies of the Knights of Labor remained, and only two were active, Musicians Assembly No. 1857 and the Bakers and Confectioners Assembly No. 1897.[22]

In 1889 delegates from the city's trade unions established the Houston Labor Council, and the city's labor movement took a new course that would carry it into the twentieth century. The goals of the Labor Council included coordinating, consolidating, and institutionalizing the bargaining strength of the city's skilled tradesmen by organizing them into craft unions.[23] This marked the introduction into Houston of the American Federation of Labor's philosophy of utilizing the strength of hard-to-replace skilled workers and mobilizing that power to advance the immediate economic interests of its members in terms of wages, hours, and conditions. The workers drawn to the Houston Labor Council's constituent unions had skills that enabled them to bargain effectively with their employers as long as they limited their demands to improved wages and working conditions. Disillusioned by defeat in the Great Southwest Strike and disenchanted with the Knights of Labor's idealistic philosophy of industrial unionism, Houston's skilled workers embraced an organizational strategy that they hoped would maximize their power and minimize their weaknesses. The council ultimately evolved into an umbrella organization for Houston's emerging craft unions that rallied them so they could focus and coordinate their efforts in reaching their objectives. It often served as an intermediary between member unions, mediated jurisdictional disputes, provided support for organizing activity, and assisted during strikes.[24]

Between 1893 and 1914 the number of craft unions associated with the Labor Council in Houston increased from seven to fifty, and membership reached approximately fifty-four hundred, nearly 22 percent of the workforce. The various crafts and skills represented among the Houston locals included plumbers, electricians, blacksmiths, machinists, iron molders, and numerous others. Houston's unionized craftsmen represented a working-class aristocracy who were basically conservative, in general agreement with the materialistic and acquisitive values of American capitalistic society and regarded their unions as vehicles for upward social mobility and entry into the middle class. Houston's craft unions made no efforts to organize the city's unskilled and semiskilled workers, which remained the least organized group in the city. While the most fully organized trades such as the plumbers, brickmasons, and printers boasted 100 percent participation, only about 10 percent of the unskilled were organized. The city's trade unions had the means, influence, and the skilled membership to keep their organizations exclusive and influential, and they saw no reason to reach out to the unskilled and semiskilled, who had little direct economic impact on craftsmen and posed no threat as strikebreakers.[25] Ninety percent of Houston's common laborers remained unorganized during this period.

The conservatism of Houston's trade unions in the nineteenth and early twentieth centuries was rooted in several factors. Houston's trade unions accepted the notion that the aspirations of "labor and capital [were] not antagonistic[,] and while the interests of capital and labor are adverse, they are not necessarily hostile and should not be." Houston did not have large, mass-production industries before the outbreak of the First World War. Thus there was no influx of unskilled immigrants from eastern and southern Europe, who might otherwise have exerted a potentially radical influence over the city's labor movement, as they did in northern industrial cities. While Houston's total population increased between 1870 and 1910, the percentage of foreign-born residents steadily declined. In 1870, 16.7 percent of the city's residents were foreign born; in 1890 that figure decreased to 11.3 percent; and in 1910, only 8 percent of the city's population claimed foreign birth. Finally, the ethnic and racial homogeneity of the white trade unions that dominated the city's labor movement were unwavering in their commitment to white supremacy, protecting white jobs, Jim Crow segregation, and relegating African Americans to primarily unskilled labor.[26]

Max Andrew, publisher of the city's labor paper, the *Houston Labor Journal*, and a member of the local typographical union, served as president of the Texas State Federation of Labor (TSFL) between 1902 and 1905. He personified the conservatism of Houston's trade unions regarding race and class struggle. Established in 1900 the Texas State Federation of Labor served the same function as the Houston Labor Council but at the state level. The primary functions of the TSFL were to lobby the legislature to pass labor friendly legislation and to act as a coordinating agency for many types of activities carried out by various Texas unions. The state federation concerned itself with such legislative issues as abolition of convict labor, prohibition of child labor under fifteen years, the eight-hour workday, and equal pay for men and women. Many of the state federation's and the Houston Labor Council's liberal political positions were rooted in the radical agrarian tradition of Texas' Grangers, Farmer's Alliances, and the Populists. Moreover, the Texas State Federation of Labor and the Houston Labor Council borrowed heavily from policies and programs introduced by the Knights of Labor.[27]

In 1911, the TSFL passed a resolution supporting a Texas minimum wage law, and after years of lobbying persuaded the legislature in 1919 to enact legislation creating an industrial welfare commission with the power to establish minimum wage rates for women and minors. The victory was remarkable for three reasons: the TSFL persuaded the Democratic party's leadership to include support for a minimum wage law as a plank in its platform; the bill became law in the virulent anti-union post–World War I era; and it was the only minimum wage law, of the four enacted at the state level between 1917 and 1919, secured almost exclusively by the efforts of organized labor. Though the legislature repealed the law under pressure from employers during the anti-union open shop era of the 1920s, the TSFL's transient victory demonstrated labor's ability to mobilize its power and influence public policy, a major reason why businessmen feared it.[28] Though the TSFL was committed to the struggle for labor's rights, it was equally committed to keeping unions racially segregated.

In 1905, during Andrew's tenure as president, the Texas State Federation of Labor issued a report that formalized the prevailing racial prejudice of the state's trade unionists. It said in part, "[a] sense of justice, to say nothing of the wisdom of the policy, would dictate organizing the Negro into separate unions."[29] The call for racially segregated unions advocated by Andrew and the TSFL ultimately guaranteed that Houston's African Americans were barred from apprenticeships and journeyman status in skilled trades such as pattern maker, machinist, molder, blacksmith, and electrician. In the twentieth century, as the Hughes Tool Company and other oil tool companies emerged in Houston and the demand for workers with these skills increased, the racial covenant of the Texas State Federation of Labor and Houston Labor Council guaranteed that blacks would be excluded from such jobs. The advance of trade unionism in Houston in the late nineteenth and early twentieth centuries thus brought little improvement to the working lives of the city's African American workers.

The city's rapidly expanding economy in the early decades of the twentieth century opened additional jobs to black workers, but the occupational status of Houston's black workers did not improve significantly since the vast majority of jobs available to them were unskilled. Many of Houston's white employers were skeptical of the ability of blacks to perform industrial labor, and this attitude served to limit African American workers to menial "Negro jobs." One white employer remarked "that it is very hard to arouse enthusiasm or pride of accomplishment in Negro workmen. They will not assume even minor responsibilities[,] resulting in shiftlessness and lack of thrift." Additionally, blacks often did not have the skills necessary to perform many of the jobs created during Houston's industrial expansion in the twentieth century, and city authorities were uninterested in supporting vocational and industrial training programs for the city's African American population.[30]

Max Andrew also advocated that organized labor in Texas accept the capitalist system, find a niche within it, and reject radicalism. He vigorously rejected the notion of class struggle and urged that organized labor and capital must work together for their mutual benefit. He emphasized that labor unions must adopt conservative policies. Andrew believed that, given the mutual dependence of capital and labor, employers should recognize that the existence of organized labor rationalized the market economy by promoting stable working conditions, shop floor contentment, and wage uniformity. He further believed that Houston's unions should promote a conservative labor ideology in order to curry public favor and to convince the citizenry that unions were merely "business organizations of the labor element." Thanks to Andrew's leadership, organized labor won considerable community favor in Houston and at the state level. Nonetheless, many Houston businessmen were unyielding opponents to organized labor.[31]

Houston's employers displayed the same animus toward organized labor as their counterparts in the country's traditional industrial regions. Beginning in the 1880s the city's economic, political, and social leadership emanated from two powerful business organizations, the Houston Business League, the forerunner of the Houston Chamber of Commerce, and the Houston Cotton Exchange and Board of Trade. Ideologically they embraced laissez faire capitalism and were committed to its dogmas of antigovernment, antiregulation, antiunion, antiplanning, antitaxes, anti-anything that seemed to place limits on the economic prerogatives and activities of the city's business community. Most importantly they believed in what they regarded as their God-given right to purchase their labor as cheaply as possible without troublesome interference from unions. The members of these organizations built Houston into the commercial center of the Texas Gulf Coast by the early twentieth century. Under their leadership the city emerged as the transportation, warehouse, distribution, and financial center for the cotton, lumber, cattle, and oil industries. As Houston prospered, these business elites were well positioned to reap the economic benefits of their efforts and to protect their class interests.[32] In order to protect those interests Houston businessmen relied on the Houston Light Guards, a local militia unit established in 1873. Two of the Light Guards' primary missions were to quell labor disturbances and race riots.

An overwhelming number of Light Guardsmen held positions of high social status as business executives, proprietors, managers, professionals, and government officials. Ambitious businessmen understood that membership in the Light Guards held the promise of advancement in Houston's economic and social community. Only a minuscule number of working-class Houstonians belonged to the Light Guards, and these men were almost all skilled tradesmen. Fewer still were drawn from the ranks of semiskilled and unskilled labor. Class distinctions between Houston's working class, the business elite, and the upwardly mobile middle class probably contributed to labor's virtual exclusion from the Light Guards. The Light Guards obviously excluded blacks and only accepted "[a]ny white eligible for membership in the Texas National Guard, [or] . . . any white man of moral good character."[33]

Between 1877 and 1898 the Houston Light Guards were called out five times to break strikes in Houston. The two most important occurred in 1880 and 1898. In October 1880 during the Texas cotton harvest 160 black laborers walked off the job at the Houston Direct Navigation Company where they loaded cotton bales onto barges at the city's wharves along Buffalo Bayou for transshipment to Galveston. They also stopped work at several cotton compresses, where cotton was compressed into bales for shipment, and the Houston and Central Texas Railroad, where they loaded cotton bales onto railroad cars. They demanded an increase in daily ages from $1.50 to $2.00. The employers refused the strikers' demand, locked them out, and brought in more than 185 Mexican strikebreakers. Strikers, some of them armed, forced the scabs to flee and successfully shut down the city's wharves, railroads, and cotton compresses. At this point the mayor called out the Houston Light Guards to restore order and break the strike. The militia's arrival forced the strikers to retreat and seek negotiations with employers. The strikers eventually returned to work without a wage increase and the strikebreakers were fired.[34]

During the strike employers played one minority group off against another. This is significant in understanding the racial caste system in Jim Crow Houston and employers' willingness to use it to their advantage. The work that striking African Americans performed was strictly "black" labor, and white Houstonians would never have considered serving as strikebreakers in this context. Equally noteworthy is that after the strike was settled employers did not hesitate to fire Mexican strikebreakers, reinstate African Americans, and reestablish the racial status quo. Houston's racial caste system pointedly dictated the racial boundaries between white and black jobs. The exploitation and prejudice suffered by Mexican workers in the Bayou City could be worse than that suffered by blacks.[35]

Though Mexicans workers were used to help break the strike, they did not represent a significant presence in Houston's working class in the last two decades of the nineteenth century. Mexican workers for the most part were not necessary or recruited by Houston's employers because of how the city's economy developed during this period. The city's businesses emerged to service the needs of East Texas agricultural production of grain, cotton, and lumber. An infrastructure of railroads, warehouses, and cotton gins emerged to facilitate the processing and shipping of these goods. For the unskilled workers necessary in these industries the city could turn to its large supply of black labor and also to the surrounding rural counties with their large African American populations. Mexican American scholar Arnoldo De León has determined that in 1900 only about five hundred Mexicans lived in Houston. They became more prominent after 1901 when the demand for workers in Houston escalated to meet the demand for the newly emerging Texas oil industry, but nonetheless by 1910 Houston could claim a Mexican population of only two thousand, whereas the black population numbered nearly twenty-four thousand. Prejudice doomed Mexicans and blacks to menial jobs, and Houston employers played Mexican labor off against black workers whenever it suited their needs.[36]

In March 1898 the Houston Light Guards played an important role in breaking a strike by 150 members of the Amalgamated Association of Street Railway Employees of America against the Houston Electric Railway Company. In this strike, organized white workers would feel the power of the militia. The union struck over a number of unresolved issues, such as wages, grievance procedures, and a closed shop. Motormen and conductors walked out, and the solid public support they enjoyed within the community alarmed management and other businessmen. The company moved quickly to assert its authority, and Houston's business leaders rallied in support of the company's position.[37]

Honorary Houston Light Guardsman John Henry Kirby, a director of the Houston Electric Railway Company and an uncompromising foe of organized labor, led the fight against the union. Kirby condemned the strike as an irresponsible disregard for the public's safety and summarily dismissed the strikers' demands. Kirby is an interesting and important figure in the economic history of Houston. A powerful presence, he came to dominate and characterize the city's economic growth. Kirby made his initial fortune in the East Texas timber industry, and his rise to economic prominence bears a striking resemblance to that of the steel magnate Andrew Carnegie. Both men came from humble backgrounds and through fortunate connections, hard work, guile, and ruthlessness made their fortunes. Much like Carnegie, John Henry Kirby believed he was a benevolent, compassionate employer, but in reality, just like the steel baron's, Kirby's outward paternalism failed to mask his tyrannical oppression in crushing efforts by his employees to unionize.[38]

Under Kirby's direction the company imported strikebreakers from other parts of the state and barricaded them in the company's office building. All the strikebreakers were white because only whites could hold motormen or conductor jobs. Strikers and strike sympathizers, at one point numbering three thousand, periodically massed outside the building, harassed those inside, and threatened the scabs. At a mass meeting on March 21, 1898, strike leaders inspired strikers and supporters with the righteousness of their cause. One blasted Kirby and the directors of the company by accusing them of union busting and undermining the supremacy of white labor. "Shall the union men of this city be organized? If we lose this strike we a go a notch lower in the scale and . . . would find ourselves on the level with the peon labor of the Southern republic that touches the border of your own states." [39] The strikers' racist hyperbole aside, Kirby and the company's directors would never have considered overthrowing Houston's white supremacy to achieve their ends in the strike. This battle would be fought only among whites, whether management or union.

When the company tried to run its streetcars with scabs, more than a thousand people gathered and prevented the cars from making their scheduled routes. Following this confrontation, Mayor Horace Baldwin Rice, a former member of the Houston Light Guards who had led a platoon during the 1880 strike, ordered out the militia to restore order, and in one instance marched at its front when it moved against a crowd. The crowd of strikers and sympathizers gave way in the face of the guardsmen's fixed bayonets. [40] As the situation worsened a citizen's committee, which included representatives from labor, the company, and those not associated with either side in the dispute, began negotiating a settlement to the dispute.

The parties reached an agreement at the end of March, 1898. The settlement granted a modest pay raise and the company's right to retain forty-nine scabs but with an understanding that the striking union men would be rehired, and management successfully avoided recognizing the union as the employees' bargaining agent. Mayor Rice's calling out the Light Guards, forbidding public assemblies, and promising to protect the company without any commensurate support for the union had strengthened management's hand, and the settlement overwhelmingly favored the Houston Electric Railway Company. The terms that ended the strike were identical to those offered by the company before the militia was called out. In the two strikes discussed, Houston's workers faced employer solidarity and intransigence, strikebreakers, and repression from the Houston Light Guards. Houston's businessmen in both strikes vigorously and successfully defeated collective action by workers. The victories reaffirmed their faith in laissez-faire economics. [41]

In addition to using the Houston Light Guards as a means of discouraging unionism, in 1904 Houston's businessmen formed a local chapter of the Citizens' Alliance. Fearing what they perceived to be the growing power of skilled craft unions, businessmen in smaller industrial cities such as Houston organized local Citizens' Alliances under the guidance of the National Association of Manufacturers (NAM) to counter organized labor. Originally established in 1895 to promote the tariff and protect American manufacturers from foreign competition, by 1903 the NAM enthusiastically assumed national leadership in resisting unions. It denounced unions as, "an enormous Labor Trust [that] is the heaviest oppressor of the independent workingman as well as the common American Citizen. . . . [T]he greatest danger lies in recognition of the union." [42]

As a condition of membership all candidates for the Citizens' Alliance were required to pledge that "I hereby make an application for the membership in the Citizens' Alliance and I affirm that I am not a member of any labor organization, which resorts to boycotting, or any form of coercion or unlawful force and fully agree to discountenance all strikes and schemes of persecution." [43] The organization's principles set forth the idea that America was made great by free enterprise and that all citizens must seek industrial peace and protect the right of workers to sell their labor to whom they pleased and for the price they could obtain.

The fact that Houston's Citizens' Alliance had 125 charter members is a striking indication of the strong hostility unions faced at the hands of the city's employers. They elected H. F. McGregor, president of the Houston Electric Railway Company, as the chapter's first president. With approval of the Citizens' Alliance, McGregor provoked a strike in June 1904 with the company's nemesis, the Amalgamated Association of Street Railway Employees of America, which still had a foothold in the company. The all-white union consisted of motormen who operated the streetcars and conductors who collected fairs. Both jobs were exclusively white. After the 1898 strike, the union had survived and remained popular with employees and the public. This time, McGregor's intention from the outset was to break the union. [44]

McGregor used a number of techniques to instigate the strike. First he fired sixteen union members over alleged complaints of poor service while at the same time hiring fifty new employees and warning them not to join the union. Another two union men were fired because they were active in union affairs, and when the local's president protested the firings the company reprimanded him for insubordination. Things worsened when management leaked information that the company had hired strikebreakers who were standing by in case the union called a strike. McGregor and the Citizens' Alliance imported white strikebreakers from other cities. As in other southern cities suffering streetcar strikes, the union stoked sectional resentment against strikebreakers who were usually recruited from northern cities. Tensions finally exploded when McGregor fired union president Oscar Miller for critical statements he made to the press about the company's oppression of the union. Immediately afterward the all white union voted unanimously to strike.[45]

The Houston Streetcar Strike of 1904 was merely one incident in a national strike wave that plagued many of the nation's cities in the first two decades of the twentieth century. Though violence characterized many of the strikes and disruption of service inconvenienced the public, striking streetcarmen nonetheless enjoyed public support that crossed class lines. As in other cities, middle- and working-class Houstonians harbored deep resentment against the streetcar companies because they were often absentee owned as in Houston, monopolized public transit, and were perceived to enjoy unfair profits at public expense. A Boston syndicate owned the Houston Electric Railway Company. Generally the public supported strikers' demands for shorter working hours for motormen because they feared that overworked, fatigued motormen were susceptible to accidents thus threatening passengers' safety. Conductors who collected carfare often engendered goodwill among the public by nurturing congenial relationships with regular riders, assisting them on and off cars and watching out for their children's safety.[46]

Undaunted by public feelings against its motives the Houston's Citizens' Alliance under McGregor's leadership immediately swung into action to break the strike. It called in the waiting strikebreakers, infiltrated the union with spies, and pressured city officials to protect the company's property from violence. In the face of these draconian measures the union girded itself for a bitter struggle, received the support of the Houston Labor Council, and—perhaps most satisfying for the union cause—enjoyed extensive public support just as it had during the 1898 strike. Mass meetings called by the union drew as many as five thousand participants. Union speakers condemned the company for being managed by outsiders not in sympathy with the Houston community. One speaker emphasized that the Boston syndicate that owned Houston's streetcar franchise supported repeal of the city's segregation ordinance, which provided separate seating arrangements for blacks and whites. At one time the company proposed removing partitions between black and white sections in a few cars, but the Citizens' Alliance quickly convinced the Boston syndicate to retract its proposal for integrating the city's streetcars because it provided fuel for the strikers and went against the values of the alliance's members. The Boston investors quickly realized their folly in trying to impose liberal northern racial values in Houston. McGregor and the Citizens' Alliance were willing to do the syndicate's bidding in battling the strikers over economic issues and union recognition, but just like the union men they were not going to let the dispute undermine white supremacy in the Bayou City.[47]

Passions against the Houston Electric Railway Company and McGregor ran high among strikers. Oscar Miller and other union leaders cautioned them to contain their anger and not resort to violence or destruction of company property because it would hurt the union and play into the hands of the company and the Citizens' Alliance. Miller and the others knew that maintaining public support was crucial. In order to help citizens in their daily commutes the union, with help from the Houston Labor Council, established hack lines to provide transportation to the city's outlying districts.[48] On both sides the stakes were high, and the union and the company hunkered down for a long fight. Victory for the strikers meant the right to have a union and a collective voice, while for management it would mean running the company as it saw fit without troublesome meddling from employees.

Shortly after the strike began, violence erupted and the union's position became increasingly untenable. A series of five dynamitings of tracks and streetcars occurred in June and July; fortunately, no one was injured. Although the police department investigated the explosions no suspects were ever arrested and a cloud of uncertainty hung over who was responsible. Union organizer C. W. Woodman accused the authorities of making a halfhearted effort to investigate the blasts, and he along with other unionists believed, though they could not prove it, that the violence was the work of agent provocateurs hired by the Citizens' Alliance. Woodman correctly surmised that the press would infer the dynamitings were the handiwork of radical unionists who disrespected the company's property rights and jeopardized public safety.

To counteract the bad publicity the Houston Trades Council offered a nine thousand dollar reward for the arrest and conviction of the person or people guilty of the dynamiting. Many citizens concluded that the surest way to end the explosions was to end the strike. At this point city officials tried to intervene and arbitrate a settlement but failed. Although some city council members gave credit to reports that the company was responsible for the explosions, they stopped short of officially blaming anyone but did pass a resolution condemning the dynamiting and authorizing the mayor to employ as many men as possible to stop further trouble. The council took steps to mediate the dispute throughout the strike but its efforts proved fruitless since the company refused to compromise or agree to an arbitrated settlement.[49]

As the dispute dragged on through August, September, and into October the inconvenience it caused citizens in daily commuting prompted many to abandon their boycott of the streetcars. As more and more people began to ride the cars, a feeling of helplessness gripped many strikers.[50] The union continued the struggle until October when it called off the strike. The union's capitulation destroyed the Amalgamated Association of Street Railway Employees in Houston and weakened the entire Houston labor movement.[51] The Citizens' Alliance effort played a major role in defeating the strike and breaking the union. Houston employers learned several important lessons from the strike. Management should not be afraid to provoke a strike in order to break a union, and should stand firm against union demands, make no concessions, denounce unionists as dangerous agitators and a threat to law and order, intimidate strikers by mobilizing local police and militia forces, enlist scabs from among so-called loyal employees opposed to the strike, encourage scabs to cross picket lines and start a back-to-work movement among their colleagues under the protection of local law enforcement agencies, generate animosity toward the strike within the local community, and be prepared to weather a long strike to wear down union resolve.

Not until 1911 would another major strike rock Houston. Trouble erupted when skilled workers in the repair shops of the Southern Pacific Railroad, one of eight lines owned by the Harriman railroad empire, joined a national strike against the company. Once again using African Americans as strikebreakers was out of the question because the shops employed skilled tradesmen in whites-only jobs such as machinists, sheet metal workers, boilermakers, blacksmiths, and car repairmen who overhauled and repaired locomotives, rolling stock, and all manner of equipment necessary to keep the trains running. The Houston strikers belonged to several whites-only unions affiliated with the American Federation of Labor. They included the International Association of Machinists, International Brotherhood of Blacksmiths and Helpers, International Brotherhood of Boilermakers and Iron Ship Builders, and the Brotherhood of Railway Carmen of America. Seeking to increase their bargaining power and to counter management's divide-and-conquer strategy of negotiating with each union singly, the individual unions confederated and formed what they called the Harriman System Federation (HSF), so they could present a united front when negotiating with management.[52] Management, which refused to recognize the newly formed Harriman System Federation, was willing "to meet representatives of individual unions, but not the Federation." Harriman officials claimed that recognizing the HSF would cripple the corporation and leave it at the mercy of the "supreme and unlimited power" of its unions. The rank and file supported the goals of the HSF and voted overwhelmingly to strike when management refused to yield. On September 30, 1911, nearly 40,000 workers struck the Harriman lines. In Houston approximately 1,200 to 1,500 joined the walkout.[53]

The first three months of the strike were the most critical. Harriman immediately employed numerous detective agencies that furnished scabs and guards. Violence flared on the picket lines between strikers and scabs in Houston and throughout the South. In Houston on October 2 pickets confronted strikebreakers; a fight broke out; and panicky scabs bolted for the fenced railroad yards. As they approached the compound, railroad guards manning the fence mistakenly identified the rushing men as unionists and fired into them. The guards' fire killed one man and seriously wounded another.[54] Three days later tragedy struck again when a Southern Pacific guard patrolling his post on company property was killed by a shotgun blast from an unknown assailant. An unidentified sniper later killed one scab and wounded three others as they were escorted through union pickets into the Southern Pacific yards. In another incident, at the Union depot in New Orleans, a traveling companion of Texas governor Oscar Colquitt was mistakenly identified as a strikebreaker and assaulted. In an effort to protect scabs from further violence, attorneys for the Southern Pacific filed suit in Houston's federal court seeking an injunction to disband the picket lines. On October 5, the federal judge Waller Burns responded by issuing an injunction and ordering the picket lines disbanded.[55]

Although the shopmen's federations were not affiliated with the Houston Labor Council, the council endorsed the strike and supplied financial aid to the strikers. In November the Labor Council increased its financial support, held mass meetings, and organized parades in support of the walkout. But the efforts by the Labor Council failed to rally public support for the strike because of the violence associated with it. The daily press strongly endorsed management's cause and refused to publicize the shopmen's side of the dispute. In desperation union officials tried to persuade the federal government to condemn railroad equipment repaired by scab labor as dangerous and unsafe to the public but to no avail.[56]

By December public opinion had turned squarely against the strike and Houston's businessmen became increasingly alarmed over the potential harm that would be done to the city's commerce if the walkout continued indefinitely. Though the Southern Pacific suffered financially from the walkout, it had sufficient resources to grind down the strikers and gradually, thanks to the injunction that protected scabs, overcame the problems of running its shops without the regular men. The strike became a grueling endurance test, and as time passed strikers were forced to seek other jobs to support their families. The strike officially continued in Houston as late as 1914 but it had long since ceased to have any meaningful effect.[57]

Houston's trade unions learned several important lessons during the strike. They learned that national industrial combinations such as the Harriman Lines were formidable adversaries and labor's only hope of competing against such power was to fashion similar federations of national unions, nurture public support of the righteousness of labor's cause, enlist the sympathies of the press, and hope for progressive and evenhanded government to arbitrate labor disputes. Another lesson learned by Houston's unionists in this strike and earlier ones was that collective action on their part would be opposed not only by national industrial combinations but also by local business combinations.

By the time Howard Hughes Sr. and his business partner William Sharp established their company to manufacture rotary drilling bits in 1908, Houston's labor movement had suffered a number of defeats but had rebounded and survived. It had experienced two discrete stages of development: one between 1865 and 1889 when the Knights of Labor and industrial unionism influenced the movement, and another from 1889 to 1914, when the Houston Labor Council consolidated the city's trade unions into a cohesive organization. During both stages Houston's unionists embraced Jim Crow segregation, racism, and white supremacy.

During major strikes that threatened to disrupt the city's commerce, unions faced a united foe that included Houston's employers, the local militia, and large national corporations. They suffered agonizing defeats but also showed a remarkable ability to bounce back, rally support among Houston's white working class, and survive. Houston's unionized skilled tradesmen demonstrated a great deal of union spirit and loyalty in the face of adversity but refused to recruit semiskilled and unskilled workers into their unions. Their racism excluded African Americans from union membership and undermined labor's power by excluding a significant portion of Houston's working class. The two factors that weakened Houston's labor movement—elitist trade unionism and Jim Crow racism—would not be seriously threatened until the Congress of Industrial Organizations arrived in Houston in the 1930s.

When Hughes and Sharp founded their company, they needed skilled machinists, blacksmiths, boilermakers, patternmakers, and other tradesmen, as well as semiskilled and unskilled labor. As the company gradually grew in size and gained a near monopoly over the manufacture of rotary drilling bits for the oil industry, it needed to hire more and more employees. Growth demanded the hiring of professional managers to run the company, and the owners abdicated the day-to-day running of the firm to a hard-nosed breed of executives and foremen.[58] Consequently worker disaffection increased. This, along with Houston's strong union tradition and Jim Crow segregation, made it inevitable that unions and race would become as much a part of the Hughes Tool Company as the famous drilling bit it manufactured.

CHAPTER TWO

How It All Began

HOUSTON, LABOR, OIL, AND WORKING
AT MR. HUGHES'S PLACE

THE HUGHES TOOL COMPANY owes its existence to the discovery of oil at Spindletop near Beaumont, Texas, in January, 1901. The spectacular oil discovery ushered in the Texas oil boom, and within weeks tens of thousands of people flocked to the Beaumont area in hopes of finding oil and instant wealth. Hundreds of wells soon jammed the vicinity as drillers, speculators, roughnecks, and the curious descended on southeast Texas. Throughout Texas, Louisiana, Oklahoma, and California, the Spindletop oil bonanza repeated itself many times over during the first decades of the twentieth century, and the focus of America's oil production shifted from Pennsylvania and Appalachia to the Southwest.[1] Oil fever infected Missourian Howard Hughes Sr. and drew him to Spindletop where he pursued opportunities as a drilling contractor and oil field speculator.[2] Hughes ultimately secured his place in the oil industry not through contract drilling or land sales but by establishing a company that manufactured rotary drilling bits that were absolutely essential to the oil industry. Born in Lancaster, Missouri, in 1869, the son of a successful attorney, Hughes was educated at the University of Iowa and Harvard Law School. After leaving Harvard, Hughes briefly practiced law in Iowa but quit the law to pursue lead and zinc mining interests in Joplin, Missouri. When Hughes heard the news of the Spindletop strike, he quickly moved to Beaumont in search of wealth.[3]

While in Beaumont, Hughes became acquainted with the drilling contractor Walter Sharp. In 1902 the two formed the Moonshine Oil Company, which specialized in revitalizing oil wells that had stopped producing. Joseph Cullinan provided the capital to get Moonshine

Oil going. Cullinan, who learned the oil business while moving up through the ranks of a Standard Oil affiliate in Pennsylvania, was president of Texaco when he invested in Moonshine Oil. His investment created a pattern for the three men's business relationship. Hughes and Sharp secured the rights to an oil field service or tool and Cullinan provided the capital to back their venture. Sharp's expertise as a master driller, Hughes's knowledge of patent law and mechanics, and Cullinan's wealth made them a formidable triumvirate.[4] The formation of Hughes Tool followed the same pattern as that of Moonshine Oil.

Oil field myth credits Howard Hughes Sr. with inventing the rotary drilling bit. Historical literature generally agrees, but the original idea emanated from Granville Humason, a Louisiana oil field worker whose inspiration for the rotary bit came from the simple workings of a coffee grinder. In 1908, while engaged in contract drilling around Oil City, Louisiana, Hughes met Humason one evening in a Shreveport bar. Humason explained the design, and Hughes, recognizing the bit's potential, bought the design from Humason for $150. Walter Sharp secured a half interest in the idea when he advanced Hughes $1,500 to patent the bit.[5]

While in Oil City, Louisiana, Hughes constructed a wooden prototype of his bit. It was a roller type bit with two cone-shaped, toothed rollers with 166 teeth. As the cones rotated with the rotary motion of the drill, the hardened steel cones ate into rock. Hughes also worked out a way to keep the bit lubricated while it cut into rock formations. Since the conical-shaped bit could drill a straight round hole rapidly and efficiently, it proved enormously superior to the inefficient fishtail bit in use at that time.[6]

Hughes and Sharp showed Joseph Cullinan the prototype and convinced him that an experimental bit should be manufactured and tested. Cullinan provided the money, and the first Hughes rotary bit, shrouded in secrecy, was manufactured by the Brown and Sharp Manufacturing Company in Providence, Rhode Island.[7] Sometime in 1908 Howard Hughes Sr. brought the bit back to Texas and tested it in the Goose Creek oil field east of Houston. He imposed strict security at the drilling sight, allowing only one trusted driller to assist him in connecting the bit to the drill pipe. The remainder of the crew was kept back until the bit disappeared from sight down the drill hole. The bit performed beyond Hughes's expectations and demonstrated its superiority over any other bits in use.[8]

A drawing of Howard Hughes Sr. preparing to lower his first prototype drilling bit into a well in Goose Creek, Texas, southwest of Houston, ca. 1908. *Photograph courtesy of the Houston Metropolitan Research Center, Houston Public Library.*

On December 11, 1908, Howard Hughes Sr. and William Sharp established the Sharp-Hughes Tool Company (later renamed Hughes Tool) to manufacture the bit. Sharp provided $15,000 to start the company, and it was agreed that Hughes would be made president and manager of operations and paid a salary. The board of directors included Joseph Cullinan, founder of Texaco; Will C. Hogg, son of former Texas governor James Hogg who was one of the founders of Humble Oil; Edgar Townes, another founding member of Humble Oil and its attorney; and Howard's brother, Felix Hughes. The new company's partners and all its board members shared interlocking oil interests through Texaco and Humble Oil, and enjoyed access to state political power through Will Hogg.[9]

In 1912, Cullinan, one of Sharp's Texaco partners, provided $300,000 worth of capital stock when the company was incorporated. Sharp received $149,000 worth of shares and Hughes was issued $151,000 worth. Cullinan and Sharp had split ownership of Sharp's interest though the transaction was never formalized. Cullinan oversaw his investment by serving as the company's chairman of the board.[10] Between 1908 and 1912, Hughes had personally secured numerous patent rights upgrading the rotary bit and his proprietary rights over it. These acquisitions were the primary reason Cullinan and Sharp agreed to let Hughes have a majority interest in the company. Cullinan and Sharp knew that the financially reckless, though legally shrewd, Hughes needed their economic backing in order to begin manufacturing the new rotary drilling bit. They recognized the bit's profitability and were willing to take a chance on Hughes in order to cash in on it.[11]

Hughes, Sharp, and the directors located the company in Houston rather than the Beaumont area, since the Bayou City enjoyed a significant advantage over Beaumont in transportation, communications, and finance. Houston's centralized location, extensive railroad network, and experience in serving the administrative, legal, and financial needs of the timber and cotton industries also made it an attractive site for the company. Joseph Cullinan had recognized Houston's advantages in 1908 and located Texaco's general offices there. With nearby Spindletop and the opening of the important Goose Creek field southeast of Houston and the Humble field northeast of the city, Houston became the primary manufacturing and distribution center for oil tools and drilling equipment.[12]

Houston's close proximity to the East Texas and Gulf Coast oil fields greatly accelerated Hughes Tool's growth as well as spawning other companies manufacturing equipment for the oil industry. The Reed Roller Bit Company and Howard Smith Company were founded in 1916. In 1919, WKM Manufacturing started operations in Houston, and in 1920 Cameron Iron Works, which would become one of the world's largest producers of oil tool supplies, began operations. Oil companies such as Texaco in 1908, Gulf in 1916, Humble in 1917, and Sinclair in 1918 established refining operations in the city. Texas' petroleum resources, the refining business, and the numerous oil-related service companies such as Hughes Tool provided the economic engine of growth that transformed Houston into a major southern manufacturing center.[13] The number of Houston manufacturing plants, many of which supplied goods and services to the oil industry, increased from 78 in 1904 to 429 in 1930.

Houston's industrial expansion clearly contributed to the growth of the population by generating a permanent demand for labor that could only be satisfied with a continuous migration from outside the area. From 1900 to 1930, Houston's population increased from 44,633 to 292,325, an incredible 655 percent. By the late 1920s, of all southern cities, only Birmingham, Alabama, the south's leading industrial center, surpassed Houston in manufacturing capacity.[14]

The drilling industry clamored for the efficient, durable Sharp-Hughes rotary-cone drilling bit, and the company had difficulty fulfilling demand. Thanks to Howard Hughes Sr.'s patents the firm enjoyed monopolistic control over the manufacture of the rotary-cone drilling bit. Initially, the company leased its bits as a means of protecting its proprietary rights over its products, but in 1913 it introduced a program whereby customers could either lease or purchase bits. Customers favored purchasing over leasing, and Hughes anticipated that selling the bits would net between 50 to 100 percent of the sale price, less commission. A purchase option allowed customers to order bits and cones and have them on hand at the drilling site, which greatly simplified drilling operations. The company flourished. By 1913 total sales amounted to $173,800, with monthly net earnings averaging $8,000.[15]

The company's first decade saw the death of cofounder William Sharp in 1913. Following his death, Howard Hughes Sr. purchased Sharp's 49 percent interest in the company from his widow. Mrs. Sharp's banker advised her to sell out to Hughes, citing Hughes's well-known reputation for fiscal irresponsibility and lavish spending,

TABLE 1   Houston's Population, 1900–1930

	Total Population	Black Population (%)
1900	44,633	14,608 (32.7)
1910	78,800	23,929 (30.4)
1920	138,276	33,960 (24.6)
1930	292,325	63,337 (21.7)

SOURCE: U.S. census data, as cited in Howard Beeth and Cary D. Wintz, eds., *Black Dixie: Afro-Texan History and Culture in Houston*, 89.

A drawing of the interior of the 20-x-40-foot space Howard Hughes Sr. rented from the Houston Car Wheel Manufacturing Company on White Street where he began production of his drilling bit. *Photograph courtesy of the Houston Metropolitan Research Center, Houston Public Library.*

both of which might one day ruin the company. Hughes became sole owner and in 1915 renamed the firm the Hughes Tool Company.[16]

Manufacturing operations began in 1909 with six employees in a twenty-by-forty-foot rented space in the Houston Car Wheel Manufacturing Company located on White Street. At the same time, Hughes contracted with the Brown and Sharp Manufacturing Company in Providence, Rhode Island, to manufacture the bit in order to meet demand until a larger Houston facility could be found.[17] In 1912, Hughes moved operations into a renovated gothic red brick building at Second and Girard Streets that had formerly housed the Armour meatpacking company. Before moving in Hughes revamped the interior, installing electrically driven machine tools and coal- and oil-fired heat treating furnaces; alongside the plant he set up a testing area, complete with oil derrick, where bits were tested in large blocks of stone.[18]

Initially thirteen employees worked in the newly renovated shop at Second and Girard. As demand for his drilling bit went up, Hughes hired more employees. Within two years of relocating, the number of employees had jumped to thirty-six, thirty-three whites and three blacks. White employees performed all machine operations, machinery repair, and product inspections, while African Americans were there for cleaning up and helping in the heat treatment department. At this point in the company's history Howard Hughes Sr. could frequently be seen out in the shop talking with employees and observing manufacturing operations. He knew his employees by name, talked with them, showed an interest in the machining operation they performed, and often shared his favorite peach-flavored hard candy with them.[19]

Seeing Hughes in the shop, taking an interest in what they did and talking with them, made a good impression with the employees. His first group of employees, the nucleus around which the company would grow, genuinely seemed to like him. Philip Page, one of the three original black employees, remembered Hughes as "a big man, so big that you could see his greatness almost [immediately]. He had that benevolent spirit of always being ready to help someone whenever he could." At times Hughes overrode decisions by his plant superintendent William Barr over wage issues. On one occasion Barr told machinist Louie Enz that his wages were going to be cut. The next time Enz saw Hughes in the shop Hughes, apparently unaware of the pay cut, asked Enz how he was doing. Smarting from the wage reduction he replied, "Mr. Hughes I don't mind working but I don't like for my pay to be cut." Afterward, in private, Hughes confronted Barr and reinstated Enz's pay rate. The next day Barr took credit for it and told Enz, "Louie I got it all fixed. They are not going to cut your pay." Enz knew Hughes had fixed it.[20] Unfortunately, the idyllic owner-employee relationship between Hughes and his small workforce could not be sustained.

The drilling industry clamored for Hughes's rotary drilling bit, and the company was forced to hire more and more employees to meet demand. Engineers were needed to devise improvements to the original drilling bit and expand the company's product line. Superintendents and foremen were needed to maintain closer supervision and accountability over the production process. Within a few years Hughes's small family-owned manufacturing company became a large one, which he was unable to run by himself. As he hired the necessary managers and supervisors to run his expanding firm, Hughes became removed from the day-to-day operations of his plant and lost touch with his employees. As his drilling bit became increasingly important in the oil and gas

In 1912 the Hughes Tool Company (then called Sharp-Hughes) moved its manufacturing operations to this renovated Swift Company packing house at Second and Girard Streets. *Photograph courtesy of the Houston Metropolitan Research Center, Houston Public Library.*

industry, Hughes became fabulously wealthy, allowing him to indulge his flamboyant lifestyle. Hughes traveled around the country in a private railroad car on marketing trips. He entertained oil men with dinners and expensive presents and was popular with everyone.[21] Success and growth distanced Hughes from his employees and eventually led to labor troubles.

Between 1915 and 1918 Hughes Tool's workforce increased to approximately eighty-five employees in response to increased demand for drilling products and federal defense contracts to develop horizontal drilling technology to be used in trench warfare. In 1915 Hughes Tool paid a daily wage of $4 to its machinists and blacksmiths, while patternmakers received $5. The U.S. Department of Labor recognized these standards as the national benchmark for wages in those particular trades throughout American industry based on the eight-hour day. But employees in those trades at Hughes Tool worked a nine-hour day, so they earned less than the national standard. During World War I

skilled workers at Hughes Tool saw their economic situation deterio-
rate for two reasons. They worked a nine-hour day for wages based
on an eight-hour national standard, and wartime inflation eroded the
value of their earnings. Conscious of the wartime labor shortage and
fearing that employers in other Texas cities like Galveston and Beaumont who paid higher wages might lure away its skilled tradesmen,
in 1918 Hughes Tool increased daily wages to $5.80 for machinists and
blacksmiths and $6 for patternmakers. Though significant, the wage
increases fell far short of keeping pace with the wartime cost of living that jumped 106 percent between 1915 and 1918. Hughes Tool's machinists and blacksmiths would have had to earn a daily wage of $8.24
and patternmakers $10.30 to keep even with inflation.[22]

In November 1918 the National War Labor Board (NWLB) issued
a ruling, called the Macy Award, over regional disparities in wages
and cost of living that reverberated among Houston's skilled tradesmen and manufacturers. America's entry into World War I and the
need to eliminate labor unrest in defense industries had prompted
Pres. Woodrow Wilson to establish the NWLB by presidential proclamation in April 1918. He charged it with maintaining labor peace
on the home front.[23] NWLB umpire V. Everit Macy (for whom the
Macy Award was named) settled a dispute between striking New York
City marine workers and shipbuilders constructing ships under defense contracts. It established a national standard daily wage rate for
skilled craftsmen employed by defense contractors. Based on an eight-
hour day, machinists, boilermakers, and blacksmiths received $6.40
and patternmakers $6.80. This ruling superseded board policy that

TABLE 2   Daily Wage Scales for Skilled Labor in Texas Cities, ca. 1918

	Machinists	Patternmakers	Boilermakers	Blacksmiths
Beaumont	$5.80	$6.00	$5.80	$4.80
Dallas	$5.44	$5.20	$5.44	$5.44
Fort Worth	$5.44	$4.44	$5.44	$5.44
Galveston	$6.40	$7.08	$6.40	$6.40
Houston	$5.80	$6.40	$5.80	$5.80
San Antonio	$5.44	$6.00	$5.44	$5.44
Waco	$5.00	n/a	$5.00	$4.44

Salaries are based on a nine-hour workday.
SOURCE: "Do You Want Houston Put Off the Map as an Industrial City?" *Houston
Post*, January 22, 1919, p. 8

had prohibited national wage scales. Macy justified his decision by arguing that federal work was exempt from regional wage scales. He reasoned federal contracting was done on a national basis and manufacturers must not be allowed to unfairly profit during the wartime crisis through low regional wage scales.[24]

Chagrined with the NWLB and the Macy Award, many employers flaunted their principles and refused to obey their directives, resulting in thousands of strikes during the war.[25] In Houston skilled tradesmen represented by unions affiliated with the Metal Trades Council struck Hughes Tool and other Houston manufacturing firms over wages and working conditions. Following the Macy Award, the council called on Houston's employers to increase wages for machinists, blacksmiths, patternmakers, and boilermakers. Hughes Tool and sixteen other manufacturers engaged in defense work vowed not to increase wages arguing that "we are convinced that payment of wages demanded would, so much in excess of wages paid in other cities competing with Houston, seriously interfere with the growth and development of manufacturing."[26] Tensions increased between Hughes Tool's management and the metal trades unions representing its machinists, blacksmiths, and patternmakers. This is the earliest evidence of union representation at the company. The two sides deadlocked, and the Metal Trades Council requested that the NWLB send a conciliator to Houston to resolve the dispute.[27]

In early December 1918 U.S. conciliator Joseph Myers arrived in Houston. Myers met separately with representatives of the council and the companies. Union representatives agreed to accept a wage increase arbitrated by Myers even if less than that established by the Macy Award. Hughes Tool and the other companies flatly refused to consider a wage increase imposed on all the cities manufacturers imposed by a federal agency. It offended their laissez-faire sensibilities concerning labor markets. They rebuffed Myers's conciliation effort and he returned to Washington, D.C., without resolving the impasse.[28] The council had hoped that the NWLB's officiating in the dispute would persuade the employers to grant some level of wage increase, but the council overestimated the persuasive powers of the NWLB and underestimated local employers' contempt for government intervention. Moreover, the war had ended and federal coercive pressure had eased. Hughes Tool and the other manufacturers organized themselves into a coalition and pledged solidarity in refusing to grant a pay raise.[29] In this dispute the strikebreaking leadership of Houston's oligarchy passed from the Houston Business League, Citizen's Alliance, and the Light Guards to the Houston Chamber of Commerce, formed by amalgamating the three groups, and to Hughes Tool. Officials from the struck companies showed their faith in Hughes Tool's unwavering antiunionism by selecting William Childs, the company's secretary-treasurer as their spokesman.[30]

Disillusioned with the NWLB's failure to effect a settlement and seeing no other way to force a wage increase and eliminate the nine-hour day, the council called a strike of machinists, patternmakers, and blacksmiths on December 18, 1918. Between 350 and 400 tradesmen struck Hughes Tool, Reed Roller Bit, Houston Car Wheel Works, Lucey Manufacturing Company, McEvoy Company, Grant Locomotive and Car Works, and nine other manufacturing firms engaged in defense production. Approximately forty-five workers walked out at Hughes Tool curtailing, but not halting, production. About forty men stayed on the job and kept the plant operating on a limited basis.[31]

The strike dragged on through the end of December and into January. In January 1919 Houston's mayor, Earl Amerman, grew concerned over reports from the Metal Trades Council that Hughes Tool and the other firms had actively recruited strikebreakers. Mayor Amerman feared that clashes between strikers and strikebreakers would lead to violence and threaten public safety. Amerman communicated his concerns to Hughes Tool's secretary-treasurer William Childs, and Childs reassured the mayor that the manufacturers had no intention of importing strikebreakers. Mayor Amerman, in an effort to allay growing public fears of strike violence, made public a letter he wrote to Childs expressing his fears over the importation of strikebreakers: "I understand from you that the Hughes Tool Company, and . . . the other concerns involved in the metal trades strike, have no intention of importing strikebreakers. . . . [O]ur experience with professional strike-breakers convinces us that they are undesirable to have in and around any plant. . . . We are glad that no effort will be made to import such strikebreakers." Amerman also offered his services to mediate the dispute and bring it to a speedy conclusion.[32] Despite Amerman's entreaties not to import scabs and the manufacturers' pronouncement that they would not, the companies launched a two-tiered initiative to bring in strikebreakers and crafted it so they could deny their involvement.

The first initiative involved the formation of a veterans' job service by the Houston Chamber of Commerce and the struck companies. Following a meeting with manufacturers, the Chamber of Commerce issued a statement endorsed by both groups expressing their desire to find employment for servicemen discharged in Houston who wanted to make the city their permanent home. The job referral service served as an incentive to attract any serviceman discharged in Houston, not specifically Houston's hometown veterans. Employer representatives from the struck companies attending the meeting heartily endorsed the Chamber of Commerce's patriotic sense of duty in forming the job service. The representatives included William Childs of Hughes Tool, who indicated that the company needed thirty machinists and fifteen helpers; A. J. Wilson, superintendent of Lucey Manufacturing Company, who could place fifteen machinists and thirty other men; J. Dore, manager of Houston Car Wheel Company, who expressed a need for thirty machinists and ten other men; and Clarence Reed, president of Reed Roller Bit Company, who needed six machinists and six helpers.[33]

The Chamber of Commerce and the manufacturers cloaked their deceptive effort at recruiting scabs in patriotism. While they cast themselves as patriotic corporate citizens trying to express their gratitude to the returning veterans the chamber and manufacturers stigmatized the strikers as dupes of un-American outside labor agitators bent on overthrowing property rights and the social order. They warned that "affiliated floaters" belonging to the radical Industrial Workers of the World (IWW) union had misled "Houston's responsible union men" and that the floaters "are now out to wreck property and to intimidate individuals in this community."[34] As with most of the thousands of strikes that plagued the country in 1919, the IWW charges by employers nationwide and in Houston were exaggerated and meant to funnel public hysteria against Communism toward unions. Houston employers used fear of the IWW as a Red-baiting tactic to stigmatize the strike as a Communist conspiracy to destroy capitalism, distract the public away from the legitimate wage issues, and throw the council on the defensive. In the employers' view, replacing strikers with veterans was not strikebreaking on their part but a patriotic duty to purge radicals from the dispute and allow reasonable unionists to bring it to an end.

In the second initiative the companies sent their agents to northern industrial cities to recruit strikebreakers. As the strike moved into February, Hughes Tool and the other manufacturers sent labor recruiters to Chicago, Cincinnati, Pittsburgh, and St. Louis to find skilled tradesmen willing to relocate to Houston as replacement workers. The biggest difficulty faced by recruiters was finding qualified candidates since striking skilled tradesmen could not easily be replaced.[35]

Hughes Tool sent a recruiter to Chicago, and he brought back ten machinists. According to William Childs, the machinists signed an agreement with Hughes Tool stating that they understood they were coming to Houston to take the place of men on strike and they would work for the prevailing wage set prior to the strike. The strikebreakers also were told the council had not sanctioned the strike and that it was being conducted by members of the IWW. Half the men Hughes Tool brought to Houston refused to scab and signed affidavits stating that the company misrepresented the Houston strike when recruiting. Lucey Manufacturing Company interviewed a thousand applicants in Pittsburgh and hired fifty. An additional twenty-eight machinists were imported from Cincinnati. Additionally, the struck plants placed help-wanted advertisements in the *Houston Post* throughout February. Of the eighty-eight machinists brought in to Houston to break the strike only nineteen refused to cross the picket lines and returned home. Though a large number of the recruited scabs crossed the picket lines, they fell far short of the number required for the firms to reach full production.[36]

The council denounced the companies' forays into northern cities to recruit strikebreakers of questionable integrity. In a full-page advertisement in the *Houston Post* on February 26, 1919, the council blamed Hughes Tool and the other companies for recruiting shiftless unemployed "floaters" and troublemakers from northern cities to break the strike. It blamed the increasing number of confrontations on the picket lines on scabs imported by the companies. In response the companies blamed picket line confrontations on a union "educational squad" composed of fifteen irresponsible outside agitators who served on picket lines as "walking delegates" charged with stirring up acts of violence and sabotage. They ran their own advertisement in the same edition of the *Houston Post* and *Chronicle* on February 26, 1919, defending the strikebreakers as "honorably discharged soldiers, sailors, marines . . . all of whom have come here for the one purpose of re-establishing themselves in peaceful industry, grateful for the opportunity, and with the intention of making this city home."

As the strike continued on through February the council resigned itself to the National War Labor Board's failure at mediating an end to the strike but proposed a daring move to force a favorable settlement. It called on the Houston Labor and Trades Council to convene a meeting of delegates from its forty-two affiliated unions to consider calling a general sympathy strike in support of the metal trades strikers. A general strike by the Labor and Trades Council's approximately six thousand members signified a desperate gamble that could enlarge the stakes of the strike and cause irreparable damage to Houston's labor unions if it failed.[37] The purpose of the proposed general strike would be to apply pressure on Houston's nonstruck companies by shutting them down with the hope that their owners and a disgruntled public would pressure William Childs and the other manufacturers originally struck to broker a compromise settlement to end the metal trades strike. Doubtful of its success and fearful of participation by IWW radicals and a public backlash against labor, W. E. Carroll, secretary of the Houston Labor and Trades Council, voiced weak support for the initiative because it would confirm charges of IWW radicalism by the struck companies, but he was bound to allow delegates from its affiliated unions to vote. Carroll and other union leaders, whose members were under contract and not out on strike, were sensitive and protective of the good reputation enjoyed by Houston's organized workers for honoring their labor agreements.[38] They reluctantly allowed delegates to vote whether to call a general strike.

On February 18 the council's 160 delegates voted down the proposal for a general strike. After the vote the delegates adopted a proposal supporting the strike and cited their reasons for rejecting a general strike. It said in part: "The trade union movement of the city of Houston does not wish to work any hardship on the people of our city because of the failure of a few autocratic employers of labor who refuse to discuss working conditions with their employees, thus causing the present metal trades strike."[39]

Following the vote, the council's member unions did agree to assess their members a dollar-per-capita fee in order to maintain the metal workers strike fund. Both the *Houston Chronicle* and the *Post* praised the delegates' decision and editorialized that Houston's labor unions deserved the highest praise for voting down the general strike and "that organized labor in Houston is very high grade, very conscientious and disposed to be fair at all times."[40] This was not a sentiment shared by executives at Hughes Tool and the other struck manufacturers. In March, as the strike entered its third month, escalating picket line confrontations threatened to erupt into wholesale violence between strikers and scabs.

On Monday morning March 3, 1919, without provocation, strikebreakers assaulted union pickets outside the Grant Locomotive and Car Works. The uproar subsided for a time, but at quitting time, pickets armed with brickbats confronted strikebreakers leaving the plant, who in turn, hastily armed themselves with nuts and bolts. Tempers flared and a melee ensued. The pickets launched a barrage of brickbats at the strikebreakers who answered in kind with a fusillade of heavy nuts and bolts. Police managed to restore order and no arrests were made. The next day, seventy nonstriking employees at Grant Locomotive and Car Works voted to stay home until the strike was settled, and the firm's president locked the gates and shut down the plant.[41]

On Wednesday March 5, a passing car fired gunshots at approximately forty strikers on the picket line at Lucey Manufacturing Company. The shots missed and a police car posted outside the plant apprehended the vehicle. Police searched it but found no weapons and released the driver. Strikers hurled bricks at the shooter's car. They missed, but hit and damaged the one following and narrowly avoided a tragic accident. The same day police arrested Lucey's nonstriking timekeeper, M. S. Lignoski, for illegally carrying firearms outside the plant. Police also arrested one of the brick-throwing strikers. J. A. Carr, Lucey's vice president, demanded that the police provide better protection for the company's property and employees or it would petition Governor Hobby, with the other manufacturers, to send the Texas National Guard to maintain order. Carr threatened to move the company out of Houston if the authorities could not protect it from strikers' intimidation and violence. His sentiments reflected those of the other struck manufacturers and indicated the length they would go in refusing to accept the union's wage and hour demands. Conversely, the Metal Trades Council criticized the employers' intransigence and castigated the police for failing to protect strikers from outlaw strikebreakers.[42]

But violence on the picket lines, employer stubbornness over wages and hours, and employers' unity and resilience sapped the strikers' resolve. Immediately following the picket line trouble, representatives of the Metal Trades Council contacted twenty-five prominent citizens representing a cross-section of Houston's business, professional, academic, and religious communities and asked them to form a committee to "hear both sides and if our demands are found to be unfair, then we request them to determine that which would be a fair settlement to both parties." The 230 remaining strikers voted unanimously to abide by the conditions that the citizens' committee arrived at to end the strike. The committee agreed to meet with labor and management separately to hear their cases and render a decision.[43] The banker John T. Scott, serving as committee chairman, members of the Metal Trades Council, and the strikers supported open meetings. Most of the manufacturers balked when faced with making their case in a public hearing. Adolphus Grant, owner of the Grant Locomotive and Car Works where violence broke out March 3 on the picket line, voiced his refusal to abide by a committee decision handed down in a public forum. James C. Garner of the Garner Bartlett Machine Works criticized the committee's call for an open hearing and demanded a private meeting.[44]

The committee met with union representatives on Sunday, March 9, at Houston's Labor Temple in an open meeting. The union men argued that since all the struck plants were engaged in government contract work, the employers should pay the NWLB-established Macy wage for an eight-hour day. When the committee met with the employers on Monday, March 10, at Central High School, it was in executive session at the employers' insistence.[45]

Ignoring the pleas of the citizens' committee and the Metal Trades Council for an open meeting, Hughes Tool's William Childs and representatives of the other companies refused to publicly meet with the committee. Company representatives refused to allow anyone other than committee members and themselves to attend, and no written minutes were kept. Afterward, it was learned that they had issued an ultimatum to the committee stating they would not agree to the strikers' demands and listed three reasons: government contracts were secured before the Macy wage scale was adopted; higher wages reduced their competitive edge in the marketplace; and the unsettled postwar financial conditions created an uncertain economic future for the manufacturers. Hughes Tool and the others made it clear that they were unified in their position and willing to allow the strike to continue.[46]

The citizens' committee announced its decision on March 11: it recommended that the strikers should return to work. In a blow to strikers, the committee declared that the workers should receive the same daily base rate for a nine-hour day that they had received at the beginning of the strike. The committee directed the employers to reinstate 25 percent of the strikers by March 17 and another 25 percent by April 1 and not blacklist any strikers. The remaining 50 percent of the strikers would be rehired as the companies needed them. No mention was made of firing scabs to make room for returning strikers. Though the committee commended the employees and employers for their "willingness to submit the matter to a committee of disinterested citizens for revision" the ruling was a devastating defeat for the strikers.[47] The committee accepted the manufacturers' arguments in toto. Though disappointed with the decision, strikers honored their pledge and obeyed it. Considering the traditional ties between Houston's business and social elites, the citizens' committee ruling in favor of the manufacturers is not surprising. At their best both groups harbored a paternalistic attitude toward Houston's working class and at worst an autocratic one. The manufacturers' loathing for federal intervention on behalf of labor was clearly borne out when they defied the National War Labor Board's effort to mediate the strike and implement the Macy Award.[48]

Following the end of the strike, William Childs of Hughes Tool recounted to reporters his remarks to the committee. He argued that Hughes Tool's wages were too high in comparison to other Texas cities and that the company had treated its employees fairly before the strike. Childs slammed the government's effort to prevent the strike and blamed the walkout on the National War Labor Board's conciliator who stirred up trouble among employees by advocating the Macy wage scale and the eight-hour day. He vented Hughes Tool's contempt for the strikers and their union by telling the committee that "[a]t the present time [our] plant is running with a full crew and [is] employing a type of men that are not typical strikebreakers. The men would be acceptable employees in any plant and they [are] actually doing more work for the company at the present time than the men who left."[49] Dismayed that some of his skilled employees had unionized and struck, Howard Hughes Sr. introduced a labor relations policy expressly intended to guarantee a union-free work environment. He implemented the antiunion open shop American Plan used extensively by American industrialists during the postwar era. Hughes regarded it as an effective means of controlling his workforce, preventing future labor unrest, and allowing him to autocratically "iron out differences that remained after the strike."[50]

The American Plan had its origins in the antiunion open shop campaign launched by the National Association of Manufacturers (NAM) during the first decade of the twentieth century. Introduced into Houston by the city's business elite during the 1904 streetcar strike, they used it as one of their weapons to destroy the Amalgamated Association of Street Railway Employees union.[51] In Houston, and nationally, the open shop campaign initially succeeded in checking union growth, but the rising tide of political Progressivism during this era weakened it. It languished until the post–World War One reaction against wartime labor reforms resurrected it. As Progressivism subsided in the postwar period, the American plan served as an effective counterstrategy to the surge of unionization encouraged by the progressive National War Labor Board. Employers regarded the American Plan as an enlightened labor relations program that balanced managerial autocracy with paternalism.[52] Following the 1918–19 strike, Howard Hughes Sr. came to regard the plan as an effective antidote against the scourge of unionism. It called for a program of welfare capitalism designed to foster employee loyalty through fringe benefits and employee representation plans (ERPs).

Fringe benefit programs fell into two categories. One offered company-operated savings plans with high interest rates or special bonuses, home ownership plans that offered employees technical assistance and financial aid, and stock purchasing plans. The second protected workmen and their families from losses resulting from accident, illness, and death; improved plant conditions and safety; provided medical services and visiting nurses; underwrote sports programs; and provided counseling for all manner of personal problems.[53]

Employee representation plans, also commonly called company unions, emanated from the realization that granting employee benefits helped guarantee labor peace. ERPs built on company welfare programs by establishing shop committees consisting of workers elected by fellow workmen to speak for them before management. Much to the chagrin of employers during World War One, elected shop committees protected by the NWLB engaged in collective bargaining and substantially improved working conditions and wage rates. Clever industrialists noticed that ERP shop committees successfully opened a dialogue between management and labor that helped ease tensions. With the National War Labor Board's postwar demise, "industrialists gambled that employee representation plans, free of government interference, could stifle the union spirit among employees" and replace it with a company-sponsored form of collective bargaining.[54]

Employers narrowly defined the power of ERPs by excluding discussions about work processes, piece rates, job classifications, and wages from shop committee agendas. Limiting shop committees' powers made them safe from management's perspective and insured that plant affairs would be collectively controlled only up to a certain point. Management personnel supervised shop committee voting and supervisors usually qualified to serve as workers' representatives on committees. As originally designed by employers, ERPs were not regarded as collective bargaining agencies but as a practical means of giving workers contact with management. Industrialists targeted unions with ERPs and in 1918–19 numerous plans had been launched nationwide to ward off organized labor.[55] Howard Hughes Sr. embraced the open shop policies of the American plan, which was popular in the Southwest, and established a welfare program that combined fringe benefits and company unionism to thwart bona fide unionism.[56] The defeat of the metal trades strike and Howard Hughes Sr.'s open shop policies succeeded in eliminating unions at the plant throughout the 1920s and into the early 1930s.[57]

Hughes had improved the working environment prior to the 1918 strike when he moved the company from its cramped quarters on Girard and Second Streets, a former Armour meatpacking plant, to a new facility on Harrisburg Street. Workers enjoyed the latest in industrial architecture in the new plant with regard to lighting, ventilation, heating, and sanitary facilities. Following the strike, each employee received an individual locker with laundry service to wash his work clothes. Additionally, Hughes provided liability insurance for employees with a minimum of six months' service and initiated an employee loan program. He launched an athletic program with baseball, football, and volleyball teams.[58] He established his first ERP with the white Mutual Welfare Organization (MWO). Hughes Tool's white company union resembled others in that it consisted of a shop committee of elected employee representatives who could meet with Howard Hughes Sr. to settle disagreements. The shop committee's final decision-making powers rested with management since it enjoyed a majority on the nine-member committee.[59]

Hughes's version of the American plan included segregating African Americans and accommodating Houston's Jim Crow society. He denied blacks membership in the MWO and refused to formally establish a black company union. Hughes, his white managers, and white employees all tacitly understood that any type of welfare plan would exclude blacks. Management and white workers were in accord that white supremacy would be maintained at Hughes Tool and that those blacks necessary for operating the plant would not enjoy welfare benefits comparable to white workers. Blacks were excluded from the loan program and participation on athletic teams. Company policy also excluded blacks from supervisory and management positions. Except for liability insurance, all welfare benefits were exclusively for white employees.[60] Nonetheless, probably aware of the fact that Houston's black longshoremen had organized two powerful unions on the city's docks, Hughes intended to circumvent any attempt by his African American employees to organize a union.[61] Consequently, Hughes tacitly supported an initiative by them to establish their own welfare organization that was unofficially associated with the company.

In 1926 black employees Richard Guess and Joe Polk, who worked as general laborers in the company's garage, organized the Hughes Tool Colored Club (HTC) as a welfare organization for black employees.[62] Hughes Tool did not contribute or assist in the formation of the HTC. The organization had no standing in the company and did not have a shop committee that presented black concerns to management even though it did assume quasi-official status when Howard Hughes Sr. allowed it use of the company name. It provided sick benefits and extended charity to members experiencing financial hardships. Members paid monthly dues of ten cents a month and were eligible to draw six dollars per week sick benefits. Approximately a hundred blacks joined the HTC.[63] Guess and Polk promoted the unsubstantiated rumor that Howard Hughes Sr. had supported their effort to organize the HTC. According to Guess and Polk, membership meant job security since "Old Man Hughes had provided that [blacks] should keep their jobs as long as they stayed with the company union, but if they did not stay with the company union they would lose their jobs."[64]

The HTC provided management with a valuable organization in monitoring and controlling black employees. As time went on HTC president Richard Guess came to serve an increasingly important role as management's unofficial liaison with black employees. Although Guess worked as a laborer in the company's garage and company policy prohibited blacks from holding supervisory or foreman positions, he was assigned two black helpers who performed all the work while he conducted HTC business. He also closely associated himself with C. W. Rice, a staunch supporter of company unions and head of the Texas Negro Business and Laboring Men's Association. Rice advised Guess on how to organize the HTC, administer it as a black self-help association, and utilize it as an antiunion organization. Rice and Guess served important roles in promoting the antiunion, open shop philosophy among blacks at Hughes Tool.[65]

A native of Jackson, Tennessee, Rice arrived in Houston in the mid-1920s from Beaumont, Texas, where he helped establish the Texas Negro Business and Laboring Men's Association. In 1925 the organization moved its offices to Houston because of the city's centralized location, and shortly afterward Rice became its president and manager. Rice's support for company unions independent of the American Federation of Labor reflected his support for the dual concepts of self-help and racial solidarity expressed by one of America's leading black spokesmen, the late Booker T. Washington. He shared Washington's contempt of organized labor because it had systematically discriminated against blacks. When unions bothered to organize blacks they were relegated to Jim Crow locals as seen in Houston's segregated longshoremen's locals. He cautioned black workers against being "used as tools for radicals to stir up labor troubles" and asserted that "Negroes in Texas held some good jobs, especially in the industries along the Gulf Coast." Casting labor unions and strikes as radical and admonishing Houston's blacks that the city's employers had their best interests at heart, Rice endeared himself to many businessmen and industrialists. Rice's calls for black self-help, racial solidarity, and criticism of unions also had a selfish motive.[66]

As president of the Texas Negro Business and Laboring Men's Association, his accommodation of Jim Crow and opposition to bona fide unions improved his agency's chances of generating fees by placing nonunion low-wage black labor with white employers. In 1931 "[a]fter studying the Negro labor situation for many years," Rice began publishing the *Houston Negro Labor News* in response to the depression and high unemployment among the city's black working class. The paper's stated purpose was to educate them about "the grave situation which seeks to destroy the very economic foundation of society."[67] In Rice's view, labor unions posed one of the greatest threats to the economic foundation of society and along with Hughes Tool's Richard Guess he diligently propagandized against them. The two eventually became Houston's leading black voices against organized labor.

After Howard Hughes Sr. established unchallenged control over his workforce Hughes Tool experienced continual growth in physical plant and personnel that correlated to the high levels of drilling throughout the 1920s. The company introduced high pressure oil field valves into its product line, which already included a wide assortment of different size drilling and reaming bits, and tool joints. Hughes Tool also did a thriving business providing specialty steel castings for oil

The first Hughes Tool Company sales meeting in 1924. Howard Hughes Jr. is fifth from right; Col. R. C. Kuldell is third from right. *Photograph courtesy of the Houston Metropolitan Research Center, Houston Public Library.*

tool companies such as Cameron Iron Works, McEvoy Company, and others.[68]

In 1920 Hughes Tool employed two hundred people. Two years later, the company added a third shift to continue manufacturing operations around the clock during the week as well as half a day on Saturday. According to former plant superintendent Louie Enz, Hughes Tool hired so many people that it seemed like "they just came in droves," with a substantial number coming from the East Texas Piney Woods. In the early 1920s, the company hired anywhere from twenty to fifty new workers a week.[69] By 1929 the company's workforce had stabilized at approximately two thousand employees.

Howard Hughes Sr.'s business and legal sense enabled him to dominate the rotary drilling bit business. When he died unexpectedly in January, 1924, Hughes Tool's estimated worth was $2 million, and it possessed extraordinary earning potential. His death marked the end of family management, though his eighteen-year-old son, Howard Hughes Jr., inherited the company. As the son's interests gravitated to aviation and filmmaking, he delegated management of the company to his father's personal assistant, Col. Rudolph C. Kuldell, who became the firm's general manager.[70]

Born in Pittsburgh in 1889, Kuldell, who became acquainted with Howard Hughes Sr. during World War I, was a lieutenant colonel in the army corps of engineers. He graduated second in his class at West Point in 1912 and earned an advanced degree from the army-affiliated United States Engineer school in 1915. During WWI he served as the army's liaison with Hughes Tool in an attempt to develop a tunneling machine that could drill from Allied trenches through no-man's-land to German trenches. Kuldell's engineering skill and effectiveness as an organizer greatly impressed Hughes. The two men developed a close relationship and mutual respect.[71]

Hughes lured Kuldell out of the army by offering him a position as assistant to the president at a guaranteed salary of $400 a month. Hughes needed an engineer with leadership abilities, the vision to see the company's place in the oil industry, and the know-how to rationalize production and streamline operations. As assistant to the president, Kuldell was given complete freedom of movement in the plant, and he quickly gained a general knowledge of the company and its production methods. Kuldell's exceptional talents immediately became obvious as he busied himself inspecting all departments, studying their operations, formulating ways to improve productivity, and filing reports directly with Hughes. Kuldell excelled, and at the end of his first year Hughes rewarded him with a new annual salary of $6,000 and an expense account of $6,000 that included a new Studebaker automobile valued at $2,000.[72] After the death of Howard Hughes Sr., Kuldell assumed responsibility for managing the company, and it prospered.

Howard Hughes Jr. also handsomely rewarded his loyal subordinate. In 1928 Kuldell's base salary stood at $16,800, but his yearly earnings topped $305,781 thanks to a bonus of $288,981. *Forbes* magazine published a list of the fifty American executives whose salaries and bonuses exceeded all others and Kuldell's remuneration from Hughes Tool placed him forty-third. His success at Hughes Tool also brought a number of social perks. Kuldell's position gained him membership in the National Association of Manufacturers, Southern States Industrial Council, American Management Association, American Petroleum Institute, and the presidency of the Houston Chamber of Commerce. As a member of Houston's elite, Kuldell socialized with society's upper crust at the Houston country, polo, and yacht clubs.[73]

R. C. Kuldell at his desk. *Photograph courtesy of the Houston Metropolitan Research Center, Houston Public Library.*

Col. R. C. Kuldell is perhaps the least-known person among those who created the economic empire that enabled Howard Hughes Jr. to become one of the wealthiest men in the United States. The younger Hughes's enormous fortune rested on the economic foundation of the Hughes Tool Company and no one deserves more credit for creating that cornerstone than Kuldell. Under his guidance in the 1920s and 1930s the company expanded, established a near monopoly in the manufacture of rotary drilling bits, and became Houston's leading manufacturing firm. Under Kuldell's able leadership plant size increased in response to growing demand for the company's products, and he introduced the Ford method of twenty-four-hour-a-day continuous flow production.[74]

The production process began in the foundry department where alloy steels were melted in several electromelt furnaces and then poured into sand molds. The roughly shaped castings were then cleaned, excess metal ground off, and shipped to the heat treating department for proper hardening. After heat treating the parts were then moved to the appropriate shop for machining. Drill bit parts went to the rock bit division; core bits, to the core bit shop; valves, to the valve division; and tool joints, to the tool joint shop. After machining, some parts once again required heat treating. The rotary cones containing the cutter teeth required hard facing and would go to the welding department. After the parts were finished with heat treating, machining, and hard facing they were assembled. Kuldell streamlined the process and ensured that the physical layout of the plant guaranteed a smooth flow of material from one operation to another without bottlenecks.[75]

As a military man Kuldell had a general's philosophy; he believed in charge and advance to obtain results. As a member of the army's officer corps, he expected obedience from his subordinates. These attitudes influenced his relationship with employees. Kuldell shared Howard Hughes Sr.'s hostility toward labor unions, and like him he combined heavy-handed control over employees with paternalism. A believer in the open shop, he had faith in himself and in the American Plan. Under Kuldell's management the company prospered, enabling employees to enjoy steady employment and stable welfare benefits. The combination of job security, welfare benefits, management's aggressive hostility toward unions, Houston's abundant job opportunities in the 1920s, and a demoralized Houston labor movement eliminated the union threat at Hughes Tool.[76] These factors proved so effective that the white company union, the Mutual Welfare Organization, was deemed unnecessary and disbanded. Welfare benefits continued but white employees lost their collective voice, though a weak one, when the shop committee was dissolved along with the MWO.[77] The Hughes Tool Colored Club continued to function mainly because it had no official status as a company union, unlike the MWO. With the MWO's demise, Hughes Tool's first era of employee representation and company unionism ended.

In the late 1920s the prospect for uninterrupted labor peace and prosperity at Hughes Tool seemed bright. At a minimal cost in welfare benefits, management enjoyed autocratic control over a docile workforce, while Hughes Tool's near monopoly over the production of rotary drilling bits promised unlimited profits.[78] The onset of the Great Depression upset this balance. It forced Hughes Tool to drastically reduce its workforce and slash wages. An atmosphere of fear and uncertainty gripped the workforce, and Hughes Tool was once more plagued with labor unrest.

Labor at Hughes Tool, 1929–1934

HARD TIMES, JIM CROW, UNIONS, AND UNCLE SAM

THE ONSET OF THE GREAT DEPRESSION following the 1929 stock market crash upset the paternalistic management environment cultivated by Howard Hughes Sr. and Col. Rudolph Kuldell. The Depression caused a downturn in the drilling industry, forcing Hughes Tool to lay off workers and slash wages. Falling revenues also forced the curtailment of welfare benefits. Management now told employees, "you are lucky to have a job." The company's remaining workers toiled under the crushing psychological burden of imminent unemployment as they worked fewer hours and took home less money. Houston's 22 percent unemployment paled in comparison to Hughes Tool's 50 percent workforce reduction.[1]

Hughes Tool survived the Depression, in large part, at the expense of its employees. Lowered wages, reduced hours, speedups (increased production quotas), stretchouts (operating several machines simultaneously), foremen doling out work to management's favorite employees, and an increasingly autocratic managerial attitude all helped rein in costs but fostered employee restlessness, distrust, and frustration. Despite the Mutual Welfare Organization's (MWO) general powerlessness before its demise, its shop committee had acted as a safety valve in airing aggrieved employees' complaints. No such venue existed during the Depression, and employee complaints festered, causing a growing sense of resentment among a sizable number of employees.

After their defeat in the 1918–19 strike, employees at Hughes Tool abandoned their union militancy in exchange for the company's paternalistic welfare capitalism. The extraordinary expansion of the 1920s meant that relatively few of the employees in the 1930s had experienced the brief period of World War I militancy. During the 1920s, Hughes

Tool's welfare capitalism succeeded in circumventing unionization, worker discontent, and strikes in large part due to management's ability to guarantee the economic well-being of its employees in return for their loyalty and goodwill. The economic collapse of 1929 upset that status quo. The Depression ended Hughes Tool's good wages and steady employment, destroyed the social contract between the company and its employees established by welfare capitalism, and nurtured disillusionment and resentment in those not laid off.[2]

White and black employees both suffered the effects of the economic catastrophe and management's response to it. Black workers lost less because their benefits never approached the level of white employees. Hughes Tool eliminated its welfare program and the whites-only Mutual Welfare Organization. White employees who escaped layoff were subjected to intense pressures from management that included speedups, stretchouts, reduced pay, and short hours. Machine operator J. B. Harris noted that during the 1930s employee morale plummeted. Full-time employment at Hughes Tool "meant working a week, being off a week" and gave many employees a "good reason to rethink [their opposition about] joining a bona fide union." Harris's observation reflected the views of many employees who had lost faith in Hughes Tool's management during the Depression and began questioning its absolute authority over their terms of employment. For black employees who escaped layoff their traditionally inferior job status worsened.[3] In addition to reduced wages and shorter hours, management discontinued liability insurance, their only company-provided welfare benefit. But the Hughes Tool Colored Club (HTC) continued to function as a welfare organization, independent of the company, dispensing what sick benefits and charity it could to its members.

Hughes Tool and Houston had prospered in the 1920s thanks to the booming oil industry. The Great Depression devastated employment in the oil industry in general and Hughes Tool in particular. The company suffered severe financial reverses between 1929–33 primarily for three reasons: the desperate national economic situation, an oil glut exacerbated by the discovery of the huge East Texas oil field in 1930, state and federal oil prorationing designed to save the oil industry by cutting back production and bringing output in line with demand.[4] The volatility in the oil economy brought dramatic drilling cutbacks. Between 1926 and 1929 the total number of oil and gas wells drilled in the United States numbered 102,149 but in the following four years dropped to 61,024 indicating the magnitude of the nation's oil glut. Wellhead prices dropped so low in comparison to production costs that they threatened to ruin oil producers and further devastate the national economy.[5]

The oil industry's economic turmoil trickled down and ravaged Houston's economy, leading to layoffs and plant closings. In April, 1930, Houston's total number of laid-off workers stood at approximately 6,000. By January, 1931, that figure had exploded to nearly 22,300 workers, more than 22 percent of the workforce. Those who encountered the most difficulty in finding jobs were laid-off blue-collar workers, manual laborers, and in particular African Americans. Black Houstonians suffered a proportionally larger share of unemployment than whites. In February, 1931, when unemployment climbed to a staggering 29,000, 20,000 were African Americans.[6]

The Houston Chamber of Commerce's 1932 annual report downplayed the Depression's damage to the city's manufacturing sector. It optimistically proclaimed that Houston manufacturing made progress during the Depression, but the opposite was true. The number of manufacturing plants in the city dropped from 429 in 1929 to 361 in 1933.[7] Hughes Tool responded to worsening economic conditions by incrementally cutting its workforce from a peak of approximately 2,150 employees in 1929 down to 900 by 1933. Additionally, many of those who remained only worked one or two days per week.[8]

Although Houston's unemployment did not approach the levels of other cites such as Chicago with its 660,000 jobless, New York City's 1 million unemployed, or Cleveland's 50 percent unemployment, there were enough visible signs to remind Houstonians of the city's economic woes. The unemployed established Hoovervilles in present-day Memorial Park and Hoover Flats along Buffalo Bayou from Milam Street to Elder near Jefferson Davis Hospital, Depression Flats on White Oak Bayou, and the Schweikert camp in the ship channel area.[9]

By 1932, Houstonians and many other Americans looked to the federal government as their salvation from the ills of the Great Depression. In the 1932 presidential election the vast majority of Americans looked to New York's reformist governor Franklin D. Roosevelt as the doctor who could cure the country's economic ills with his unspecified New Deal for the American people. Swept into the presidency with 58 percent of the popular vote, Roosevelt received a resounding mandate for action.[10]

One of the first pieces of legislation enacted during the New Deal was the National Industrial Recovery Act (NIRA), which implemented economic and labor policies aimed at salvaging the nation's crippled industrial economy. The NIRA established the National Recovery Administration (NRA) to administer the act, and the NRA allowed industries to draft codes that established production and pricing levels without facing the threat of prosecution for antitrust violations. The NRA generously granted companies the right to collude and fix prices and production levels in an attempt to deal with the glut of industrial goods saturating the market, which depressed prices and stalled recovery. Industrialists hailed the NRA's efforts, but the NIRA also included two labor provisions meant to stabilize wages and maintain employment levels that they were not too excited about. Section 7(a) gave workers the right to organize unions without retribution from management, and section 7(b) called for minimum wage levels and maximum working hours.[11] Section 7(a) galvanized the moribund labor movement and workers nationwide, including in Houston, organized unions, and demanded recognition from their employers. Despite the NIRA's labor protections, industrialists were unwilling to stand aside and let unions undergo a renaissance. Many employers disregarded section 7(a) and persecuted employees who exerted their right to unionize. Workers responded with a flurry of strikes between 1933 and 1934 demanding union recognition in the belief that they now had the federal government on their side.

In response to the enormous number of strikes and the violence associated with many of them, Roosevelt established the National Labor Board (NLB) to serve as a referee to peacefully and equitably arbitrate the disturbances. The NLB was composed of three members each from labor and industry with Sen. Robert Wagner serving as chairman. Like the First World War's National War Labor Board, the NLB possessed no coercive powers to enforce its decisions and was forced to rely on appeals to public opinion to help discipline recalcitrant employers or failing that on the U.S. attorney general to prosecute offending companies.[12]

The NLB's most significant contribution in settling labor disputes and strikes was in its formulation of what became known as the Reading Formula. The Reading Formula established a process for terminating strikes in a fair and equitable manner. The formula forced the parties to call a truce while the NLB investigated the issues; required employers to reinstate all strikers without prejudice; provided for secret ballot union representation elections conducted by the NLB; and ordered employers to bargain with a representative selected by a majority of their employees. Union representation elections, shop floor democracy, became the essence of the NLB's approach to protecting workers' rights under section 7(a). The notion of shop floor democracy through a free election by a secret ballot and majority rule appealed to the basic fundamentals of America's democratic traditions.[13] Labor reforms brought by the NIRA, NLB, and Reading Formula energized worker militancy at Hughes Tool. In the summer of 1933, a group of white employees led by machinist P. F. Kennedy and molder W. F. Heickman formed a steering committee to organize a machinist and molders union at Hughes Tool.

They contacted Houston AFL organizer Robert Cole for assistance. With Cole's help they chartered two Hughes Tool AFL locals, IAM (International Association of Machinists) Blue Eagle Lodge No. 1303, and International Molders and Foundry Workers Union, Local No. 259. Kennedy concentrated on recruiting machine operators, machinists, and repairmen from the main machine shop, the plant's largest department, as new members of Lodge No. 1303, Heickman focused on molders and coremakers in the company's much smaller foundry department.[14] In its organizing drive at Hughes Tool, the IAM exploited employees' restlessness and abandoned its elitist tradition of only organizing skilled workers. It courted the company's hundreds of machine operators as a means of insuring victory in a National Labor Board–sponsored union certification election.[15]

Between August and November, 1933, more than six hundred employees joined Blue Eagle Lodge No. 1303. During the same period, Heickman recruited forty-four of the foundry's seventy-seven white employees into the molders union.[16] Though the IAM and the molders union broke with AFL tradition and recruited semiskilled and unskilled workers, they upheld the federation's traditional racism and denied blacks membership.

The IAM and the molders unions excluded blacks because to admit them would be, in the minds of many white employees, tantamount to admitting that African Americans shared equal status in the unions. For this reason, Houston's AFL leadership, which coordinated the Hughes Tool campaign, never considered allowing blacks membership. Class interests and class solidarity could not overcome the virulent racism that infected Houston's labor establishment.[17] Despite

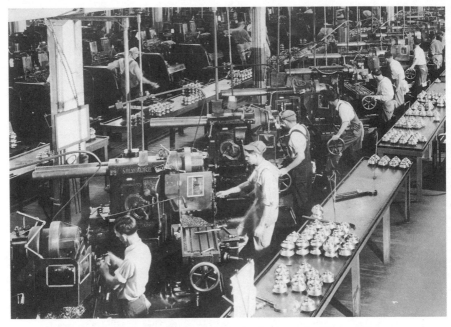

Machine operators such as these men running horizontal mills were drawn to membership in IAM Blue Eagle Lodge 1303. *Photograph courtesy of the Houston Metropolitan Research Center, Houston Public Library.*

racial discrimination that weakened the city's unions, Houston's businessmen and industrialists regarded labor's resurgence under the NIRA as a dangerous threat to their authority.

Jacob Wolters, who headed the city's National Recovery Administration committee, did not appoint a labor representative on the oil tool industry codemaking board until the AFL registered a strong complaint. When Wolters did appoint labor representative, he denied him a vote in the codemaking process. His antipathy and contempt for unions dated back to World War I when he served as a brigadier general in the Texas National Guard and strongly supported using military force to break strikes by Gulf Coast oil field workers and Galveston longshoremen.[18]

Colonel Kuldell offered a blunt and unequivocal assessment of section 7(a) in a bulletin issued to the company's employees after the IAM launched its organizing drive: "This act [NIRA] does not require, nor even encourage the organization of employee unions, especially in plants where conditions have been as satisfactory as those of the

Hughes Tool molders prepare to tap a heat from a one-ton electro-melt furnace. Men such as these served as the nucleus of International Molders and Foundry Workers, Local No. 259. *Photograph courtesy of the Houston Metropolitan Research Center, Houston Public Library.*

Hughes Tool Company, and it is the belief of the officers of the company that the employees of this company will serve their own interests to the fullest extent by reposing complete confidence in the . . . officers and executives of the Hughes Tool Company." [19] IAM official Thomas Carroll responded by pointing out that working conditions at Hughes Tool were unsatisfactory and that Kuldell's haughty attitude dismissed employee discontent and attempted to undermine their democratic right to organize. Many employees joined the IAM and Molders Union to secure a strong bargaining voice and to protest against Kuldell's violation of NRA industrial codes in rehiring laid-off workers and setting wages and working hours. [20]

From October, 1929, through August, 1933, Hughes Tool reduced its workforce from approximately twenty-one hundred to nine hundred and slashed wages 25 percent. The weekly schedule called for employees to work forty-five hours spread evenly over a five-day week.

The figures are misleading, however, since the employees frequently worked only one or two days per week and often less than nine hours per day while suffering speedups and stretchouts.[21] Between August and November, 1933, Hughes Tool implemented NRA codes governing employment, wages, and working hours for the oil tool industry, codes it helped write, and rehired approximately twelve hundred employees. But Hughes Tool, in violation of its own NRA codes, arbitrarily changed working hours, wage schedules, and shift assignments, and continued speedups and stretchouts that resulted in employees' being forced to produce more in fewer hours while their pay fell below the oil tool industry's minimum standard.[22]

Kuldell justified the company's draconian violation of the codes by stating that "although the company has had a remarkable increase in gross business" it had not recovered from the Depression and must carefully control costs to remain profitable. Union official Thomas Carroll offered a more cynical view of management's motivation: "This past summer and fall the force of workers at Hughes Tool Company was increased. This was not a benevolent gesture of the Hughes Tool Company in response to the government's recovery program, but it was to take advantage of a profitable market."[23] Renewed drilling activity stimulated demand for Hughes Tool's products and seemed to bear out Carroll's assessment. Six thousand new wells were drilled between 1933 and 1934, and this upward trend continued, surpassing pre-Depression levels by 1936. The total number of oil and gas wells drilled in 1933 stood at 12,312; by 1936 the number had increased to 25,167.[24]

Colonel Kuldell's manipulation of NRA codes and his animus toward unions reflected the policies of other Houston industrialists. They wanted to reap the benefits of the NRA's economic reforms without honoring its labor provisions. Most regarded the NRA as a temporary expedient to allow industry to rebound and offset the damaging effects of the Depression. Afterward they planned to continue business as usual. Kuldell publicly claimed that "under the terms of the National Recovery Act . . . we will give our employees every opportunity to select representatives of their own choosing."[25] He further stated that in an effort to protect his employees' right to organize, "Any employee threatening or intimidating any other employee either to join or refrain from joining any union will be discharged."[26] But his public expressions of support for the NRA's labor reforms were contradicted by his reactionary antiunion policies within the plant.

Aerial view of Hughes Tool Company plant, ca. 1930s–1940s. *Photograph courtesy of the Houston Metropolitan Research Center, Houston Public Library.*

When the AFL began its organizing drive, Kuldell posted an anti-union bulletin throughout the plant. It stated that "the fact is nonetheless real that there exists in the minds and hearts of your foremen, superintendent, manager, and general manager, an antipathy toward the professional organizer and representative." [27] Shortly after posting the bulletin, management fired IAM organizer J. W. Crittenden as a warning to employees not to join the union. [28]

AFL staff man Thomas Carroll arranged a meeting with Kuldell and tried to persuade him to reinstate Crittenden. Carroll argued that the company unfairly fired him because he had exercised his rights as an organizer. Kuldell disagreed and reminded him that company rules prohibited "union activities" on company property. Carroll responded by saying it was Kuldell's attitude, actions, and company policy that had disaffected employees and prompted them to organize. Kuldell dismissed the accusations claiming "that relations between management and employees have never been more cordial." [29]

Carroll appealed Crittenden's firing to the San Antonio Regional Labor Board in November, 1933, and argued that Hughes Tool had violated Crittenden's rights under section 7(a) by firing him for union activities. He succeeded in convincing the Labor Board that Crittenden should be reinstated and also persuaded the board that a union certification election was necessary to determine if the employees wanted independent representation. In light of the disagreement between the union and management over labor's support among the company's employees, the Labor Board ordered an election.[30] Angered over the National Labor Board ruling and the union's successful challenge to his authority, Kuldell now faced the unsavory prospect of a government-ordered union certification election on December 1, 1933, in which his employees might democratically choose union representation and repudiate the company's open shop tradition.[31] Industrial democracy under the auspices of the NLB now threatened Hughes Tool's autocratic labor relations policies.

Kuldell issued a press statement downplaying NLB inferences that Hughes Tool was suffering from labor strife. He declared that employees were satisfied with the company's implementation of NRA codes and the Labor Board had involved itself at the request of a union official "who is not a member of our organization, therefore the request for [Labor Board help] did not come from the Hughes Tool Company or any of its employees."[32] The colonel clearly wanted to stigmatize the IAM as a group of troublesome outsiders seeking to disrupt the harmonious relationship between management and its workers.

Kuldell's rhetoric embraced a democratically selected collective bargaining agent, but he took steps to insure that the employees voted for a management-approved union. In mid-November, with two weeks remaining before the scheduled NLB election, he resurrected Hughes Tool's defunct Employee Representation Plan (ERP), the Mutual Welfare Organization, to counter the IAM's organizing drive. Kuldell's decision to rejuvenate the company union was part of a national trend among America's industrialists to co-opt workers from voting for bona fide unions. Between 1933 and 1934, hundreds of company unions appeared under the auspices of the NRA. These classic ERPs were designed to allow CEOs to remain masters in their own plants and demonstrated their resolve to stay free of unions.[33] Favoring a semblance of collective bargaining with ERPs and rejecting genuine negotiations with unions, industrialists asserted that "[i]ndustry is not without experience in bargaining with American Federation of Labor unions . . . and [it] has not been conducive to satisfaction, either to employees or to management. Employee representation is a cooperative, constructive effort on the part of all employees of the company, both management and men." Industrialists bristled at critics who called ERPs company unions and rejected criticism that management controlled them and made their decisions.[34] Such industry denials, could not, however, disguise the fact that industrialists dominated most ERPs.

But company unions did indeed have an appeal for employees. Since the company paid the bills, dues were not usually required. Company unions were risk free for management and employees. Although management encouraged and in some cases coerced their employees to participate, in the eyes of many industrial workers, company unions were not necessarily less legitimate or effective than so-called bona fide unions, especially since "unlike the AFL, they did not fragment workers into arcane craft compartments."[35] Nonetheless, Kuldell faced several dilemmas in his hurried effort to reestablish the company union and defeat the AFL. The effort had to appear as an employee initiative in order to squash anticipated AFL charges that the organization was a management-dominated sham union. It needed officers and a bureaucratic structure. Finally, the membership had to be quickly recruited before the election. Kuldell found a willing ally in hourly employee E. M. Ramsey.

Ramsey, who began working at Hughes Tool in 1923, was a skilled toolmaker in the machine shop. On November 14, 1933, Ramsey wrote Kuldell a letter outlining a plan to organize a company union.[36] Ramsey's letter expressed a preference among a number of Hughes Tool's most highly skilled employees for an organization along the lines of an ERP rather than an IAM-established union. Skilled tradesmen such as Ramsey, though a minority, were an elite in the plant and exerted a measure of influence over working conditions and wages. They opposed the IAM's plan to organize unskilled, semiskilled, and skilled workers into one union, fearing that it would undermine their elite position within the plant. Ramsey and his fellow tradesmen felt that aligning themselves with management and forming a company union favorable to Kuldell would safeguard their status while still allowing unskilled and semiskilled employees into the organization. The NLB-ordered union certification election steeled them into action.[37]

The crux of Ramsey's letter was that he and a group of senior employees were interested in forming a welfare organization as an alternative to the IAM. Troubled over the IAM's increasing popularity and recruiting success, Ramsey and his associates proposed forming a welfare group that could function as a labor organization but one "more satisfactory and helpful" to Hughes Tool than the machinist's union.

Ramsey made it clear that he needed Kuldell's help in persuading employees to join and asked the colonel to endorse the EWO (Employees Welfare Organization) because what Kuldell "suggests or that they know you approve, will be a success with the majority of the personnel in the shop. So for your consideration, the following is my idea [for a welfare group] that will be of more direct help, to all Hughes employees, both financially and morally."[38] Several days after receiving the letter, Kuldell sent for Ramsey and they discussed the proposal. Kuldell told Ramsey that "the Company and I personally [have] no objection whatsoever to [you] proceeding along the line suggested in the letter." He also expressed concern over the growing IAM threat.[39]

Ramsey and seven other employees formed an organizing committee and, using a borrowed copy of the constitution and by-laws of the Southwestern Bell Telephone Workers company union as a guide, created the Employees Welfare Organization. One of its first initiatives was to segregate blacks.[40] The EWO instituted racial segregation as a means to maintain white supremacy in the workforce. Management approved of the EWO's discrimination because experience had shown that racial prejudice was profitable. Blacks had traditionally been kept in lower wage scales than whites and relegated to the most menial jobs. Excluding them from EWO membership guaranteed that they could not demand wage and working conditions comparable to those granted to white workers. Equally important, from management's standpoint, the EWO would preserve the occupational and social distance between races and make collective action difficult. Much like the AFL's racial discrimination, the EWO sanctioned it because the vast majority of whites supported it.[41] During the initial organizing work, neither Kuldell nor Ramsey considered contacting HTC president Richard Guess and suggesting that the black welfare union be rejuvenated into a company union.

The committee appointed Ramsey EWO chairman and over his signature issued a bulletin addressed "To All Hourly Employees." The notice, published at company expense, introduced the group and the reason for organizing it. Posted throughout the plant, it stated that section 7(a) granted employees the right to organize; the EWO would serve employees better than the IAM; and employees would have an opportunity to vote whether they wanted the EWO to represent them. Ramsey chose his words carefully. On the one hand, he solemnly pledged the EWO's independence from management. On the other he emphatically announced management's endorsement of the group.

The notice stated that the EWO "is not sponsored by the Hughes Tool Company, nor any officer of the Company, but has the assurance of the Company that it will cooperate with an organization of this kind in every way humanly possible as long as the officers elected are strictly Hughes Tool Company men. So let your conscience be your guide and vote for the one that you think will help you the most and not the other fellow."[42] Ignoring the bulletin's neutrality pronouncements, Ramsey and the committee embarked on a recruiting drive within the plant with management's full support and assistance.

Kuldell granted Ramsey permission to call an employee meeting in the plant's dining room to discuss the EWO and formulate its constitution and by-laws. He authorized personnel director, John "Daddy" Rohlf, to grant Ramsey and the committee two weeks' leave with pay to get the organization functioning, and also allowed Matt Boehm, general plant superintendent, to furnish them with permanent office space. Paying EWO organizers and granting them office space violated the spirit of the NIRA. The law's intention was to allow workers to organize unions free from management's influence, otherwise they could not enjoy the benefits of independent representation. On November 22, 1933, Ramsey posted a notice that all employees should attend a mandatory EWO information meeting in the dining hall after their shift on November 24.[43]

Management fully participated and pressured employees into attending the quasi-mandatory meetings. The general plant foreman Henry Hogan told his foreman to notify the men that they would knock off work early and attend the meetings while still on company time. The meetings lasted about an hour and consisted of an EWO and management propaganda blitz aimed at denigrating the IAM and persuading employees to join the EWO. Ramsey and Jimmy Delmar, the company's athletic director and personnel manager at the Hughes-owned Gulf Brewing Company, harangued the men about the many benefits that the company granted them and the importance of displaying their loyalty to Hughes Tool.[44]

Ramsey and Delmar reminded them that the company paid high wages, provided an athletic program, and arranged to sell employees gasoline at wholesale prices. In trumpeting the EWO, they argued that being a member would be cheaper than membership in the IAM with its expensive dues, that EWO funds would be readily available to members as sick benefits, and that Hughes Tool was a family and its employees were intelligent enough to represent their own interests without the help of IAM. IAM organizer P. F. Kennedy, who attended one of the meetings, objected to Delmar and Ramsey's criticisms of the machinists union and tried to respond but was not allowed to speak. Though Kennedy was "very much displeased about the remarks and considered them untrue" he and other union members were forced to listen to them.[45]

Despite the efforts of Ramsey, the organizing committee, and management, the EWO was not fully functioning by the date of the NLB union certification election. Though the EWO lacked a constitution, by-laws, elected officers, and members, and only consisted of Ramsey and the seven committeemen, the NLB's representative overseeing the election allowed it to be placed on the ballot.[46]

Labor's weekly news journal, the *Houston Labor Messenger,* responded to Hughes Tool's overt support for the EWO and hostility toward the IAM with a series of articles that leveled stinging criticism of Kuldell's labor policies. One stated that "Colonel Kuldell is a dyed-in-the-wool open-shopper and frankly admits his hatred of anything resembling a labor union. He has ruled Hughes Tool Company with an iron fist heretofore and prevented all efforts to unionize the plant. . . . The Baron of Hughes Street proclaims himself lord and master of all who seek a livelihood inside the gates of the Hughes Tool Company."[47]

The journal chronicled a litany of harassment and intimidation against union members in violation of their rights under section 7(a). It argued that Hughes Tool's six hundred union members and another four hundred expressing their sympathy substantiated reports of widespread employee dissatisfaction with Kuldell and his policies. The journal reminded readers of union organizer J. W. Crittenden, who had been unjustly fired, and the IAM's successful effort in reinstating him. The union promised employees that "[w]e the members of Blue Eagle Lodge pledge ourselves and the workers of Hughes Tool Company, whether enrolled under our banner or not, that we will faithfully promote their interests in every lawful manner."[48] The journal's broadsides against Kuldell and the company's labor policies roused a fiery response.

Resentful of both the *Labor Messenger*'s personal attacks against him and public exposure of his intimidation of union sympathizers in the week before the election, Kuldell issued two bulletins formulated to denigrate Blue Eagle Lodge No. 1303 and persuade employees to vote for the EWO. In the first, "To the Employees of Hughes Tool Company," Kuldell issued a terse appeal reminding employees that management disdained labor unions and harbored "antipathy to the professional organizer and representative." The statement also included an unsubstantiated charge that the IAM's local would cost $58,000 a year in dues to maintain and the EWO would operate for one-tenth that amount.[49] Kuldell warned employees against supporting unionists, "persons who are out of favor with your foremen and all management officials." He particularly resented their public attacks against him and his labor policies, which eliminated them from "any consideration of gentlemanly courtesy."[50] Kuldell's second statement, titled "A Farm Parable," appealed to employees' loyalty and reassured them that they could freely bring their grievances to management without fear of retribution.[51]

In both bulletins Kuldell passionately argued that his employees were extremely satisfied with management's policies and that the company's labor conditions were entirely satisfactory "to all concerned except [for a] few professional organizers." Kuldell welcomed the upcoming election between the EWO and IAM and expressed absolute confidence in his employees' loyalty. He predicted an overwhelming EWO victory on election day and arrogantly promised that he would join Blue Eagle Lodge No. 1303 if it won the election.[52]

The results of the election held on December 1, 1933, vindicated Kuldell's assessment of his employees' loyalty. The victorious EWO garnered 1,026 votes to the IAM's 602. Though disappointing for union partisans, the result demonstrated a strong core of union strength among the plant's employees, who proved willing to come forward and express their sentiments.[53] Federal protection under the NIRA's section 7(a) had emboldened IAM sympathizers to challenge Kuldell's claim that all was well under the company's open shop regime and that the election was fair.

This marked a major turning point in the labor history of Hughes Tool. Beginning with this election, union-minded employees, even in defeat, continued to challenge management's right to impose autocratic labor policies upon them. They took to heart the New Deal's promise that workers could organize and represent themselves on an equal basis with management. Moreover, Hughes Tool's unionists rejected defeatism and the company's retrograde open shop heritage, and most importantly, refused to be bound by weak-kneed collective bargaining under the auspices of a company union such as the EWO. Following the defeat, union officials appealed the results to the NLB, alleging that Kuldell and management had gerrymandered the election by creating an atmosphere of fear that coerced employees into voting for the EWO.[54]

The IAM argued that the EWO enjoyed an unfair advantage because the voting took place at the company rather than at a neutral site, Ramsey and EWO committee members served as election clerks, and management personnel presided at the polling places which influenced workers to vote for the company union.[55] While the NLB launched an investigation into the complaints, the union continued recruiting. Its determined efforts served as a reminder to "Colonel Kuldell and others who think they have broken the back of the labor movement." Hughes Tool's unionists remained optimistic considering that a year earlier Hughes Tool militantly barred unions. Union officials hoped that the NLB would invalidate the election and order another that would be closely monitored for fairness by the Labor Board.[56] Meanwhile, management and the EWO rapidly worked to consolidate their victory.

At the time of the election, technically, the EWO did not exist. Since it possessed no permanent organizational structure prior to the election, employees had actually voted for the EWO concept of company unionism rather than the organization itself. It consisted only of the organizing committee chaired by Ramsey, had no elected officers, possessed neither a constitution nor by-laws, and had no membership. Consequently, Ramsey and the committee quickly called a general meeting for December 10 to elect officers, draft a constitution and by-laws, and enlist members. Approximately 700 employees, 300 less than voted for the EWO, attended the meeting held in the shipping department.[57]

Ramsey and Jimmy Delmar, a member of management, presided over the meeting. It began with a talk by Ramsey that included drafting a formal resolution thanking management for throwing a party for the EWO the evening before the meeting. Ramsey then deferred to Delmar who guided the meeting through signing up members, distributing copies of the constitution and by-laws drafted by Ramsey and the committeemen, electing officers, and signing authorization slips for payroll deduction of membership dues. Management provided the meeting space and all the EWO's forms without charge. That, along with Jimmy Delmar's directing the meeting, clearly demonstrated management's control over the organization. Following the first meeting, regular meetings were held on the second and fourth

Sunday of the month. The company also provided permanent business offices for the EWO in the plant.[58]

A short time later Colonel Kuldell sent a letter to Ramsey and the EWO's officers for doing "a very fine piece of work" in getting the organization going but interjected a cautionary warning. He expressed management's willingness "to assist you in any way we can but the organization must remain entirely independent of control or approval of management . . . but we stand ready to give such advice or assistance as may be asked." IAM charges to the NLB that the company created, funded, and dominated the EWO prompted Kuldell's warning. The colonel's duplicity in establishing the EWO was borne out in a memo sent him from Ramsey.[59]

The memo included the EWO's financial records and expressed Ramsey's desire for Kuldell to "see what the Organization of which you and Management are directly responsible for the existence of has been doing for the welfare of the employees of the Hughes Tool Company . . . and . . . to do everything I [can] do to show my appreciation and respect and courtesy to management [for not] raising an antagonistic barrier over which to deal." Despite his rhetoric to the contrary, Kuldell clearly exerted control over the EWO through hourly employees trying to curry his favor, such as Ramsey, as well as through managers like Jimmy Delmar and shop foremen. Leaving nothing to chance, Kuldell also reconsidered his earlier decision not to form a black company union and decided to enlist black support in thwarting unionization at Hughes Tool.[60]

In January, 1934, Kuldell contacted John Rohlf, Hughes Tool's personnel director and suggested that Rohlf discuss with the HTC's president Richard Guess the possibility of converting the Hughes Tool Colored Club into a company union. Kuldell wanted "our colored employees" to "organize a welfare organization patterned somewhat along the white men's association."[61] Management wanted to convert the HTC from a black charitable organization into a company union that would serve as an effective deterrent to the threats of either black unionization or biracial unions.

Biracial unionization at a southern Jim Crow factory, though unlikely, could happen. In Alabama, where Jim Crow segregated workers, the Union of Mine, Mill, and Smelter Workers organized five thousand miners into biracial unions between 1934 and 1938. Alabama mine operators, faced with a strong biracial union, made concessions to the miners. Kuldell intended to circumvent a similar occurrence by continuing Hughes Tool's tradition of segregation in its company unions. Personnel director Rohlf contacted HTC president Richard Guess and directed him to form a committee from the HTC's membership and reorganize the group into a company union.[62]

During his eleven years at Hughes Tool and eight as HTC president, Guess had often demonstrated his loyalty to management through his support of the open shop and company unions and opposition to independent unions. Management deemed him the ideal man to head Hughes Tool's black company union because Guess could be relied upon to push antiunionism among black workers. Guess was also well known and active in Houston's black community. Besides his involvement with the HTC, Guess served as deacon and financial secretary of the Fourth Missionary Baptist Church, as a director of the Third Ward Civic Club, a board member of the colored YMCA, one of the vice presidents of the Houston Negro Chamber of Commerce, and he occasionally contributed articles to the *Houston Negro Labor News*.[63] Guess's animosity toward independent unions originated in his disgust over the AFL's racism.

In his recruiting pitch, Guess emphasized that the AFL's racial discrimination left the HTC as black workers' only medium as a collective bargaining agent. At this point in Hughes Tool's labor history, Guess rightly observed that without the HTC "there would have been no organization representing Negroes, which admitted Negroes to membership."[64] Nonetheless it did not change the fact that management dominated and interfered with the organization through Guess and the HTC's officers. Union-minded blacks from that time were skeptical of the HTC's role as an employee advocate and they regarded Guess as an Uncle Tom.[65] The difference of opinion between blacks over their role in organized labor at Hughes Tool was easily contained by management and Guess because no union in Houston, black or white, had ever dreamed of organizing its black employees. But all that changed in 1937 when the Committee of Industrial Organizations (CIO) began organizing the plant. Then the controversy erupted into a passionate, full-blown public debate within the plant and Houston's black community because for the first time a union attempting to organize Hughes Tool openly courted black support and welcomed African Americans as members.[66]

The result of the meeting between Guess and his committee included his selection as HTC president and the adoption of a constitution and by-laws patterned after the EWO. A copy of the HTC's constitution and by-laws were submitted to Kuldell for his approval. Kuldell voiced his satisfaction with the committee's work and offered his help. But just as he had done when the EWO made the same request, Kuldell refused to sign the HTC constitution. Kuldell sensed that his overt public support for either the EWO or HTC would violate section 7(a).

In April, 1934, Guess and the committee presented the constitution and by-laws to two hundred of Hughes Tool's approximately four hundred black workers at a meeting in the company's dining hall. Guess secured management's permission to use the company's facilities, and Hughes Tool furnished printed copies of membership applications, by-laws, and the constitution. Those at the meeting also approved a dues checkoff for paying monthly membership dues. Unlike the EWO's organizational meeting, no managers or foremen attended the HTC's gathering. In order to prevent any possibility of African Americans wielding power over white workers, Hughes Tool's Jim Crow policies forbade blacks from holding managerial and supervisory positions.[67]

In addition to his prominent role at Hughes Tool, Guess was an activist who enjoyed a certain measure of influence in Houston's black community. He was an associate of fellow black conservative C. W. Rice, the publisher and editor of the *Houston Negro Labor News*. Rice also served as business manager of the Texas Negro Business and Working Man's Association, a group that promoted "the industrial, commercial, financial, and agricultural development of the Negro race." It also served as a job placement service for black domestic and industrial workers. Additionally, Rice used his newspaper and the Working Man's Association as mediums to level criticism at the AFL. Like Guess, Rice opposed organized labor, except for company unions.[68] Rice and Guess became staunch allies in promoting the HTC.

Houston's African American working class held mixed opinions about Rice. While many praised him, others, especially proponents of organized labor, accused his Working Man's Association of charging excessive fees for placing workers. Blacks who regarded labor as a potential ally in empowering black workers believed that Rice regarded organized labor as a threat to his lucrative job placement service.[69]

In addition to sponsoring the black and white company unions as bulwarks against the IAM, Kuldell issued a warning to machinist union agitators who challenged the validity of the EWO's election victory. EWO vice president A. J. Keith alerted Kuldell to the IAM's agitation against the company union. Keith stated in a letter dated January 18, 1934, "We still have a few in the shop that are causing trouble, but we think that if we get the cooperation of the Company we can have everybody working in harmony. . . . Believing that these purposes could be more easily accomplished if you would make us a talk at your earliest convenience, we are writing this letter to you, asking you to make such a talk on any subject of your own choosing."[70] Five days later, Kuldell responded to Keith's request in a memorandum that was posted throughout the plant. The notice clearly stated that employees who continued to persist in favoring AFL representation jeopardized their jobs.

Although stating that employees were perfectly free to join any organization they liked, the memo warned that membership in a group that caused tensions and interfered with nonmembers was "ample grounds for dismissal." In thinly veiled anti-IAM prose, he asserted that complaints against unionists by other employees justified dismissal and "relieves management of any responsibility for continuing such undesirable persons in the employ of the company." Kuldell reminded union members of the spirit of American democracy and admonished them to accept the election results, forget their personal views, and wholeheartedly support the EWO.[71]

Meanwhile, Roger Bushfield, the secretary for the regional NLB that included Houston, conducted an investigation of the IAM's charges against Hughes Tool. He found election irregularities that violated section 7(a), including Kuldell's statements on the eve of the election that threatened discrimination against employees voting for the IAM, polling done at the plant rather than a neutral site, EWO officers serving as election officials, and shop foremen loitering at the polling places as a reminder of the company's hostility toward the IAM. Bushfield ordered a new election to be supervised by the San Antonio Regional Labor Board and scheduled it for April, 1934.[72] Kuldell indignantly replied to Bushfield's ruling: "We don't care if it was voided. We didn't care about there being an election. The NRA calls for collective bargaining, and that is agreeable to us. It does not require that the bargaining be done through a union affiliated with the American Federation of Labor."[73] His contempt for the new industrial democracy established under section 7(a) reflected the attitude of most industrialists. Though Kuldell could not ignore the NLB's order for a new election, he felt confident that his company unions would triumph once again. At the urging of Roger Bushfield, Kuldell and IAM officials agreed not to resort to underhanded tactics to influence the vote. Shortly thereafter, Kuldell broke his pledge.

In March, 1934, Kuldell announced that the company and EWO had negotiated a pay raise and eliminated stretchouts. The raise would increase wages to their peak 1929 levels, but that exceeded limits established by NRA industrial codes. The IAM regarded the announcement as a management ploy to force union opposition to the raise because it violated NRA standards. To that extent the tactic worked. The union protested the size of the raise as well as its timing seeing as it came during the preelection period in which both sides pledged not to engage in questionable tactics. Union officials also charged that the move was calculated to embellish the EWO's reputation as a strong employee bargaining agent.[74] But the company's strategy backfired.

Management had overestimated its employees' support. A significant number of employees expressed skepticism over management's motives for the raise and ending stretchouts. Management confirmed their cynicism when it reneged on the raise and the elimination of stretchouts and promptly blamed the IAM and NRA. Disgruntled employees ignored the company's version and placed the blame squarely with management.[75] One employee, angered by the company's actions and arrogance, remarked that "he had never heard of a union opposing a raise before." The damage to Hughes Tool and the EWO's credibility reached dangerous levels and EWO officials warned Kuldell that employees' anger might cause the "whole welfare plan to crumble."[76]

Employee discontent over the pay raise controversy carried over to the second election held on April 26, 1934. Conducted at Houston's Fields Lumber Company under the supervision of the San Antonio Regional Labor Board, the IAM won a substantial victory, polling 718 votes to 515 for the EWO. But following the election, Kuldell notified the Labor Board that the company would not recognize the IAM as the employees' representative and collective bargaining agent. The union appealed to the New Orleans Regional Labor Board to force Kuldell to honor the majority rule provision of section 7(a).[77]

Majority rule meant that if workers voted for an AFL or other outside union the employer was bound to deal with that union as the employees' representative. When confronted with a union electoral victory, Kuldell and other industrialists, on the advice of the National Association of Manufacturers and the National Chamber of Commerce, dodged negotiating with unions through a process of multiple representation. Multiple representation meant that management negotiated with all groups representing employees or with individual employees. It circumvented section 7(a) and worked to dilute worker solidarity.[78]

Hughes Tool defended its action by arguing that the IAM did not represent a majority of employees and that it would be unfair for the union to speak for those who opposed it. Using the election results as verification, Kuldell defended the company's position on multiple representation by claiming that the IAM's 718 votes represented only about one-third of the company's approximately two thousand employees and it would be unfair to force union representation on the remaining two-thirds. He further declared, "In view of the fact that the result of the election indicates the existence among employees of other organizations, for collective bargaining, it shall be the policy of the management to deal with individuals directly or with such organization as may choose to deal with management themselves." He bolstered his position with an unsubstantiated claim that more than seven hundred members failed to vote and if they had voted the IAM would have lost the election.[79]

Colonel Kuldell proposed establishing a workers' council comprised of eight members from the EWO and four representing the IAM. The council's proportional mix, according to Kuldell, reflected the true membership percentages for each organization. Kuldell unequivocally declared that the council would be the only collective bargaining agent that the company would recognize. Incredible as it may seem, the Labor Board accepted his proposal. It denied the IAM's demand to be recognized as the employees' collective bargaining agent.[80] Colonel Kuldell's successful defiance of section 7(a)'s majority rule provision clearly demonstrated the NLB's critical weakness. It lacked the coercive power to force recalcitrant employers to bargain with unions that won Labor Board certification elections.

When the EWO won the December, 1933, certification election, Kuldell warned IAM supporters that they must recognize the company union as their exclusive bargaining agent regardless of their personal preference. He inferred that it was un-American not to accept majority rule in democratically held elections. He quickly reversed his position when the EWO lost the second certification election held in April, 1934. Following that election Colonel Kuldell refused to recognize the IAM's victory and subverted it with multiple representation that favored the EWO.[81]

The union's standing also fell among employees because it betrayed the workers most responsible for its election victory, Hughes Tool's white semiskilled and unskilled workers. The IAM's representatives on the workers' council would only represent skilled tool room employees and machinery repairmen, who numbered approximately 150.[82] The union's behavior validated criticism from the EWO, HTC, and management that IAM Blue Eagle Lodge No. 1303 was an elitist, racist, outside organization that could not protect employees' interests. Even faithful union men acknowledged that "the AFL just did not care about the regular workers at Hughes Tool."[83]

Exploiting the IAM's weakness and the NLB's impotence, Kuldell solidified the EWO and HTC's position at the company. With the assistance of the EWO's and HTC's officers he successfully nullified the unionization threat posed by the IAM. Kuldell rewarded the EWO and HTC by ordering an increase in the amount of advice, financial aid, supplies, meeting space, and legal counsel that Hughes Tool provided them.[84] However, Kuldell's reassertion of management's autocratic control did not relieve worker discontent over wages, working conditions, and lack of representation, which had prompted employees to organize. But two important events occurred in 1935 that would upset the labor relations status quo carefully crafted by Kuldell: in July, 1935, President Roosevelt signed into law the National Labor Relations Act, commonly known as the Wagner Act, to replace the NIRA, and United Mine Workers president John L. Lewis broke from the AFL and formed the Congress of Industrial Organizations (CIO).

The Wagner Act strengthened workers' protection and the right to organize. Lewis, disgusted with the AFL's failure to organize America's workers in the mass-producing industries under the NIRA, organized the CIO and launched a new campaign to unionize industrial workers. The Wagner Act would bring the full coercive force of the federal government onto the side of workers' rights, and the CIO offered them new hope with its pledge of inclusive, biracial, industrial unionism, as opposed to the AFL's elitist, racist, craft unionism. Many Hughes Tool employees regarded the two events as a second chance to organize a bona fide union.

CHAPTER FOUR

Industrial Democracy Comes
to the Monarchy of Hughes Street

THE WAGNER ACT, THE CIO,
AND HUGHES TOOL, 1935–1940

THE WAGNER ACT irrevocably changed labor-management relations at Hughes Tool. It democratized the company's labor relations by protecting the right of employees to freely choose their representatives through NLRB-conducted union certification elections. Equally important, it outlawed company dominated unions such as the EWO and the HTC. Unlike the federal government's first two experiments with industrial democracy that failed, the First World War's National War Labor Board and the National Industrial Recovery Act, the Wagner Act succeeded in empowering workers at Hughes Tool.[1]

In March, 1934, Sen. Robert Wagner of New York, an old guard Progressive and liberal friend of labor, introduced the NLRA, commonly known as the Wagner Act. Senator Wagner drafted his labor legislation when it became evident that the NIRA had failed to protect workers and the Supreme Court would probably nullify it. In 1935, the Wagner Act passed both houses of Congress and President Roosevelt signed it into law on July 5, 1935, two months after the Supreme Court had declared the NIRA unconstitutional. The Wagner Act replaced the NIRA; it also enlarged the government's role in protecting the rights of organized labor from industrialists who were organized in powerful trade associations.[2] Wagner had designed his legislation to equalize power between labor and management so that neither side would enjoy an unfair advantage in negotiations.

The Wagner Act guaranteed workers the right to organize unions, prohibited companies from interfering with the operation of unions, outlawed employer-dominated company unions, gave the NLRB the authority to conduct union certification elections, and empowered the NLRB to enforce the provisions of the Wagner Act by taking punitive action against companies that violated the law. Though the Wagner Act codified labor law and promised industrial workers liberation from oppressive employers, it nearly failed to pass Congress when Senator Wagner suggested that it should include provisions striking down racial discrimination in labor unions.[3]

The AFL successfully lobbied Senator Wagner against including an antidiscrimination amendment. Wagner bowed to AFL pressure against racial equality out of fear that his prolabor legislation would be defeated through the efforts of organized labor. Wagner's aide Leon Keyserling remarked that "much against his will," the senator had to strike a clause prohibiting union discrimination and exclusion of blacks "in order to prevent scuttling the whole bill."[4] Though not with its author's blessing, the Wagner Act had sanctioned Jim Crow unionism.

Black civil rights organizations vigorously opposed the Wagner Act because it excluded provisions explicitly protecting blacks from racial discrimination in organized labor. The National Association for the Advancement of Colored People and the Urban League lobbied hard against its passage. At the time of the Wagner Act's passage in 1935, most unions affiliated with the AFL, except for the United Mine Workers led by John L. Lewis, enforced rigid segregation. African American opponents of the Wagner Act argued that AFL unions would use the law to establish closed shop contracts with employers that would exclude blacks from employment opportunities.[5]

Trade associations and business groups voiced nearly unanimous opposition to the Wagner Act. They branded the law as un-American and heavily biased in favor of labor. One reason they particularly despised the Wagner Act was because it outlawed employee representation plans, that is, company unions. Employers regarded company unions as effective and fair mediums for settling grievances and giving employees a say over their governance, and as a means to maintain a union-free workplace. They loathed the right of employees to vote for representatives of their choice because they did not control the process, thus the election outcomes would be uncertain. Employers denounced the Wagner Act's majority rule provision in union certification elections as "clash legislation of the worst kind."[6]

Two weeks after President Roosevelt signed the Wagner Act into law, the lawyers committee of the antiunion American Liberty League published a brief signed by fifty-eight lawyers pronouncing the Wagner Act unconstitutional. Earl Reed, chairman of the Liberty League lawyers committee, advised industrialists that "[w]hen a lawyer tells a client that a law is unconstitutional, it is then a nullity and he need no longer obey that law."[7] As the constitutionality of the Wagner Act slowly made its way to the Supreme Court between 1935 and 1937, most companies, including Hughes Tool, took Reed's astonishing advice, and ignored the law.

The Houston-based law firm of Andrews, Kelly, Kurth, and Campbell represented Hughes Tool and kept Colonel Kuldell abreast of the legal controversy surrounding the Wagner Act. Kuldell was advised to continue maintaining the company unions without any changes. The firm believed that the NLRB would not, on its own, take any action against Hughes Tool's domination of the EWO and HTC and that the AFL probably would not lodge a formal complaint. Hughes Tool's legal counsel anticipated that the Supreme Court would eventually rule the Wagner Act unconstitutional. Accordingly, Kuldell advised the EWO not to worry about its ties to management because the Labor Board "will probably never bother you."[8]

Since its inception in 1933, the EWO had kept management informed of shop floor discontent and union activity. It worked closely with management in defeating the AFL's 1933–34 organizing drive. In 1935 EWO president E. M. Ramsey thanked Kuldell for management's help in routing the AFL and for the "splendid cooperation received from you in all matters taken before you by the officers of our Organization and to assure you of our sincerest cooperation in any and all matters that might arise in the future."[9] EWO officers functioned as unofficial adjunct members of management though they retained their hourly jobs. They received time off with pay to take care of the organization's business affairs and handle what grievances employees submitted. Supervisors and foremen continued to be eligible for membership and enjoyed voting rights in the EWO.[10] Hughes Tool's white power structure excluded president Richard Guess and his fellow HTC officers from any decision-making processes in the company unions, though they received paid time off for conducting the organization's business. Management permitted Guess to serve as HTC president because of his effectiveness in monitoring black union activity and in spreading the company's antiunion propaganda to black employees. Union-minded blacks regarded Guess's behavior as management "pimping," but many were afraid to defy him for fear of losing their jobs.[11]

Management continued supplying both organizations with office space, supplies, legal advice, telephones, printing services, and a bi-weekly newspaper. Management and the EWO's domination over shop floor affairs caused growing discontent among employees who resented management's favoritism of EWO members and not having a vigorous advocate to represent them.[12] An economic downturn in 1935 heightened tensions.

Hughes Tool, like many other companies, responded to the business slump by cutting work hours. In April, 1934, the EWO and management had agreed to a system of employee seniority governing lay-offs and cutbacks, but ignored it during the 1935 downturn. Employees feared being laid off or having their hours reduced primarily on the whims of their foremen rather than on years of service and ability to perform the work. Employees frequently lost their jobs to those with fewer years' service because a junior employee happened to be the foreman's friend, relative, or because the foreman simply "didn't like the way you combed your hair."[13] The EWO registered no complaint and accepted no grievances over management's disregard of the seniority agreement. Management also made the situation worse by giving EWO members preferential treatment during the downturn.

Shop foremen received instructions to cut nonmembers hours or lay them off before selecting EWO members. W. Jones served as foreman in the machining department and gave his assistant C. Prescott an employee roster on which red Xs marked EWO members. Jones instructed Prescott to cut the hours of employees without a red X by their names. This outward show of favoritism and disregard of seniority caused bitter resentment among non-EWO members.[14]

The EWO's failure to represent employees raised the ire of members and nonmembers alike. EWO grievance men who conscientiously tried to adjust grievances, often found themselves dealing with condescending foremen who warned them against pursuing grievances too aggressively. Moreover, since Hughes Tool and the EWO did not have a contract that enunciated a grievance process, grievances were settled arbitrarily, and such settlements never established guiding precedents for resolving similar complaints in the future. The case of forge shop employee Ward Clark provides an example of the EWO's ineffective grievance procedure. Clark's case is noteworthy because he was an EWO member in good standing and served as the organization's forge shop grievance man.[15]

In 1936, Clark filed a grievance on an employee's behalf concerning wages and a promised pay raise. Failing to adjust the grievance with his foreman, J. W. Stewart, Clark went over his head and met with Colonel Kuldell where he also failed to secure an equitable settlement. But Clark's meeting with Kuldell earned his foreman's enmity. Stewart warned Clark against filing too many grievances and noted that his meeting with Colonel Kuldell made the supervisor look bad and as if he were losing control of the forge shop. Clark's boss branded him a troublemaker who was "trying to organize the boys against me." Clark retorted that it was his duty as an EWO grievance man to protect the workers he represented, and if he had wanted to organize the forge shop's employees it would be into a real union and not "the Welfare [which is] nothing but a fake union." Stewart warned Clark to be careful about voicing his union sympathies since the EWO was the only kind of union Hughes Tool would allow.[16]

Disgusted, Clark withdrew from the EWO after its officers refused to support him in the dispute. He then disassociated himself from Stewart by transferring to the foundry. After starting his new job, Clark joined the AFL's molders union, which had a small white following in the foundry department and actively recruited new members into the union.[17]

But Clark faced more trouble in the foundry. After settling in, he requested a week's vacation. Clark frankly, but foolishly, told the foundry foreman W. L. Fleming that he wanted time off "to do a little organizing, the boys here want a union." Fleming denied his request even though Clark made it clear that the organizing would be done off company property and that he was eligible for vacation. Clark's foreman retorted that "they don't need no union here, we have the Welfare, that is got good benefits, that is all we are going to have or recognize."[18] Employees wanted representation, but management's control of the EWO prevented it from being an effective employee advocate.

Employee discontent with the EWO and management's hostility to unions was also manifested in 1936 with the publication of a biweekly, underground newspaper titled the *Fighting Hughes Worker*. Published by a small group of Hughes Tool employees who were also members of the Texas Communist party, the *Fighting Hughes Worker* contained articles criticizing Kuldell, his labor policies, and management in general. Mimeographed in the home of machinist P. F. Kennedy, it was distributed at the company's gates by Communists who were not Hughes Tool employees.[19] Upon reading articles attacking him, Kuldell hired the Pinkerton Detective Agency to discover who published them and to infiltrate Hughes Tool's Communist contingent. In the past, Kuldell had used detective agencies to spy on his employees while at work and at home.[20]

The Pinkertons successfully infiltrated the group. Attending meetings at Kennedy's home, they discovered who published the *Fighting Hughes Worker* and how it was distributed. After the Pinkertons reported their findings to Kuldell, in July, 1936, he called Kennedy into his office and confronted him over his Communist activity and the newsletter. Though there is disagreement between Kuldell and Kennedy over what was actually said in the meeting, it seems that Kuldell admitted to spying on Kennedy and his group, threatened to fire him, and then stopped short when Kennedy demanded to see the Pinkerton's report to substantiate Kuldell's charges.[21] Kennedy kept his job but the record is clear that Hughes Tool paid the Pinkerton Detective Agency to spy on Kennedy and his colleagues. Although Kennedy denied being a member of the Communist party, following the incident the AFL discharged him.[22]

In 1937, Hughes Tool had to confront two threats to its autocratic labor relations policy: the Supreme Court validated the Wagner Act and the CIO launched an organizing campaign. Colonel Kuldell posted bulletins notifying employees of the Supreme Court's decision. He assured employees that they faced no discrimination due to union membership and that the company had never engaged in the unfair labor practices outlawed by the Wagner Act. But Kuldell's major concern in 1937, much like the majority of American industrialists, was the CIO.[23] The CIO, founded by United Mine Workers president John L. Lewis in October, 1935, coupled with the Wagner Act, posed a serious threat to management's hegemony over its workers. The CIO's guiding principles were the radical ideals of industrial and interracial unionism.

The CIO's philosophy advocated organizing workers into one big union plantwide and eventually industrywide regardless of occupation. Known as industrial unionism the goal was to empower workers by using their collective strength and combining the unskilled, semiskilled, and skilled workers into the same union, for example, to organize all workers in the steel industry regardless of occupation and demand the same reforms for all steelworkers regardless of the steel company that employed them. The same held true for the auto, rubber, and America's other basic industries. This differed dramatically from the AFL's elitist approach of organizing only skilled tradesmen and ignoring the unskilled and semiskilled workers. The weakness of the AFL's approach can be seen in the failure of the machinist and molders' unions at Hughes Tool. Before the 1930s, attempts at industrial unionism by the Knights of Labor, Eugene Debs's American Railway Union, and the Industrial Workers of the World had all failed. But a combination of Lewis's drive and charisma, coupled with the Wagner Act, allowed the CIO to flourish where the others had failed.[24] The CIO's racial egalitarianism stemmed from altruism and practicality.

John L. Lewis supported civil rights and promoted black membership in the CIO. He earned the respect of black leaders and spokesmen by insisting that African American workers be organized on an equal basis with whites. But he had a practical reason for welcoming blacks into the CIO. The CIO also embraced interracial unionism as a practical matter because of the large numbers of black workers toiling in the mass-producing industries. As victims of organized labor's traditional racism in the past, African Americans had often willingly served as strikebreakers and Lewis wanted to eliminate that threat to the CIO by welcoming blacks into the union. They were also potential votes in union certification elections.[25] The CIO needed black support but it also hedged on its commitment to racial equality. The CIO regarded blacks as workers needing union representation first and victims of racial discrimination second. In making their pitch to industrial workers, union organizers often minimized the CIO's racial egalitarianism, except when addressing African Americans.[26]

In July, 1936, Lewis formed the Steel Workers Organizing Committee (SWOC) of the CIO. The SWOC headed by UMW vice president Philip Murray, organized steelworkers in Pennsylvania, Ohio, Illinois, and Alabama. Its greatest triumph came on March 1, 1937, when U.S. Steel, America's bastion of the open shop, signed a collective bargaining agreement with the union that won workers a 10 percent wage increase, a forty-hour week, and union recognition. The SWOC's triumph at U.S. Steel was the high-water mark of the union's 1937 organizing campaign. Though the SWOC was a direct arm of the CIO, members referred to their union as the CIO, not SWOC.[27]

The CIO subsequently sent organizers to Houston. In April, 1937, the CIO's SWOC chartered Local No. 1742 at Hughes Tool. Between 1937 and 1939, the CIO attempted to recruit whites and blacks into Local No. 1742 and resisted pressure from white workers who called for a separate local for blacks. The issue of segregation seriously hampered the CIO's organizing efforts. During this two-year period, the CIO recruited approximately 425 workers from among Hughes Tool's nearly 3,000 hourly employees. Many white workers sympathetic to the CIO's class issues refused to join because of the union's biracial philosophy.[28]

The CIO's opposition to race-based discrimination cast it in a favorable light in Houston's black community, and the union actively tried to establish bridges to Houston's black working class. Though the mainstream white press was relatively indifferent to the CIO's activities in Houston between 1937 and 1939, African Americans stayed well informed about the union's activities through community events and Houston's black newspapers. For example, in May, 1937, the Houston chapter of the NAACP sponsored an open labor forum at the Antioch Baptist Church. Representatives from the CIO and the AFL extolled the advantages of their respective unions. The CIO spokesman, Roy Sessions, declared that his union offered blacks the best opportunity to better conditions in the workplace. AFL representative George Wilson's remarks received a cool reception since blacks were well acquainted with the AFL's record of racial discrimination.[29]

C. W. Rice, the publisher of the *Houston Negro Labor News* and an ardent supporter of the Hughes Tool Colored Club (HTC), spoke in favor of independent unions. He challenged the CIO's assertion that it was the best labor organization to represent blacks at Hughes Tool. Rice warned the audience that both union spokesmen were ignorant of the workings of their respective unions. He advised the audience to be cautious of the AFL and CIO and questioned their motivation for wanting to save the Negro worker.[30] In previous speeches, Rice had criticized the CIO and dismissed its official policy of racial equality and warned that the union was "too young and controversial for Negro workers to accept for their only salvation."[31] He suggested that black workers should form their own organizations and then bargain with their employers. He opposed black participation in organized labor based on the AFL's record of racial discrimination in its numerous Houston locals. Rice also implied that blacks who joined the CIO would probably lose their jobs if the union negotiated closed shop agreements with employers. Correctly pointing out that "thousands of Negro workers [were] overworked and underpaid and have no redress," he accurately prophesied that the CIO could not be trusted to protect black working-class interests.[32]

Rice and Carter Wesley, a strong supporter of the CIO and publisher of Houston's leading black newspaper, the *Informer,* became bitter enemies as they debated over which labor union best served the interests of black workers. Considering his paper the official black voice for organized labor in Texas, Wesley used it as a platform to support the CIO and criticize Rice. In an editorial directed against Rice, Wesley denounced "narrow-brained Negroes who argue that the Negroes should not join the AFL or the CIO." Wesley supported the CIO because it was making an effort to organize a biracial union at Hughes Tool. He appeared willing to give the CIO a chance, because the only other union alternative for blacks at Hughes Tool was the HTC. Moreover, Wesley noted that C. W. Rice and Richard Guess, president of the HTC, were quick to denigrate racism in organized labor but were conspicuously silent concerning Hughes Tool's racism.[33] In addition to carrying the burden of integration, the CIO faced management-directed attacks from supervisors, foremen, and the EWO.

Colonel Kuldell wanted to smash the CIO before it attracted a loyal following. Between May, 1937, and April, 1939, Kuldell collaborated closely with EWO president E. M. Ramsey and his successor, Clarence Ramby, in using the EWO as an employee spy network, a medium to disseminate company propaganda, and a tool to discredit the CIO. Additionally, Colonel Kuldell encouraged Ramsey and later Ramby to collaborate with other Houston-area company unions in perfecting strategies and techniques in order to present a unified anti-CIO front throughout Texas' upper Gulf Coast industries.

Acting on Kuldell's advice, Ramsey collaborated with W. A. Thomas, a company union activist working in Humble Oil's massive refinery at Baytown, Texas, who had orchestrated that company's successful anti-CIO campaign. Thomas helped Ramsey secure copies of literature opposing both the CIO and the Wagner Act, and briefed him on how he and fifty other loyal employees formed Humble Oil's company union, the Employees Federation, and used it to defeat the CIO's organizing drive at the refinery.[34] Kuldell and Ramsey recognized that Thomas had defeated the CIO by making the victory seem to be a groundswell of employee loyalty to the company. In fact, the CIO's defeat resulted from collusion between management and the Employees Federation, employee intimidation, and a smear campaign of Red-baiting and race-baiting.[35]

Ramsey's meeting with Thomas produced a Houston-based anti-CIO company union coalition called the American Association of Independent Labor Unions (AAILU) dedicated to "sane and sensible means of settling any issue between employees and employers." The AAILU included company unions from Hughes Tool; Humble Oil; the

Texas Company; Crown Central Petroleum; Jefferson Lake Oil Company; three soft drink bottling companies, Coca Cola, Nehi, and Barq's; Southwestern Bell Telephone Employees' Union; and the Western Union Employees Union. Ramsey served as its president, and under his leadership the members networked, lobbied politicians in Austin, and promoted "matters affecting general policies of independent unions in the State of Texas."[36]

The EWO inundated employees with anti-CIO and anti–Wagner Act literature. In May, 1937, Kuldell granted the EWO permission to distribute pamphlets, secured with the help of the AAILU, at all plant gates and clock houses. One such pamphlet, *What the Supreme Court Does Not Require,* was published by the national lawyers committee of the American Liberty League and lambasted the Wagner Act's unconstitutionality. One by the American Iron and Steel Institute, *The Men Who Make Steel,* was a highly partisan work extolling company unions over professional labor organizations. The last, published by the anti-union Constitutional Educational League and titled *Join the CIO and Help Build a Soviet America,* branded John L. Lewis a Communist and CIO membership as un-American. The distribution of such literature violated the company's stated policy prohibiting soliciting and hand-billing by special interest groups on company property. Nonetheless, all employees received copies while clocking in or out. At the same time Houstonian Vance Muse, a fundamentalist right-wing Christian preacher and cofounder of the reactionary antilabor and anti–civil rights group the Christian American Association, joined Hughes Tool's campaign against the CIO.[37]

The Christian American Association called for the twelve-hour workday, six days a week, and less pay for overtime. It opposed the CIO as a "dangerous subversive organization" that embraced socialistic labor reforms, Communism, and racial mixing.[38] As the self-professed protector of the American worker, Muse warned Hughes Tool's workers that if the CIO triumphed at Hughes Tool it would bring socialism and force "white men and women into organizations with black African apes whom they shall have to call brother or lose their jobs." Management issued no disclaimers to Muses's charges. Muse and his group also served industry's interest by vigorously supporting rabid antilabor Texas politicians such as Rep. Martin Dies and Gov. W. Lee O'Daniel and restrictive labor legislation.[39]

Acting on the advice of Hughes Tool's legal counsel, Kuldell informed the EWO how to avoid NLRB scrutiny. He listed five questions that must be answered in the affirmative if an organization claimed to be a bona fide union: Do the members of the organization pay dues? Does the organization hold regular membership meetings? Has it written agreements with the company? Does it have contract with other working organizations? Has it the right to demand arbitration of differences whereby management abandons absolute veto power?[40] Kuldell's list neglected to mention that a contract was supposed to be the result of collective bargaining and that real unions selected their own leaders by majority vote. The EWO did not even meet the last three criteria on the stunted list, although Kuldell assured the EWO that it met all five requirements.

Kuldell also listed the characteristics of an illegal union: The employer has taken an active part in forming the organization. The company has suggested the form of the constitution. A few picked employees have been urged to create the organization. Management has been both willing and eager to sign agreements with the organization it helped create. Membership is automatic as soon as a worker is hired. Foremen have brought pressure on employees to join. The company union is praised by officials and given a printed publication, credit for settling grievances, establishing recreation facilities, and so on.[41] Hughes Tool violated all except making membership automatic at the time an employee was hired. Sensitive to the CIO's aggressive nature in bringing charges against illegal company unions to the Labor Board, Kuldell decided to enter into a formal written agreement with the EWO and HTC and make them appear to be bona fide unions independent of management. Management drafted the agreement and submitted it to Ramsey and the HTC's Richard Guess for their ratification.

Signed in July, 1937, the quasi contract recognized the company unions as the exclusive collective bargaining agents for its white and black employees. Employees knew nothing about the agreement making the EWO and HTC their collective bargaining agent until it went into effect on October 1, 1937. They were denied a voice in its formulation and a ratification vote.[42]

The agreement, Hughes Tool's first published labor accord, gave the appearance of a negotiated contract between management and its company unions. Kuldell's recognition of the EWO and HTC as exclusive collecting bargaining agents for white and black employees broke with management's historical commitment to the open shop. He defended his action by claiming that since a substantial number of employees belonged to the company unions, the Wagner Act required him to bargain with them exclusively.[43] But Kuldell had recognized them without an election to validate that they represented a majority of employees, a direct violation of the Wagner Act.[44]

The document granted management control over major labor issues: the production process, grievance procedure, seniority, wages, and recognition. Management retained control over the production process by allowing it to set piecework rates. Workers could appeal to the EWO's executive committee if they felt the company's production rates were excessive, but the committee, staffed by Hughes Tool's hand-picked men, often sided with management in supporting speedups and stretchouts.[45]

The grievance procedure allowed workers who felt they had been treated unfairly under the rules and regulations of the company to file complaints. But the agreement did not list the company's rules and regulations nor a step-by-step grievance procedure, making the so-called grievance process a farce. Refusing to establish seniority rules because they would "break Hughes Tool," management maintained arbitrary control over seniority rights. In the event of layoffs, Hughes Tool reserved the right to handpick individuals, regardless of seniority or ability, and keep them on the job. Equally important, the agreement excluded a detailed job classification system and rates of pay for various jobs, major components of any legitimate collective bargaining agreement.[46] Following execution of the agreement, Kuldell directed his managers, at various times, to post notices instructing employees that all grievances must be handled through the EWO. Kuldell warned in one plantwide bulletin that any employee who does not use the "usual channels" for grievances, namely the EWO, "cannot long continue in the employ of the company."[47]

The agreement also codified Hughes Tool's racist labor relations for the first time. The agreement excluded all mention of wages except to say, "The minimum beginners wage for semi-skilled (white) men is forty-five cents (45¢) per hour; for unskilled (black) men, forty cents (40¢) per hour." Moreover, blacks had to wait two years for a five-hundred-dollar insurance policy while newly hired whites received a one-thousand-dollar policy after six months. The agreement's racist nature also manifested itself in the EWO executive committee, which was given the power to negotiate all labor matters with management. The agreement thus rendered the HTC powerless and validated Hughes Tool's traditional policy of white supremacy by excluding the black company union from negotiations and forcing it to negotiate through the EWO. The EWO exercised full veto power over any HTC proposals.[48]

Hughes Tool's recognition and domination of the EWO and HTC and its quasi contract with them denigrated the spirit of industrial democracy inherent in the Wagner Act. Nonetheless, Hughes Tool's company union proved popular among a large number of employees who opposed the CIO. Many employees rejected the CIO because of its racial policy or the Red-baiting campaign waged against it. The formation of the American Association of Independent Labor Unions, and the creation of the EWO and HTC at Hughes Tool, reflected a broad movement on the Upper Texas Gulf Coast by employers to find a CIO alternative and maintain a management-based, procompany approach to labor relations.[49] Hughes Tool recognized the value of the EWO and HTC as an employee rallying point against the CIO and a means for maintaining autocratic control over its workforce. Kuldell also used the EWO as an employee spy network and encouraged its officers to identify CIO members and report their activities to management.

In May, 1938, Clarence Ramby reported the recruiting activities of three CIO men to personnel director John "Daddy" Rohlf. Ramby informed Rohlf that the CIO men had been recruiting on company property during working hours and it was disrupting production in the machine shop department.[50] The Wagner Act protected the right to organize but it did not specify where or when. At this time, Hughes Tool did not have a specific policy prohibiting union recruiting. Since its inception, the EWO had recruited on company property during working hours with management's approval; CIO organizers were merely following that precedent. Nonetheless, Rohlf called the men into his office and confronted them over Ramby's allegations. When asked to reveal his source, Rohlf glibly replied, "You know, you boys know how that is, just through the grapevine."[51]

J. C. Caffal, one of the CIO men, reminded Rohlf that the Wagner Act gave them the right to organize without management harassment. Rohlf retorted that the Wagner Act favored labor unions and company policy superseded federal law. He sent them on their way with a warning: "I want it to be known that the company will not keep a man that goes through the plant talking union." Rohlf passed their names on to Kuldell with a note saying that he had "talked to these men" about their union activities.[52] While CIO unionists faced harassment for organizing, management encouraged supervisors and foremen to actively recruit EWO members.

Setup man "Honey Bear" Steinman, a supervisor and EWO member, approached machine operator Irving Tuck several times while on the job and tried to pressure him into joining the company union. Tuck refused, telling Steinman that he had joined the CIO because management's domination of the EWO made it useless as an employee advocate. Tuck defended the CIO and told Steinman that it "would do the American working class a lot of good." Steinman warned Tuck, "You ought to be very careful about what you get into out here" and suggested that Tuck should read *Join the CIO and Help Build a Soviet America* and the *Fighting Hughes Worker*.[53] Tuck had read them both and rejected the former's Red-baiting and the latter's anticapitalism, and he told Steinman that he could make up his own mind without the help of pamphlets. Following the confrontation, Tuck faced increased hostility from his setup man for "talking CIO" on the job.[54]

Tuck had helped charter CIO Local No. 1742 and served on its grievance committee. Though Hughes Tool had promised that it would deal with all employee representatives regardless of affiliation, management snubbed the CIO's grievance men. After Kuldell recognized the EWO and HTC as exclusive employee collective bargaining agents it proved impossible for CIO members to have their grievances adjusted. Shortly after the CIO received its charter, the grievance committee met with plant superintendent Matt Boehm.[55]

During the meeting they identified their responsibilities as CIO grievance men and informed him they had a number of CIO grievances they wanted to discuss with him. Boehm refused to recognize their official status. Instead, he lectured them on the foolishness of being in the CIO. He told them they should try and "boost production and study how to make ourselves better workman rather than taking up labor matters." Boehm also inferred that they were dupes for big shot labor bosses whose only concern was to enrich themselves by squeezing members for dues payments. Shortly after meeting with Boehm, the committee called on Colonel Kuldell and attempted to persuade him to recognize them as CIO grievance men. Rather than recognizing their status, Kuldell launched into a tirade about the CIO's Communist connection at Hughes Tool. Kuldell confronted the committeemen with a copy of the *Fighting Hughes Worker* and ridiculed the union for granting its publishers' membership. The colonel slammed Hughes Tool's CIO local for tolerating Communism and refused to recognize the committee as a legitimate employee representative.[56]

CIO members C. D. Wilson, and his older brother, Nathan, were warned by the general foreman Henry "Hy" Hogan to be careful about associating with the Communist-dominated CIO. Hogan warned the Wilsons that "they better not get caught talking CIO on the job." Hogan's warning came in part because the Wilsons were vocal critics of the EWO. Nathan had been an EWO member in the early 1930s, but he withdrew when he realized it was a sham dominated by management. When C. D. began his forty-four year career at Hughes Tool in 1936, he did not join the EWO because Nathan had "wised him up about the company union." C. D. Wilson recalled that during the late 1930s, "If you were sympathetic to the [CIO] the foreman would try to hide behind columns and keep an eye on you while you were working. I didn't care, I wore my [CIO] button because I believed it was my right."[57]

Management also launched a systematic crusade to intimidate CIO shop stewards. The CIO's shop stewards served critically important leadership roles as the union's immediate shop floor representatives. They were highly visible people who served as grievance men and were responsible for collecting union dues. CIO shop stewards encountered enormous difficulties collecting dues from members and often had to resort to dues picket lines outside the plant to collect delinquent dues from members entering or leaving the plant.[58] CIO organizer David McDonald characterized the dilemma that Hughes Tool shop stewards faced by observing that steelworkers would "go out and die for the union in the excitement of the picket line, but they'll be damned if they'll pay another dollar to that 'lousy shop steward.'"[59] Kuldell, who knew of the CIO's difficulty in collecting dues and remaining solvent, sanctioned management's harassment of CIO shop stewards. At the same time, Kuldell denied a CIO request to have dues collected through payroll deduction, a service provided to the EWO and HTC since 1933.[60]

CIO shop stewards faced pressure from their foremen to stop collecting union dues on company property.[61] Their bosses warned them to stop wearing their union steward badges on the job or face being fired. Wearing steward badges in the plant identified them as CIO officials so that union members could recognize their grievance men and also know who was authorized to collect dues. While on the job, their setup men, foremen, and EWO loyalists attempted to persuade them to quit the union and join the EWO. They warned the CIO men that wearing their steward badges put them "on the spot" with management and they better be careful with their union activities.[62] Some shop stewards joined the EWO to cover themselves while continuing their CIO activities in secret. J. B. Harris joined the company union because he "felt a little fear" and "kept riding the [EWO] until I felt all fear of being discharged was over." Targeting CIO shop stewards brought a measure of success in discouraging employees contemplating CIO membership. Welder E. E. Jeter, though sympathetic to the CIO, would not publicly "associate with them because I was afraid" of management retribution.[63]

An economic downturn between 1937 and 1939 offered management one last opportunity to purge the CIO from Hughes Tool. Caused primarily by President Roosevelt's drastic withdrawal of federal funding for relief projects, the "Roosevelt recession" plunged the country's economy back into a depression. The stock market collapsed in August, 1937, and by March, 1938, unemployment climbed to 20 percent. The recession hampered CIO organizing work between 1937 and 1940 and halted its national momentum. But the union also scored its first victory at Hughes Tool during this period.[64]

Between March and May, 1939, management laid off four hundred employees, orchestrating the layoffs in such a way that they affected younger employees who were the CIO's support base.[65] Management recognized no seniority rules in its 1937 labor agreement with the EWO and HTC and continued that policy when it renewed the agreement in March, 1939. When CIO members filed grievances over being unfairly laid off, Clarence Ramby ignored them.[66] Frustrated, CIO chief grievance man Woody Clayton tried to meet with Tom Mobley, Hughes Tool's personnel director, in hopes of persuading him to recall CIO members unfairly laid off. After Mobley refused to see him, in July, 1939, Clayton took the matter over Mobley's head and arranged a meeting with Stanley Brown, Hughes Tool's new general manager.

Brown had succeeded Kuldell as the head of Hughes Tool after the colonel unexpectedly announced his retirement in July, 1939. Many CIO loyalists regarded Brown as a fair-minded, progressive, and enlightened manager.[67] An executive in the sales division, Brown seemed unaffected by the company's ongoing labor upheavals. Whether Brown agreed to meet the committee out of an idealistic sense of fairness or over concern for a pending Labor Board investigation against the company initiated by the CIO is not clear. Regardless of motivation, Brown's meeting with Clayton and the CIO's grievance committee earned him the respect of CIO members.[68]

Clayton persuaded Brown that management had unfairly targeted

CIO members in the layoff and persuaded him to reinstate sixty CIO members. Though not all CIO members were recalled, Clayton's success and the Labor Board's ongoing investigation of Hughes Tool emboldened many more employees to publicly support the CIO by becoming members. Nonetheless, due to management's unrelenting pressure against it, the CIO measured recruiting success in small increments. At the end of 1939 the CIO mustered only 425 dues-paying members. Management eventually recalled all the laid off employees by the spring of 1941 when the company expanded in order to fill military contracts during the pre–World War II defense buildup.[69]

Woody Clayton's success in reinstating sixty laid off CIO members had raised the union's standing among employees, but not enough to offset management's actions against it. Hughes Tool's continued domination and manipulation of its company unions, which the Wagner Act outlawed, undermined the CIO's recruiting efforts. Frustrated, the CIO filed unfair labor charges against Hughes Tool with the Labor Board in June, 1939.[70]

The CIO's unfair labor charges against Hughes Tool reflected a key part of its overall strategy in confronting antiunion employers who used company-dominated unions to thwart organizing drives. Between 1937 and 1939, the CIO filed numerous charges against companies claiming that their company unions interfered with their employees' right to freely choose their own representatives without management interference. The NLRB found that unions dominated by management were often used to spy on employees and intimidate CIO members. The Labor Board disestablished numerous company unions to stop illegal and unfair labor practices. The rulings represented critically important CIO legal victories that energized its organizational drives, and the union used them in the face of Hughes Tool's onslaught against it.[71]

The CIO's case revolved around the EWO and HTC and rested on allegations that Hughes Tool's company unions primarily served as company-driven antiunion organizations and only secondarily as employee representatives. The charges specified that management guaranteed their existence through preferential treatment, financial support, legal advice, free office and meeting space, office supplies, and the publication of a biweekly newspaper. The NLRB conducted its hearing from July 17 to July 26 and from September 8 to September 14, 1939. Hughes Tool found itself in the dock and in the unprecedented position of having its labor relations policy opened to public scrutiny.[72]

Sensing the loss of absolute power over its labor relations and fearing that the Labor Board would probably substantiate the charges, Hughes Tool distanced itself from the charges by abandoning those most responsible for them, Colonel Kuldell and the company unions.

On July 17, 1939, the first day of the hearing, Kuldell surprised everyone, except Hughes Tool's attorneys, by announcing that he had retired from the company. Appearing as the Labor Board's first witness, Kuldell immediately revealed that he had resigned as president and general manager of Hughes Tool effective April 1, 1939. When asked by Labor Board attorney Nat Wells if he had any connection to the company Kuldell replied, "No, sir, not at all. I have retired."[73] Vice President Stanley Brown had replaced Kuldell, though Brown was gravely ill with pleurisy and died in August. Kuldell's sudden revelation at the beginning of the hearing instantly removed from scrutiny the person who seemed most responsible for orchestrating Hughes Tool's virulent antiunionism, creating the EWO and HTC, and directing the attack against the CIO. Kuldell's abrupt departure served to absolve Hughes Tool of responsibility for its actions since he no longer directed the company and appeared at the hearing as a private citizen unconnected with the company.[74] The company took the position that it could not be held responsible for Kuldell's actions while he was in charge.

Though the company shared an important stake in the hearing, it was the EWO and HTC that were fighting for survival, not Hughes Tool. The worst that Hughes Tool could suffer from the hearing was the disestablishment of its company unions. But company union loyalists faced the loss of their organizations and favored status with management. Hughes Tool's attorneys, William M. Streetman and Tom Mobley, for the most part played a passive role in the hearing except to argue that the company bargained in good faith with the EWO and HTC and executed two contracts with them, and that Hughes Tool had not violated the Wagner Act.

Attorney Tom Davis represented the EWO and HTC and upon his shoulders fell the responsibility of proving that his clients were bona fide unions as defined by the Wagner Act. Davis focused his defense around three issues: management treated the CIO and AFL the same as the EWO and HTC; the Labor Board favored the CIO over other unions, which disqualified it as an impartial arbitrator of labor disputes; and the vast majority of employees favored the EWO and HTC and the Labor Board should conduct a certification election to settle the dispute.[75]

Labor Board attorney Nat Wells focused his case against the EWO and HTC around several issues: Hughes Tool's domination of the EWO and HTC; providing them offices and meeting rooms, office supplies, and administrative support, and financial aid; cosigning for EWO bank loans; and intimidating the CIO. Wells called Colonel Kuldell and a series of employees as witnesses. Using their testimony, he chronicled the evolution of the company's open shop philosophy, formation and domination of the EWO and HTC, management's disregard of the NIRA and the Wagner Act, flaunting workers' rights protected under the NIRA and Wagner Act, domination of the company unions, and its collusion with the EWO and HTC to drive the CIO from Hughes Tool.

The testimony revealed that the company had continued to dominate the EWO and HTC following passage of the Wagner Act and after its validation by the U.S. Supreme Court. It became clear that Kuldell relied on the EWO's officers and the 215 managers, foremen, and supervisors holding membership to discourage organizing efforts.[76] Kuldell's policy defied the spirit and intention of the Wagner Act and denied his employees the right to freely choose their own representatives. Rather than divesting itself from the EWO and HTC following validation of the Wagner Act, management expanded their role in the company's anti-CIO campaign.

Kuldell, John Rohlf, and EWO officials all testified that the company's agreements with the EWO and HTC, first negotiated in 1937 and renewed in 1939, demonstrated that the company unions and management "bargained at arms length" and represented bona fide labor agreements. They argued that the negotiations took weeks and that the EWO and management had engaged in the normal give-and-take process of contract talks and that at one point they stalled and the EWO threatened to strike.[77] In a memorandum, Kuldell told Ramsey and Guess that the agreements simply articulated labor policies that had proven their worth over the years and had worked "to the satisfaction of all concerned." The agreements also recognized the EWO and HTC as the exclusive collective bargaining agents at Hughes Tool, but no evidence was produced to show that they represented a majority of employees between 1937 and 1939.[78] Wells painstakingly brought all this out, building his case that the agreements were shams that gave the appearance of contracts while in essence merely validated rules that had always been company policy.

The trial examiner William Webb played a critical role in the proceedings. The NLRB in Washington had empowered him to conduct the hearing, gather testimony and evidence, and use the data to determine if Hughes Tool dominated the EWO and HTC and violated the Wagner Act. If Webb so determined, he was required to recommend appropriate punitive action against Hughes Tool and its company unions to the NLRB in Washington. During the two weeks of testimony, Webb queried Nat Wells, Tom Davis, and William M. Streetman over management's association with the EWO and HTC and their responsibilities under the law.

A crucial factor in Labor Board attorney Wells's case that sparked particular interest in Labor Board Trial Examiner Webb was bank president John Scott's testimony concerning loans made to the EWO by his bank. Scott served as president of the First National Bank, which handled Hughes Tool's account. The EWO did its banking with the South Texas Commercial National Bank.[79]

Webb took particular interest in Kuldell and Scott's relationship in insuring the EWO's economic survival. On the morning that Scott testified, he perjured himself by denying that he had spoken to Kuldell about an EWO loan application. Unconvinced by Scott's morning testimony, Wells subpoenaed bank records during the noon recess that showed Scott's involvement in the loan process. Scott had initially disapproved the unsecured EWO loan. But after realizing that the organization was associated with Hughes Tool, he telephoned his friend Colonel Kuldell who told Scott that the EWO was "all right and that the bank would be safe making a thousand-dollar loan and that he would personally see that they paid it back." On the reassurance of his Galveston Bay neighbor and friend, and not the EWO's ability to repay the loan, Scott approved the application.[80]

Shortly after receiving the first loan, the EWO requested that the loan be increased to three thousand dollars. Once again, after conferring with Kuldell, Scott granted a thousand-dollar increase after the colonel recommended "that probably they could get along on less." In 1938 and 1939 the First National Bank continued to make loans to the EWO.[81]

When bank officials informed Scott that Wells had inquired about securing the loan records, Scott returned to the hearing that afternoon and corrected his earlier statement. Retaking the stand, Scott still maintained that "I have no recollection of having telephoned Colonel

Kuldell about the thousand dollar loan" but bank officials "far more careful than I was produced records showing [I] did." The record clearly showed that Scott had talked to Kuldell about the loan and then approved it.[82]

Scott's testimony severely damaged Tom Davis's defense because it directly linked management's financial support to the EWO. The testimony seemed to catch Davis off guard. He did his best to minimize the damage, but from that point onward his argument that management supported all labor organizations equally fell apart.[83] It also seems likely that Kuldell's backing of the EWO loans forced his retirement, since it directly linked company support to the EWO, a clear violation of the Wagner Act. Davis cut his losses on the issue and moved on to other arguments.

Davis's attack on the credibility and unfairness of the NLRB echoed that of many American industrialists, who criticized the Labor Board as being the complainant, prosecutor, and judge in labor disputes and complained that the Wagner Act gave it dictatorial powers over industry. They argued that labor's right to brand employer practices as unfair without a corresponding right to label union practices as unfair smacked of labor favoritism by the federal government.[84] The AFL also attacked the Labor Board for its alleged pro-CIO leanings. The AFL charged that the Labor Board's application of the Wagner Act would destroy its craft unions in the mass-producing industries where craftsmen were outnumbered by the semiskilled and unskilled workers who favored the CIO's industrial unionism.[85] Davis lashed out at the Labor Board's unfairness arguing that "[i]n this case the Board has consistently refused to place anything in evidence that would be favorable to the EWO. In fact, the NLRB constitutes itself as grand jury, judge, jury, and appellate court in labor matters."[86] The basis of Davis's fury was that the Labor Board provided Nat Wells to argue the CIO's case before Trial Examiner Webb. It irked Davis that the CIO had no lawyer and that Wells argued its case. Davis slammed the hearing's format saying that "the best attorney you can think of having is the attorney on the same payroll as the people who are ultimately going to decide the case."[87] His rancor found basis in fact.

Between 1937, when the Wagner Act was validated, and 1941, the NLRB and its staff ruled in the CIO's favor in a majority of cases. Part of the reason for this was the Labor Board's own internal troubles: funds were short; the predominantly young, inexperienced staff was sometimes injudicious; and the NLRB's first members had little intellectual distinction. But to overcome and neutralize the historic hard practices of antiunion American employers, Labor Board attorneys aggressively prosecuted their cases on behalf of American workers. Overall, the short-staffed and underfunded agency put out an enormous amount of work and succeeded in evolving the common law of the Wagner Act concerning industry's use of company unions, espionage, provocateurs, strikebreakers, private police, and the stockpiling of munitions.[88]

In his third line of defense, Davis attempted to convince Trial Examiner Webb that "one of the ultimate issues in this case is whether the employees of the Hughes Tool Company joined the EWO . . . of their own free will." Davis argued that if employees joined the EWO and the HTC of their own free will, then the NLRB did not have the authority to order them dissolved, even if it appeared that both organizations received assistance from Hughes Tool. The only just means to settle the dispute between the CIO and company unions would be to conduct a representation election.[89] To that end, Davis presented in evidence authorization cards signed by EWO members and HTC members. Webb allowed Davis to develop his argument and admitted the authorizations as evidence but chastised Davis for his timing and their relevance to the case.

Davis composed the authorization cards two weeks before the hearing started, and EWO and HTC officers hurriedly collected the signatures before Webb began hearing testimony. The EWO collected 1,396 signed authorization cards and the HTC 611. But the cards had been collected long after the charges were filed, making them irrelevant to the case, and none of them had been checked against Hughes Tool's rolls to verify employment. Webb instructed Davis that under these circumstances the authorization cards did not meet the standards necessary for the Labor Board to call an election.[90]

Davis had pushed Ramby and Guess to collect the signatures in order to have them included in the record and prove that employees overwhelmingly supported the company unions. He doubted that Webb's handling of the hearing was legal and wanted the cards entered as evidence in anticipation of an appeal to the federal appellate court. Wells rebuked Davis's defense and his criticism of the Labor Board. He counseled Davis that his only business in the hearing was to address whether or not the management dominated the EWO and HTC, not to establish how many employees were members.[91]

Trial Examiner Webb concluded the hearing on September 14, 1939.

Tom Davis moved to dismiss the complaint against the EWO and HTC, as did Hughes Tool's William M. Streetman. Both attorneys argued that there was insufficient proof to sustain the charges and that they should be dropped. Webb denied their motions, adjourned the meeting, and retired to consider the evidence gathered.[92]

In his intermediate report to the NLRB issued on February 12, 1940, Webb found that Hughes Tool had violated the Wagner Act by dominating the EWO and HTC, which in turn interfered with its employees' right to free association and independent representation. He based his decision on Hughes Tool's initiative in starting the organization, management's solicitation of membership, employees' lack of opportunity to accept or reject establishment of the organizations, management's attitude toward the CIO, management's linkage to financial and other support, and the participation of supervisors in the affairs of the EWO.[93]

Webb's report recommended that Hughes Tool immediately end its domination of the EWO and HTC, nullify its labor agreement with the company unions, and stop interfering with its employees in selecting their representatives. To implement his recommendations Webb suggested that the following actions be taken: management should withdraw recognition of the EWO and HTC as bargaining agents, reimburse EWO and HTC dues money collected through payroll deduction since July 5, 1935, and post notices in the plant for sixty days listing Webb's recommendations and remedies.[94] It would take time before the Labor Board rendered its decision on Webb's intermediate report, in the interim period, Hughes Tool appealed Webb's report directly to the Labor Board in Washington.

On April 25, 1940, William M. Streetman, Hughes Tool's attorney, appeared before the three-member NLRB and pleaded that the charges be dropped. Streetman refuted the allegation that management had dominated the EWO and HTC and asserted that dues reimbursement was impossible. Streetman argued that the company's "development of labor policies and handling of labor has been a continual one" and that "we are still learning" to adjust to the industrial democracy granted by the Wagner Act. Chairman J. Warren Madden seemed most concerned about Hughes Tool's traditional hostility toward unions and why management had interfered with employees who had chosen to join the CIO. Streetman replied that between 1933 and 1939 as labor law evolved, former president Kuldell had "[tried] to do the right thing and properly interpret the law, and obey the law in letter and spirit."[95]

Madden reminded Streetman that in 1933 Colonel Kuldell posted a bulletin stating, "Whether justified or not, the fact is nonetheless real that there exists in the minds of foreman, superintendents, manager, and general manager an antipathy toward the professional organizer and representative." "I do not see," said Madden, "how you can claim that there was anything neutral about that attitude."[96] Tom Davis did not appeal Webb's intermediate report, but EWO president Clarence Ramby made his position clear.

Ramby rejected Webb's report, reminding members that it did not have the force of law. Only the NLRB could issue an order forcing the EWO and Hughes Tool to comply with Webb's findings. Until that happened, Ramby vowed that the EWO would honor its labor agreement with Hughes Tool.[97] Hughes Tool did not act on Webb's recommendations either, guaranteeing that the NLRB would review the case and issue an order. A Labor Board decision and order could have been avoided simply by disestablishing the EWO and HTC.

Many employers disestablished their company unions in a preemptive move to avoid Labor Board hearings or when facing an unfavorable NLRB decision. When employers disestablished company unions that had large memberships, the former company unionists often formed independent unions, gathered signed authorization cards, verified them with management rosters, and petitioned the Labor Board for a representation election. The CIO questioned the legitimacy of the hastily formed independent unions and noted that they usually had the same officers, structure, assets, and employer favoritism of the defunct company unions. Despite the controversy surrounding the new independent unions, the Labor Board recognized the vast majority of them as labor organizations within the meaning of the Wagner Act, and the majority of company unions made the switch to independent unions by 1940.[98]

Humble Oil followed this strategy and disestablished its company union, the Joint Conference, before the CIO filed charges. The Joint Conference's large membership promptly formed a new independent union called the Employees Federation, voted it their representative, and defeated a CIO organizing drive.[99] It is surprising that Hughes Tool and the EWO did not initiate the same process since it had worked at Humble Oil's Baytown refinery, especially since during the hearing it came to light that Humble's Employee Federation and the EWO coordinated their anti-CIO campaigns.[100] On the contrary, while waiting for the Labor Board's decision, Hughes Tool and its company unions signed a new labor agreement on March 1, 1940. The new agreement resembled the 1937 and 1939 agreements with one major difference, it contained the company's first public listing of job titles and hourly pay rates. This marked a major reform. Hughes Tool had never before published its pay scales or paid uniform rates for individual job classifications, although unequal pay differentials and promotional ladders based on race remained in effect.[101]

On October 14, 1940, the NLRB ruled that Hughes Tool had dominated and interfered with the administration of the EWO and HTC, and it rejected claims by management that Hughes Tool maintained a policy of strict impartiality toward all labor organizations in the plant. It ordered Hughes Tool to stop interfering with its employees' right to organize, to nullify the EWO and HTC labor agreement, and to collectively bargain with representatives freely chosen by its employees. It required the company to withdraw its recognition of the EWO and HTC and disestablish them, reimburse all dues money paid by members through payroll deduction since July 5, 1935, and immediately post throughout the plant for sixty days the NLRB's decision and order.[102] Hughes Tool requested permission to adopt the provisions of the 1940 contract as the company's labor policy. The NLRB and the Fifth U.S. Circuit Court of Appeals consented, since the removal of the company unions abrogated the agreement and the document no longer enjoyed the force of contract.[103]

Officials and members of the EWO and HTC expressed considerable outrage over the NLRB decision. They believed that the Labor Board unjustly dissolved their organizations and showed favoritism for the CIO throughout the ordeal. Company union sympathizers also feared that the favorable ruling for the CIO threatened their jobs. Management fanned their fears by declaring that it "would just as soon close the company and let the NLRB give 4,000 men employment."[104] Former officers and members of the company unions urged workers not already in the CIO to refrain from joining. Their exhortations were not particularly effective: CIO membership jumped from 740 at the time of the decision to 1,065 in the following six months.[105]

The favorable CIO ruling in the case was a watershed in Hughes Tool's labor history. The decision ended thirty years of management's autocratic control; Hughes Tool no longer wielded absolute power over its workers. Under the Wagner Act, employees and the federal government now had a voice in shop floor affairs. The Labor Board's decision insured that industrial unionism would become a permanent part of Hughes Tool's environment. Management faced the unprecedented prospect of having to share power with its employees in formulating labor relations policies and negotiating contracts.

Hughes Tool had difficulty in adjusting to the Wagner Act's industrial democracy. This was evident in the plea of Hughes Tool's attorney, William M. Streetman, to the Labor Board. Streetman told the board that management was "trying to do the right thing and properly interpret the law, and properly obey the law in letter and in spirit."[106] Streetman and management were trying to adjust to the new balance of power at Hughes Tool, but they had no experience with industrial democracy, and proved unwilling to surrender management prerogatives to employees without a fight. On the other hand, employees exploited their new power under the Wagner Act, and not necessarily in the CIO's favor.

Resentment against the CIO created an ideal atmosphere for EWO and HTC partisans to organize an independent union. Authorization cards, presented as evidence by attorney Tom Davis during the Labor Board hearing, indicated that an overwhelming majority of employees favored the company unions over the CIO. The Wagner Act guaranteed them the right to organize a union unaffiliated with the CIO or AFL. In late 1940, the disaffected company unionists formed the Independent Metal Workers (IMW) Union. The IMW attracted an enthusiastic following and devoted itself to four things: recruiting a majority of employees, maintaining Jim Crow unionism, winning the collective bargaining rights through a representation election, and purging the CIO from Hughes Tool. The IMW sharply criticized the CIO's call for racial equality, and race eclipsed class as the major battleground between the two unions. The following chapter examines how race dominated the struggle between the IMW and CIO.

CHAPTER FIVE

Jim Crow Wearing Steel-Toed Shoes and Safety Glasses

HUGHES TOOL'S RACE-BASED UNIONISM, 1940–1943

LABOR RELATIONS AT HUGHES TOOL entered a transitional period following the Labor Board's dissolution, in October, 1941, of its company unions, the Employees Welfare Organization and Hughes Tool Colored Club. The company lost two allies in its campaign against the CIO, but company union loyalists formed the Independent Metal Workers Union to replace them. The IMW, a single-firm union associated with the Confederated Unions of America (CUA), established a strong foothold at Hughes Tool in late 1940. Though it distanced itself from management, many CIO loyalists regarded it as merely a new version of the defunct EWO and HTC.[1] More importantly for the CIO, the IMW stood as the only obstacle in its way to eventually securing the collective bargaining rights at Hughes Tool.

IMW unionists claimed they spurned the CIO because they believed that "big shot labor dictators and their stooges" dominated the union.[2] They trumpeted the IMW's loose affiliation with the CUA and its unique status as a union that existed only at Hughes Tool. As such, the IMW was supposedly keenly aware of employees' needs, attitudes, and customs, and was best suited to represent them. IMW officers promised strong union representation that would bring fair and equitable labor agreements without introducing radical notions such as the CIO's interracial unionism.[3] The IMW's constitution established two racially segregated locals. It mandated that "Local No. 1 shall have complete, final and exclusive authority to negotiate [for] all white employees. . . . Local No. 2 shall have complete, final and exclusive authority to negotiate [for] all colored employees. Each Local shall have full authority to handle its own affairs without interference from the other Local."[4]

The Wagner Act allowed the IMW to maintain Hughes Tool's traditional Jim Crow unionism, while at the same time empowering it to democratically seek the bargaining rights through a Labor Board certification election. Although the IMW and the CIO discriminated, to varying degrees, against blacks at Hughes Tool, African Americans represented an important voting bloc and had the power to determine the outcome of any election. Both unions lobbied hard for their support.

Former EWO president Clarence Ramby formed a steering committee to organize IMW Local No. 1. Between August and December, 1940, it worked to "form a union of their own choice for the purpose of collective bargaining, grievances, wages, working conditions, and so forth." Local No. 1 quickly attracted a loyal following; by early 1941 it had recruited more than 1,300 members. Many had been members of the EWO.[5] Richard Guess, former HTC president, volunteered to form a committee and organize IMW Local No. 2, the Jim Crow local. On November 10, 1940, more than 200 blacks, out of the 806 employed by Hughes Tool at the time, attended an organizational meeting, formed a union, and agreed to affiliate with the white local.[6] It is unclear how many of the HTC's former 611 members joined Local No. 2.[7]

Local No. 1's steering committee decided to affiliate with the Confederated Unions of America, which was a loose confederation of independent unions. The CUA was modeled after the CIO and AFL but had several important differences: it maintained no full-time staff, did not provide help to its affiliated unions in negotiating contracts, had no legal department, did not have a strike fund, and collected a 2 percent per capita tax to fund itself. The CUA's tax system allowed 98 percent of Local No. 1's dues money to remain in its Houston bank account.[8] In comparison, the highly bureaucratic International CIO collected a 75 percent per capita tax from Hughes Tool Local No. 1742. Only 25 percent of Local No. 1742's dues money stayed in its Houston bank account; the balance was transferred to the International CIO's Pittsburgh treasury to fund national organizing campaigns, legal counsel, salaries, and a strike fund.[9] The CUA was segregated and refused to charter IMW Local No. 2 or allow it an affiliation. African Americans in Local No. 2 voted to affiliate with the Confederation of Independent Unions. The Confederation of Independent Unions was a Jim Crow labor organization similar to the CUA.[10] Led by Ramby and Guess, the IMW's steering committees came out in support of Hughes Tool's Jim

One of the jobs reserved for blacks only, charging reheat furnaces in the forge shop. *Photograph courtesy of the Houston Metropolitan Research Center, Houston Public Library.*

Crow labor policy that had formerly been part of its contract with the EWO and HTC.

The provisions of that contract regarded the EWO and HTC as two separate entities, though they executed a joint contract that codified the company's Jim Crow labor relations policy. Management endorsed Jim Crow because experience had demonstrated that Hughes Tool's color barrier helped undermine union solidarity along racial lines and also provided the company with a relatively cheap pool of black workers reserved for the hottest, dirtiest, and most menial jobs in the plant.[11]

Though blacks comprised 25 percent of Hughes Tool's workforce and worked in all six of the company's major departments, they could hold only a limited range of jobs.[12] In 1940, blacks could work in only 26 of the company's 270 hourly job categories, and company policy mandated: "We don't use colored employees to perform work that white employees perform and we don't use white employees to perform the work that colored employees perform."[13] The company di-

TABLE 3   Hughes Tool Company, Segregated Pay Grades and Pay Scales,
Effective May 1, 1941

Department	No. of Pay Grades, White	Pay Scales, White (per hour)	No. of Pay Grades, Black	Pay Scales, Black (per hour)
Machine Shop	6	$.65–1.28	3	$.48–.62
Pattern Shop	4	$.80–1.30	1	$.54
Foundry	4	$.80–1.00	3	$.48–.60
Heat Treat	1	$1.08	2	$.54–.60
Shipping	3	$.74–.87	3	$.48–.62
Storeroom	n/a	n/a	3	$.48–.62

SOURCE: Contract between the Employees Welfare Organization and the
H.T.C. Club of the Hughes Tool Company and the Hughes Tool Company,
Houston Plant, 1940–41, NARACP, RNLRB, RG 25, CF 3066, "Official Report
of Proceedings before the National Labor Relations Board: In the Matter of
Hughes Tool Company and Independent Metal Workers Union, Locals Nos. 1
and 2," Exhibit B-5.

vided its six production units—machine shop, pattern shop, foundry,
heat treat, shipping, and storeroom—into pay brackets based on occupation. Black pay scales peaked below the lowest white levels. Whites
also enjoyed more numerous pay brackets covering a much wider
range of pay, allowing them opportunities for advancement. Segregated from whites by occupation, blacks performed unskilled and menial tasks. Throughout all six departments blacks were required to
address Hughes Tool's whites, regardless of age or occupation, with the
formal greeting "Mister." Whites commonly addressed blacks by last
name or "boy," though "nigger" was frequently used.[14]

In the machine shop department, 424 blacks served as common laborers pulling metal chips, handling material, doing all the heavy lifting, fetching and carrying, and cleaning, while whites operated all machines. One black employee's duty consisted of simply washing
"spittoons." The highest-paid white occupations in the machine shop,
such as tool room mechanics (tool and die makers), and machine rebuilders, received 66 cents per hour more than the highest paid blacks
in the department, a 103 percent differential.[15] Moreover, white tool
room mechanics and machine rebuilders enjoyed the prestige, perks,
and autonomy that come with being skilled tradesmen.

The 163 blacks in the heat treat department and the 129 in the foundry performed the heaviest work and toiled in the hottest jobs in the plant. In heat treat, they worked in the "hot box gang," which was responsible for charging and emptying parts from furnaces, in which temperatures ranged from 1700 to 2500 degrees F.[16] They also performed all cleanup duties. In the foundry, blacks charged electric furnaces in which temperatures reached more than 2900 degrees and performed all the heavy carrying, material handling, and cleanup for white melters, molders, ladlemen, and core makers.[17]

The 25 blacks in the shipping department and 63 in receiving handled material, did heavy lifting, and all cleanup. The one black assigned to the pattern shop was responsible for moving materials and for cleaning machines, work areas, and the locker room, and he served white workers as a general handyman.[18] The white-dominated occupational hierarchy guaranteed that blacks served secondary, though necessary, unskilled or semiskilled functions throughout the plant.

While the IMW adopted Hughes Tool's traditional Jim Crow segregation, it diligently tried to remain aloof from Hughes Tool's management. Former officers of the EWO who served as IMW organizers fastidiously avoided contact with management to forestall accusations by the CIO that Hughes Tool had anything to do with forming the new union. They retained Tom Davis, the EWO and HTC's former attorney, to compose the union's constitution and by-laws so the organization would meet the requirements of a labor union articulated in the Wagner Act.[19] Nonetheless, Davis cautioned the committee that "whenever a new independent [union] follows one that has been disestablished," even if it meets Wagner Act standards, the CIO will accuse it of being company dominated. Davis expressed his doubts about the new union's viability because of the Labor Board's apparent hostility to independent unions. Davis told Local No. 1's organizing committee that "[t]he attitude of the Labor Board toward an Independent [union] was hostile and it had to be clean as a whistle to have a chance to live, the people who had anything to do with the [EWO] would have to have hands off on the formation of a new one."[20] IMW organizers, for the most part, heeded Davis's advice. Shortly after the union was formed, the membership elected officers who had never held office in the company unions, although they had been members.[21] The only exception was former HTC president Richard Guess, who was appointed Local No. 2's business agent. Shortly after the IMW was formed, Clarence Ramby, former EWO president and IMW charter member, accepted a position with management as the assistant personnel director of Hughes Tool's Aircraft Strut Plant.[22]

The IMW had quickly established itself as a labor union and in the process kept its relationship with Hughes Tool formal and limited to labor matters. But a controversy arose over how the IMW had funded its organizing campaign. Former EWO member and IMW organizer H. T. Abbey related that in the late summer of 1940, EWO president Clarence Ramby called him into the organization's office in the plant and asked him to help organize the new union. Abbey agreed and worked hard for a time as a recruiter but eventually he quit because "things were happening that looked quite funny to me."[23] Abbey suspected that Ramby and the EWO's treasurer were funneling money from the organization's bank account into a secret fund to finance the IMW.

When the NLRB disestablished the EWO and HTC on October 14, 1940, it ordered that all dues money collected from payroll deductions since July 5, 1935, be reimbursed to the members. At the time of the Labor Board decision the EWO had $96,000 on deposit and the HTC $33,000.[24] According to membership figures presented at the hearing, the EWO had 1,396 members and the HTC 611.[25] The Labor Board recognized those figures as official, accordingly each EWO member should have been reimbursed $69 and HTC members should have received $59. But each white received $2.05 while black company unionists were issued checks for $2.18. The balance of the money disappeared and never was accounted for.[26]

Abbey had been asked to cash an EWO check by R. W. Harrup the organization's secretary and then bring the money back to Harrup. He received the check in an envelope that bore his name. When Abbey took it, he noticed a stack of envelopes with other people's names on Harrup's desk. Shortly after the check-cashing incident, Clarence Ramby formed the IMW steering committee, funded its educational committee, retained Tom Davis's legal services, rented office space for the IMW across the street from the plant, and began paying organizers' expenses. Abbey believed, although it was never proven, that the EWO had funded all these IMW initiatives with money that had been earmarked for refunds.[27]

After the disestablishment of the EWO and HTC, Abbey received his $2.05 reimbursement check and concluded that Ramby and the other EWO officers had embezzled the remaining funds from the membership. When Abbey confronted Ramby over his suspicion, Ramby dismissed his accusation by saying that the money had somehow been stolen from the account and no more could be paid. Abbey agreed with the first part of Ramby's reply, but called him a "damned liar" over the second. Frustrated, Abbey quit the IMW and joined the CIO.[28]

Richard Guess oversaw the dispersal of the HTC's funds. George Duncan, a former HTC activist, accused Guess and the HTC treasurer, Philip Page, of drawing down the organizations $33,000 bank account while the Labor Board conducted its hearing and during the interim period before the NLRB issued its intermediate report. Duncan, along with IMW Local No. 2 organizer Ernest Martin, suspected that Guess siphoned the money to C. W. Rice, the publisher of the *Houston Negro Labor News*.[29] Rice, a staunch supporter of the defunct HTC and the new IMW, allegedly channeled the money into organizing the IMW.

Guess and Rice strongly supported the IMW, worked to recruit black members, and denigrated the CIO. Using Rice's paper as a platform, Guess argued that since 1937 Hughes Tool's blacks had opposed the CIO and the union would be nothing but trouble for African Americans. In an article in the *Houston Negro Labor News*, Guess defended the IMW's Jim Crow unionism by stating, "The work done by the Negroes [at Hughes Tool] is of a different nature from that done by the white men, and it is entirely appropriate to place them in a separate unit so they could bargain for themselves."[30] Guess saw no reason for blacks to turn their "[dues] money and affairs" over to strangers in the CIO. He urged African Americans to stick with the IMW and urged them to exercise their rights under the Wagner Act and vote against the CIO.[31]

Rice frequently wrote editorials against the CIO. He was a Booker T. Washington accommodationist. Rice believed that the CIO's calls for racial equality would lead to agitation between the races, with dire consequences for blacks. Rice urged blacks to reject the CIO and said that "Negroes in the South can best improve their conditions through the formula handed down by Booker T. Washington nearly fifty years ago, that is, to make friends with the white people in their respective communities, and win their confidence through the practices of honesty, intelligence, thrift, sane and sober living."[32] He condemned "white CIO bosses" for exploiting racial prejudice as a ploy to win black support in union certification elections and to bilk them for union dues.[33]

Rice based his criticism of the CIO on the AFL's record of racial discrimination. Rice often reminded his readers that the AFL, a large national labor organization, discriminated against tens of thousands of black craftsmen by denying them membership and claimed that the CIO, another national labor organization, would discriminate against blacks in the mass-producing industries.[34] He dismissed the CIO's rhetoric of racial equality and warned, "Where contracts have been entered into with the CIO, it is found that a differential wage scale exists with white workers, legislating Negroes out of jobs they formerly held." Rice championed the IMW because it was independent of the AFL and CIO. He admired and supported Richard Guess and black IMW members because they understood that at Hughes Tool "racial progress must be made by evolution rather than revolution."[35]

Carter Wesley, publisher of Houston's leading black newspaper, the *Informer,* and Robert Grovey, who owned a barber shop on Dowling Street and served as president of the Third Ward Civic Club, supported the CIO and countered Guess's and Rice's attacks against the union.[36] Wesley often questioned Rice's and Guess's motives for supporting racist independent unions. He editorialized that "[l]ike all men who have no justification for their acts, Messrs. Rice and Guess are attempting to confuse the issue. Rice organizes company unions for the purpose of ingratiating himself into the good graces of employers and has no sincere intentions of fighting for the rights of Negro employees."[37]

Grovey also engaged in a running battle of words with Rice and Guess over the CIO. He regarded them as the "master enemy of Negro workers," who sought to advance themselves at the expense of other blacks. Grovey believed that the CIO's national clout, with several million members and considerable financial assets, could promote and protect black interests better than the IMW, with its fewer than two thousand members and its avowed commitment to Jim Crow.[38] Grovey suggested that "[t]he question of Negroes organizing independent unions is unsound. He is the minority in industry and in no way can organize plants where he will become the bargaining agent. Therefore, at present, an independent union can only become a specific Negro set-up dominated by those who hire the Negro." He urged blacks to do the "logical thing" and join a bona fide union, such as the CIO.[39] But in accepting the CIO, Grovey and Wesley both downplayed its racism.

They served as apologists for the CIO in much the same way that Guess and Rice did for the IMW. All four made excuses for their particular unions' white supremacy and Jim Crow unionism. Rice published numerous articles in the *Houston Negro Labor News* that attacked the CIO's racism, while Wesley's *Houston Informer* responded in kind against the IMW. Neither Rice or Wesley would promote the fact that all labor unions, whether independent, CIO, or AFL, treated blacks as second-class unionists unworthy of parity with whites.

The CIO promised blacks racial equality because it desperately needed their votes if it hoped to win a certification election at Hughes Tool. Evidence at the Labor Board hearing that had led to the disestablishment of the EWO and HTC showed the company unions had overwhelming employee support. CIO Local No. 1742 president Paul Gardner and recording secretary Woody Clayton tried to offset that imbalance by reaching out to blacks. In an open letter addressed to African American organizer Ernest Martin, who had formerly been with the IMW, they declared, "We of the CIO know that unless we organize our colored co-employees the employer shall always be able to create friction between white and colored in order to lower the standard of living of all of us. It is, therefore, not only a Christian Act to help and associate all workers regardless of color and creed, but it is good sound business protection for all workers." [40] Their egalitarian rhetoric belied the fact that they were reaching out to blacks as potential voters rather than oppressed workers deserving racial justice. Race frustrated the CIO's organizing drive.

On the other hand, the IMW's racial stand was uncompromising and was popular with whites. It unabashedly embraced the Jim Crow "traditions of the Southland." [41] The vast majority of Hughes Tool's white employees were comfortable with Jim Crow segregation since Houston's segregated society regarded racial discrimination as normal. This contributed a great deal to the IMW's successful recruiting campaign between August, 1940, and March, 1941.

Though figures are unavailable showing the breakdown between whites and blacks, the combined membership of Local Nos. 1 and 2 was 1,391. Sensing that it enjoyed majority support, the IMW requested that Hughes Tool recognize it as the collective bargaining agent at Hughes Tool. Management refused to recognize the IMW until it had been certified as the employees' collective bargaining agency by the Labor Board. In April, 1941, the IMW petitioned the NLRB to conduct a representation election. [42]

Along with its petition to the NLRB, the IMW submitted 1,391 signed authorization cards, 37 percent of Hughes Tool's 3,787 employees. The IMW's boldness and popularity threw the CIO on the defensive. The CIO had not kept pace with the IMW's recruiting efforts and did not want an election. Since there were no unfair labor charges pending against Hughes Tool, there was no legal bar to an election as long as one union demonstrated that it enjoyed the support of at least 30 percent of the workforce. The IMW had clearly met this requirement. In order to get on the ballot, the CIO had no other alternative but to submit its own authorization cards showing employee interest. The CIO submitted 1,065 cards, 29 percent, but after checking company records 190 were invalidated because the signatories no longer worked at Hughes Tool. The IMW lost 141 after verification with the employment office, which made the adjusted totals, 1,250 for the IMW, 33 percent, and 850 CIO, 22 percent.[43]

Since both unions had demonstrated that they enjoyed considerable support, the Labor Board deemed it necessary to conduct a hearing and identify eligible voters before the election took place. The NLRB conducted a hearing in Houston on May 15 and 16, 1941. The important difference between this hearing and the one that disestablished Hughes Tool's company unions was that this was a representation, rather than an unfair labor practices, hearing. A representation hearing establishes only two things: what unions should be included on the ballot and what employees should be allowed to vote. The trial examiner, James Whittmore, was only charged with conducting a hearing and passed the transcript on to the NLRB since intermediate reports were not required after a representation hearing.[44]

In comparison to the passion that marked the earlier unfair labor case, in which the CIO and Hughes Tool's company unions had engaged in a bitter legal battle, the representation hearing was characterized by tedium as the IMW and CIO quibbled over who should be eligible to vote. The IMW wanted to include all Hughes Tool's hourly employees and salaried nonsupervisory personnel, while the CIO insisted that only hourly people should be eligible to vote.[45] Hughes Tool cooperated in the hearing by presenting data to the NLRB, IMW, and CIO that listed job classifications, a brief description of each job, and in what department it was performed, which made it easier for the Labor Board to determine who should be eligible to vote. Labor Board attorney Lee McMahon thanked Hughes Tool for "very generously" supplying the parties with the eighteen-page document. The document explained the promotional/demotional ladders for Hughes Tool's 270 job classifications. The job classification system was extensive and complicated. A major reason for this, apart from the company's complex manufacturing processes, was management's work assignments for black workers.[46]

Although Hughes Tool's African Americans worked in all six departments, they were assigned to individual departments from one large black labor pool. Unlike white employees, who held permanent departmental jobs, blacks were temporarily assigned to one of Hughes Tool's six major departments. The personnel director Tom Mobley testified that African Americans "[m]ight be transferred from day to day or week-to-week, and are often moved from one department to another. In one department they might sweep . . . then they might be sent out to the yard to mow grass, then dig ditches to lay pipes. . . . They don't operate machines, but they will do the handy work and heavy work around the machine."[47]

Management wanted the flexibility of moving unskilled black labor between departments without posting job bids. During the production process, the need for unskilled labor ebbed and flowed in the company's different departments. For example, in heat treat and the foundry, where lag times in the production process were common, management would transfer black laborers from those departments, during slack periods, to the machine shop where the production schedule was continuous and required a large number of unskilled blacks to serve as handymen, oilers, cleaners, and porters. Due to a shortage of skilled white workmen in Houston, Hughes Tool usually kept whites in one department, where they were trained and promoted through a "system of upgrading" in which they progressed from unskilled to semiskilled to skilled jobs.[48]

Mobley testified that Hughes Tool's policy of training whites for particular jobs was "highly desirable" and provided the semiskilled and skilled white workers the company needed and "reduced turnover" of personnel. Mobley stated that Hughes Tool had developed its policy of upgrading whites and keeping blacks in a large labor pool in 1919; it had been in place ever since. The IMW supported, and the CIO acquiesced, to Hughes Tool's white upgrading system and black labor pool. It satisfied their white members because it kept job classifications strictly segregated and denied African Americans promotions that would have given them parity with whites.[49]

The NLRB issued its decision on August 5, 1941. It ruled that all hourly employees, whether black or white would be eligible to vote. The decision excluded executive, supervisory, engineering, and professional employees, and those strictly engaged in clerical work. The Labor Board's decision meant that 3,297, of Hughes Tool's 3,787 employees were eligible to cast ballots. It also ordered that an NLRB-supervised election should be conducted within thirty days of the decision.[50]

Although neither union offered protection against the racial discrimination at Hughes Tool, African American support was crucial for the IMW and CIO if they hoped to win the election. African Americans constituted 21 percent of Hughes Tool's workforce and were a powerful voting bloc that could sway the election either way. Despite their racism, the IMW and CIO wooed black voters through their respective black allies.

Rice attacked the CIO by telling blacks that they would lose their jobs if the CIO won the bargaining rights at Hughes Tool. He surmised that if CIO won the election, it would negotiate a closed shop contract in which union membership would be required for employment. This meant that African Americans would be forced, against their will, to join the CIO to keep their jobs.[51] Rice based his speculation on the AFL's record of closed shop contracts. His argument accurately characterized some of the AFL's unions at the time, but exaggerated the affect of its closed shop contracts. Only a relatively small number of skilled craft workers were covered by AFL closed shop agreements in the mass-producing industries, while unskilled and semiskilled workers were not.[52] Rice was joined in his attack against the CIO by black IMW organizer George Duncan. Duncan leveled a shot at Carter Wesley and the CIO by rhetorically asking, "The *Informer* has urged us to join the CIO. Who are the people that makeup that organization? The same faction that kept us out of the AFL. I believe in the saying, a leopard can't change its spots."[53] Duncan called on the CIO to "clean its own house" on the race issue before seeking to represent black interests at Hughes Tool.

Carter Wesley put up a spirited defense of the CIO. He told his readers that the CIO had a 50–50 chance to win the election if "Negro workers at Hughes Tool Company would support the CIO in large numbers." Wesley speculated that if the CIO won the election with African American support, their loyalty would be rewarded with better wages, seniority rights, wider promotions, and greater improvement in the general welfare of African Americans. Wesley urged blacks to vote for the CIO because it was better suited than the IMW to protect African Americans and would be completely free of management influence.[54]

He reminded blacks that they already had one bad experience with a company-dominated union, the HTC, and urged them not to make the same mistake by supporting the IMW. Wesley believed that the IMW was a "Rice type of independent union which is a company union under the guise of an independent union" and was worthless in uplifting black workers. He called Rice's charges that blacks would lose their jobs if the CIO won the election "a lot of hooey and poppycock." Wesley astutely noted that blacks had secure jobs at Hughes Tool because "[t]hey can be hired cheaper than whites can be hired to do that type of work, and they will keep their jobs because that will be true after the election. . . . There is a shortage of skilled workers, so whites don't need to take the jobs of Negroes in unskilled work."[55]

Robert Grovey joined Wesley in his defense of the CIO. Grovey regarded the CIO, with its national policy of nondiscrimination, as the best hope for black unskilled and semiskilled workers to enjoy the benefits of unionism. He regarded it as "criminal neglect" if blacks did not join the CIO. According to Grovey, the CIO's nondiscriminatory approach to unionism would standardize wages for whites and blacks and protect black seniority rights. He "honestly believed" the CIO would resolve many of Hughes Tool's racial problems that the IMW "had no desire to solve."[56] Grovey also became involved in a controversy surrounding allegations that foremen had tried to intimidate blacks into voting for the IMW.

Black CIO member Ray Grant reported to Robert Grovey that a number of African American employees in the heat treat department had been warned by their foremen Jack Lawson to vote against the CIO. Lawson told them to pick up a copy of an IMW circular being handbilled at the plant gates and told them that the IMW "is the best thing for you." It was also alleged that W. L. Fleming, a white foundry foreman with a reputation for teasing the foundry's "old Negroes," asked one of his black employees, "Say, boy, how are you going to vote, are you going to vote for the CIO?" The black employee replied, "No, I am going to vote Hughes Tool Company." Francis Chargois's foreman bluntly told him, "You have a good job and are doing all right. You better vote for the Independent if you want to keep it."[57]

Grovey brought the allegations to the attention of Clifford Potter, an official with the regional Labor Board in Dallas. Potter interviewed Grovey and Grant concerning the allegations; he wanted them to bring forward their informants and have them testify. Unfortunately, Grovey and Grant could not persuade the black employees who had allegedly been harangued into making a sworn statement. Grovey told Potter they would not testify because they were afraid that in retribution Hughes Tool would fire them. Without their testimony, Grovey's and Grant's allegations were hearsay and had no weight. Potter correctly dismissed them. In his report to the NLRB, Potter dismissed Grant's and Grovey's allegations and noted that "[t]he Company has taken every reasonable step possible to anticipate and prevent any interference in the election by its supervisory officials and employees. . . . [T]he objections filed by the CIO do not raise a substantial and material issue with respect to the conduct of the ballot."[58]

The election was held on August 28 and 29, 1941. The IMW handily won the election with 1,601 votes; the CIO received 950. The IMW's victory indicated that a considerable majority of voters supported the IMW's concept of independent unionism as opposed to the nationally affiliated CIO. The vote conclusively showed that an overwhelming number of Hughes Tool's employees supported labor unions. Of the 3,297 employees eligible to vote, 2,736 voted either for the IMW, CIO, or an affiliated AFL union, an impressive 83 percent.[59] The election ended Hughes Tool's open shop era. From 1941 onward employees would be covered by collective bargaining agreements negotiated by bona fide labor unions. But African Americans had little to celebrate since the IMW and CIO both discriminated against them.

Although the vote count was not broken down by race, the general feeling was that the IMW had attracted a majority of black voters. The CIO leaders regarded its loss as proof that its idea to organize a biracial union at Hughes Tool was a failure.[60] In the aftermath of its defeat, the CIO revised its racial policy to correspond with Hughes Tool's Jim Crow tradition, hoping to attract more white members and to reassure blacks that it was not a dangerous, radical organization that would cost them their jobs. In late 1941, the CIO chartered Local No. 2457 for Hughes Tool's African Americans. Local No. 1742's black and white membership voted on the issue and approved the measure to segregate.[61]

The CIO easily adjusted to Jim Crow unionism. It segregated union meetings, and each local operated independently of the other except for assignments on three committees. On the other hand, the IMW had a segregated dual committee system in which there was no inter-action between committees from Local No. 1 and Local No. 2. Al-though blacks were segregated in all other CIO union activities, they enjoyed parity on two committees and representation on another. Blacks and whites shared equal representation on the bargaining and the policy-fixing committees, and blacks held a minority on the griev-ance committee. This arrangement proved satisfactory to CIO whites and blacks and had three practical results: it silenced white members who criticized the union's racial mixing; black unionists shared a mea-sure of power by serving as committee members with whites; and black membership increased.[62] With the formation of Local No. 2457, the CIO accepted Jim Crow unionism and supposedly thought it solved the dilemma of trying to work for black improvement while not alien-ating white workers.

Robert Grovey regarded the formation of Local No. 2457 as a tem-porary, but necessary, setback for black workers and the CIO. In an article in the *Houston Informer,* Grovey acknowledged that there were CIO members who were not "willing to concede to the Negro his full share and rights as an American citizen." Nonetheless, Grovey urged African Americans to stay with the CIO and give it time to fulfill its promise of nondiscrimination. Grovey regarded the interracial com-position of the CIO's three committees as proof that the union had not fully conceded to Jim Crow unionism and still deserved black sup-port.[63] Carter Wesley also sprang to the CIO's defense. Despite his dis-appointment over the need to form Local No. 2457, Wesley stayed loyal to the CIO and told his readers that "it is not the policy of the CIO to discriminate against any worker be he white or black, but the human element [of prejudice] enters into all considerations."[64] Rather than regard the formation of Local No. 2457 as a defeat, black CIO unionists launched an aggressive recruiting campaign.

Robert Grovey had a high public profile during the drive. He served as a paid CIO organizer and vigorously defended its policies. At an organizing rally, Grovey told the crowd that the CIO had a "policy of fairness and would not hesitate to enforce it whenever challenged." He challenged blacks to rise above the small number of "pin-headed men in the CIO" who were racists and focus their attention on the union's class issues that would benefit blacks and whites.[65] Grovey recruited two hundred blacks in between running his barber shop on Dowling Street and his duties as president of the Third Ward Civic Club.[66]

Ernest Martin, president of CIO Local No. 2457, took a five-week leave of absence to devote his full attentions to organizing. Though Martin and other black CIO officials publicly attacked black IMW leaders, they muted criticism against members of IMW Local No. 2. Instead, they extended an olive branch to its rank and file and asked them to join the CIO. In an article in the *Houston Informer,* Martin and the CIO's African American leaders urged the IMW's "fine group of [black] men" to join the CIO and help build a real union that would win better jobs and higher pay.[67]

The nation's entry into World War II helped the CIO's effort at Hughes Tool. The company needed to hire an unprecedented number of workers to fill its defense contracts, and Hughes Tool's workforce more than doubled during the war, increasing from approximately thirty-six hundred in 1941 to sixty-eight hundred in 1946.[68] During the war, Hughes Tool operated three plants. It continued to run the main Houston plant that manufactured the vast majority of the country's oil drilling equipment and in 1941 began operations at the Aircraft Strut Plant on Wallisville Road and the Dickson Gun Plant on Clinton Drive.[69] All three plants produced critically important products for the war effort, and the CIO and IMW vied for bargaining rights in all three.

The new hires between the fall of 1941 and the summer of 1942 were for the most part indifferent to unionization and mostly unaware of the labor strife between the company, the IMW, and the CIO. They did not have a tradition of belonging to unions, and the opportunity for full-time employment was their major concern. The CIO recruited heavily from this group, asking each member to recruit several new employees into the union. It proved an effective organizing strategy and the union's membership steadily increased.[70]

In contrast, the IMW experienced little growth. After winning the collective bargaining rights, the IMW negotiated and executed a one-year contract with Hughes Tool on January 12, 1942, that was nearly identical to the 1940–41 contract between the EWO/HTC and management. With few exceptions the agreement merely validated the labor relations policy that Hughes Tool had put into effect when its company unions were disestablished. It reaffirmed Jim Crow unionism and vested Local No. 1 with full bargaining power. The contract provided for a ten-cents-per-hour raise for all employees and also that "[n]o white employee shall be employed at a rate of less than sixty cents per hour, and no colored employee shall be employed at a rate of less than fifty cents per hour." It maintained a segregated wage scale and job classification system that denied African Americans advancement and parity with whites.[71]

The IMW became complacent and did not match the CIO's success in recruiting new hires. After the IMW registered a decisive election win by garnering 61 percent of the vote to the CIO's 38 percent, the union's officers were lulled into a false sense of security. The CIO's persistent recruiting efforts surpassed the IMW's, and in July, 1942, it presented signed authorization cards from 56 percent of the workforce to the Labor Board and requested a certification election. In comparison the IMW offered authorization cards signed by 53 percent of Hughes Tool's employees. The vast majority of the CIO's signatures were gathered in 1942 while only 25 percent of the IMW's were dated 1942, suggesting the CIO's success in establishing a Jim Crow local and ambitiously recruiting new employees.[72]

Since the combined totals of the unions' authorization cards totaled 109 percent, the Labor Board deemed it imperative to hold a hearing and try to sort out the CIO's and IMW's conflicting claims. The NLRB held a hearing in Houston on October 23 and 24, 1942, to determine if an election was warranted. The IMW argued that the CIO did not deserve an election while the IMW's contract with Hughes Tool remained in effect. This would have been the case if the IMW had had an unfair labor charge pending against Hughes Tool. In cases where a union holding a contract filed an unfair labor charge against the contracted company, the Labor Board would not hold a representation election requested by a competing union until the unfair labor charge was resolved.[73]

The NLRB in Washington issued its decision on November 27, 1942. It ruled that since both unions showed strong employee support and that the IMW's contract would expire in two months, a union certification election should be held within thirty days.[74] For the most part, electioneering was subdued because employees were busy working long hours and their energies were devoted to keeping defense production going. Neither union engaged in a last-ditch recruiting effort before the election; both the CIO and IMW felt that their support had been solidified long before the Labor Board issued its order for an election. The NLRB conducted the election between December 10–12, 1942, and the CIO triumphed with 1,680 votes to the IMW's 1,538.[75]

The results were not broken down along racial lines, so it was impossible to calculate how many blacks voted for either union. C. W. Rice published an unsubstantiated report that stated only sixty of Hughes Tool's eleven hundred black employees voted for the CIO. Carter Wesley regarded the IMW's defeat as a vote of no-confidence against the IMW's leadership "who for years had enjoyed a lucrative career at the expense of the advancement of the rank-and-file."[76] Robert Grovey took great delight in pointing out that Hughes Tool "did not close down following the CIO victory as was predicted by C. W. Rice and his stalwarts." Grovey reported that "colored workers who last year voted for the metal workers, or stayed away from the polls, have denounced C. W. Rice and his regime" and were joining CIO Local No. 2457 in large numbers.[77]

After several months of negotiations the CIO and Hughes Tool signed an agreement on April 6, 1943. The contract covered employees in the Hughes Tool's main and aircraft strut plants and introduced some improvements for blacks. It eliminated white/black pay differential for entry-level employees, now all new hires received sixty cents per hour, and no mention of the words colored or white appeared in the contract.[78] The contract also improved the pay of African Americans. Under the CIO's contract, when an African American was pulled from the labor pool and temporarily assigned to a department he would receive the rate of pay for the job he filled rather than the lower pay rate for common black labor. This new system increased black pay by four to six cents an hour.[79] Though management grudgingly conceded these minor improvements for African Americans during negotiations with the CIO, it did so only because the contract did not substantially change the occupational status of blacks in any way.

A comparison of the job classification systems in the EWO/HTC's 1941 contract in table 3, and the CIO's 1943 contract in table 4 clearly shows that the CIO's agreement firmly kept job discrimination in place. The CIO's contract identified white jobs as part I and black jobs as part II; the EWO/HTC contract simply called black jobs "colored"; and the IMW's 1942 agreement listed white jobs as group I, and blacks as group II. An examination of the two tables shows that the CIO's contract continued to limit lines of promotion and demotion available to blacks and kept their wages at significantly lower levels than whites.[80]

During negotiations Hughes Tool had been tough in its demand to maintain racial segregation. Jim Crow had been a cornerstone of the company's labor relations policy since 1909, and company officials feared that any tinkering with the company's system of segregation would heighten racial hatred among whites, lead to rioting in the

TABLE 4 Hughes Tool Company, Main Plant, Segregated Pay Grades and Pay Scales, Effective April 6, 1943

Department	No. of Part I Pay Grades*	Part I Pay Scales (per hour)	No. of Part II Pay Grades	Part II Pay Scales (per hour)
Machine Shop	7	$1.485–.855	3	$.825–.685
Pattern Shop	4	Salaried	1	$.745
Foundry	4	$1.265–1.005	3	$.805–.685
Heat Treat	1	$1.285	2	$.865–.805
Shipping Dept.	3	$1.075–.945	3	$.825–.685
Storeroom	5	$1.365–1.115	3	$.825–.685

*Part I applied to white employees; part II, to black employees.
SOURCE: Contract Covering Wages, Hours, and Conditions of Employment between United Steel Workers of America C.I.O., Locals 1742 and 2457, and the Hughes Tool Company, NARACP, RNLRB, RG 25, CF 6288, "Official Report of Proceedings before the National Labor Relations Board in the Matter of Hughes Tool Company (Dickson Gun Plant) and the United Steelworkers of America Locals 1742 and 2457," Exhibit Pet. 2.

plant, and possibly provoke a race war.[81] CIO officials welcomed management's minor concessions over the racial issue and dared not push for more because they could take credit for what had been achieved while at the same time reassuring the majority white membership that Jim Crow was still securely in place.

Several major issues remained unresolved, but the CIO agreed to put the contract into effect with the understanding that it would present the issues to the National War Labor Board (NWLB) for arbitration. The CIO wanted a maintenance of membership clause with a fifteen-day escape period. It also wanted a cessation of management's settling grievances with the IMW and collecting IMW dues through payroll deduction.[82] The NWLB, a panel comprised of labor, industry, and public representatives, established the controversial maintenance of membership as a means of preventing disruptive strikes during World War II. Normally, in return for a union's agreement to enforce a no-strike pledge, a maintenance of membership clause would be included in contracts that required all employees covered by the contract to become members of the union for the duration of the agreement. The NWLB required a fifteen-day escape period in which a new member or an old member under a new contract could withdraw from the union, but few workers took the time to withdraw in their first hectic weeks on the job.[83]

Once enrolled under a maintenance of membership contract, members were required to pay their dues, usually under a checkoff arrangement, and abide by all union regulations. Otherwise they would be expelled from the union and then fired by the company. In practice, this policy dramatically increased the size and financial stability of the CIO, since its new union members were covered by government-sponsored maintenance of membership contracts.[84] Hughes Tool adamantly refused to recognize the procedure in its CIO contract. In a letter to the NWLB's chairman, Hughes Tool's legal counsel William M. Streetman argued that because of the certification election's close vote, no maintenance-of membership provision "even of the mildest form" should be required in the contract.[85]

Maintenance of membership and the two other unresolved contract issues, Hughes Tool's continuing to negotiate with the IMW's grievance committee and deducting IMW membership dues through payroll deduction, would cause a great deal of trouble between the CIO and Hughes Tool during World War II. The race issue would also resurface during the war and further complicate matters. The CIO and IMW remained committed to maintaining white supremacy, though the CIO did make efforts to ameliorate its worst effects. Although the NLRB insured the peaceful transition of bargaining rights from one union to another, the Labor Board did not guarantee civil rights for blacks in unions that it certified. During World War II, as the federal government tried to settle the three unresolved contract issues through the National War Labor Board, African Americans in the CIO would also demand that the federal government use its powers to put an end to racial discrimination at Hughes Tool.

CHAPTER SIX

The Battle for Union Security and Civil Rights

LABOR'S WAR AT HUGHES TOOL, 1943–1946

THE CIO'S ASCENDANCY as the collective bargaining agent at Hughes Tool marked the end of a five-year struggle. But the CIO's selection by the majority of employees' as their collective bargaining agent did not bring labor peace to Hughes Tool. Management refused to recognize the CIO as the collective bargaining agent of its employees due to the narrowness of its election victory over the Independent Metal Workers Union and in direct violation of the Wagner Act continued to negotiate with IMW officials and process their grievances. But the two issues that caused the widest rift between the CIO and Hughes Tool were maintenance of membership and racial discrimination. The company adamantly refused to implement the former or abolish the latter.

The National War Labor Board's maintenance of membership policy meant that if a union had a contract with an employer, all newly hired workers would automatically become dues-paying members after their first fifteen days on the job had elapsed. If they did not want to join, they had to declare that before the fifteen-day waiver period ended. Having failed to exercise this option, workers were required to remain members in good standing and pay dues for the length of the contract, at which time they could once again exercise their fifteen-day escape option. Labor leaders hailed maintenance of membership because it greatly enhanced union security by increasing membership and dues money. In return for the NWLB's enforcing maintenance of membership, CIO leaders agreed to give up the right to strike. They took responsibility for preventing wildcat strikes and disciplining rank-and-file radicalism that might disrupt defense production. The no-strike pledge produced immediate benefits for unions such as public approval and government goodwill, but experienced unionists worried that giving up the right to strike deprived them of their most important weapon.[1]

Given the wartime emergency, most employers cooperated with the NWLB's maintenance of membership and generally implemented its rulings. That did not mean they approved of the policy. As far as Hughes Tool and other Houston manufacturers were concerned, compulsory union membership was a violation of basic principles of individual freedom. Hughes Tool had the city's largest CIO membership, and during World War Two the company played a singularly important role in leading the city's industrialists against the union and maintenance of membership.[2]

In addition to these tensions, the CIO suffered from internal upheaval between whites and blacks over its unfulfilled pledge of racial equality. A majority of Hughes Tool's black workers supported the CIO due to its philosophical commitment to racial egalitarianism, and their support proved to be the margin of victory for CIO's triumph over the IMW. In return for African American support, the CIO had promised to eliminate racial discrimination at Hughes Tool once it became the collective bargaining agent. But the CIO's contract with the company enacted in April, 1943, proved that the CIO had no more intention of upsetting Hughes Tool's Jim Crow status quo than the Independent Metal Workers Union had. Of the two volatile issues, the first that exploded into a confrontation was maintenance of membership.

During contract negotiations with the CIO in April, 1943, Hughes Tool adamantly refused to accept a maintenance of membership clause in the contract. Faced with management's uncompromising stand, union negotiators decided to pass the issue on to the National War Labor Board for arbitration. CIO negotiators fully expected a favorable ruling from the board, and if Hughes Tool continued to resist, the Smith-Connally War Labor Disputes Act empowered the board with three remedies to resolve the dispute. It could impose economic sanctions by withdrawing Hughes Tool's priority for receiving natural resources or it could cancel the company's defense contracts.[3] Neither of these options was feasible since Hughes Tool enjoyed a near monopoly on vital oil drilling equipment and was the country's primary supplier of these products. The third option would be for President Roosevelt to issue an executive order directing the army to seize the plant and force Hughes Tool's compliance.[4] The NWLB preferred not to use this option unless absolutely necessary. A hearing was quickly convened in Houston in April, 1943, to sort out the issues and rule if the union deserved the benefit of maintenance of membership. A three-member panel appointed by the War Labor Board presided over the hearing.

The attorneys William Streetman and Tom Mobley represented Hughes Tool. Streetman argued that the company had not violated the law by rejecting the NWLB's standard maintenance of membership. He challenged the legality of the Smith-Connally Act and the NWLB's legitimacy by declaring that "the War Labor Board does not have any power to rule" on the disputed issues. He based his argument on the fact that the Supreme Court had yet to rule on the legality of the NWLB or the Smith-Connally Act, so consequently they had no legal authority over the dispute between the company and the CIO.[5]

Mobley testified that maintenance of membership violated the company's long-standing policy of not recognizing one union as the exclusive collective bargaining agent. He argued that the narrow CIO victory in the December, 1942, certification election, 1,680 votes for the CIO as opposed to the IMW's 1,538, indicated widespread IMW support. Mobley warned that if the NWLB forced Hughes Tool to implement maintenance of membership it would cause terrible resentment in the IMW and lead to a shop floor revolt that would disrupt production.[6]

Management believed that every employee had the right to make his own decision whether to join or not to join a labor union and asserted that Hughes Tool would not be a party in abrogating that right. Both attorneys warned the panelists that finding experienced help was difficult during the war and Hughes Tool, like other Houston industries, suffered from a labor shortage and chronic absenteeism. Mobley and Streetman argued that if CIO members were forced to stay in the union as a condition of employment then many would quit and go work somewhere else, making it impossible for Hughes Tool to satisfy its defense contracts.[7]

Arthur Mandell the CIO's lawyer dismissed Streetman and Mobley's arguments by stressing that the CIO's certification by the National Labor Relations Board following the December, 1942, election validated the union's standing as the "duly elected and exclusive bargaining agent" at Hughes Tool. Consequently, under NWLB policies the CIO deserved maintenance of membership. In response to the closeness of the election Mandell argued that their near parity in membership made it all the more important for the CIO to be granted maintenance of membership to keep the IMW from raiding its membership. He reasoned that with CIO membership stabilized for the duration of the contract, members could devote their full energies to production and not be distracted by competition between unions.[8]

Due to an enormous backlog of similar cases, the panel members were unable to issue their report to the full NWLB in Washington, D.C., until September, 1943. They ruled in favor of Hughes Tool and did not order it to implement maintenance of membership. The public and industry representatives voted against, while the labor member voted in favor.[9] The majority stated that it would be inappropriate to grant the CIO special privileges since both unions had relatively equal membership. They explained that in this case it would be unfair to grant something to the CIO without making the same offer to the IMW.[10] The labor member dissented arguing that a majority of employees supported maintenance of membership, otherwise they would not have voted for the CIO in the December, 1942, union certification election. He also dismissed the argument that the relatively equal strength of the CIO and IMW was a barrier. The CIO appealed the report to the NWLB in Washington, D.C.

Disappointment over the decision unleashed a groundswell of resentment and distrust of the War Labor Board among CIO unionists. As the appeals process ran its course, the rank and file agitated for a wildcat strike. Keeping union members on the job was very important for CIO leaders; there was concern among the union's leaders and the NWLB that Hughes Tool was trying to provoke a strike in order to discredit the union.[11] The board had obtained information that identified Hughes Tool and Mosher Steel, one of Houston's larger steel fabricating plants, as the city's leadership against the CIO and maintenance of membership.[12]

The CIO organized workers at Mosher Steel in 1943. The major differences between the CIO's successful campaign at Mosher Steel and its successful drive at Hughes Tool was that at Mosher the CIO did not face a challenge from a strong independent union nor did it have to overcome a tradition of company unions. CIO organizers found employees at Mosher Steel receptive to the union and successfully organized the company in the face of determined management opposition. The company unequivocally refused to include maintenance of membership in its contract with the CIO. The union filed charges against Mosher Steel with the War Labor Board, and William Streetman, Hughes Tool's attorney, represented the company at the hearing. Unlike in the Hughes Tool case, the board ruled in favor of the CIO since the union enjoyed strong employee support and ordered Mosher Steel to grant maintenance of membership. It refused.[13]

Floyd McGowan, chairman of the Dallas Regional War Labor Board believed that Hughes Tool and Mosher Steel meant to test the board's resolve over maintenance of membership. He contacted Leonard Berliner, the board's dispute director, in Washington, D.C. and warned him that although both companies denied there was a concerted effort by Houston and Gulf Coast employers to resist their orders, he believed "that such a concerted plan is either in existence or that the effect could be the same as though such a plan was in existence." McGowan found no legal reason why the companies should not comply with the War Labor Board's policy. He concluded that Hughes Tool and Mosher Steel made every possible effort to confuse, undermine, and delay the program. McGowan regarded their actions as a "clear cut case" of violating NWLB orders, and strongly recommended that steps be taken to force Hughes Tool and Mosher Steel to comply.[14] McGowan worried that if "immediate action [is] not taken" against both companies "serious labor trouble may result."[15]

In a letter to Berliner, Noah Dietrich, Hughes Tool's executive vice president, denied any collusion with Mosher Steel in disobeying the NWLB. According to Dietrich, "We have no knowledge as to what the ultimate attitude of Mosher Steel Company may be, except that our attorney, Mr. W. M. Streetman happens to be also the attorney for Mosher Steel Company. . . . Certainly there is no connection between the action taken by the two companies."[16] Though it was never proven that Hughes Tool and Mosher Steel colluded in defying the NWLB, McGowan feared that their disobedience of its orders would lead to a rash of wildcat strikes in industries on the upper Texas Gulf Coast.[17] In order to avoid labor trouble, McGowan recommended that the NWLB make an example of Hughes Tool. He believed that forcing it to comply would maintain shop floor peace, keep people on the job, and serve as an example to other Houston manufacturers who planned to defy the board's authority. McGowan chose Hughes Tool rather than Mosher Steel because it was the city's largest manufacturing plant, had the largest CIO membership at 2,636 strong (an increase of 1,056 since the December, 1942, certification election), and its products were "100 percent essential" for the war effort.[18]

Hughes Tool produced 75 percent of the rotary drilling bits and 40 percent of the tool joints for the drilling industry. In the face of unprecedented wartime oil demand, the Petroleum Administration for War (PAW) warned that "any slackening of the production of rock bits and tool joints would seriously endanger the drilling program seeking a minimum of 24,000 oil wells" by the end of 1944. As matters stood, the drilling industry already suffered from a ten-month backlog of tool joints, and the PAW could not meet the country's wartime petroleum needs if a labor dispute at Hughes Tool erupted into a wildcat strike.[19] Production needed to be raised by 30 percent in order to meet the armed forces' petroleum needs. Even without labor unrest, Hughes Tool suffered a chronic labor shortage, making it nearly impossible to meet production quotas.[20] McGowan's warning and the PAW's worries over meeting production quotas seem to have affected the board's decision concerning the CIO's appeal.

In February, 1944, the full nine-member national board in Washington, D.C., ruled on the appeal. In a majority decision in which the three public and three labor members concurred and the three industry representatives dissented, the board ordered Hughes Tool to implement maintenance of membership. Hughes Tool ignored the directive.[21] Between March and June, 1944, the board made several appeals to the company to comply and each time it refused. William Streetman responded to the order by restating Hughes Tool's position that it "does not recognize the authority of the Board . . . [which] does not have the authority to issue such an order." McGowan confided that he believed Hughes Tool's intention was to provoke a strike by the CIO and force the War Labor Board to take drastic action. If events unfolded as he feared, the company would score a major public relations coup by blaming the selfish, unpatriotic union and the meddling War Labor Board for causing the strike.[22] At this point, black unionists, disillusioned with the failed promise of racial equality, filed discrimination charges against the company and union with the Fair Employment Practices Committee (FEPC).

President Roosevelt created the FEPC with Executive Order No. 8802. The formation of the FEPC marked the first time since Reconstruction that the nation had had a federal agency devoted to minority problems.[23] Roosevelt's order declared, "The duty of employers and labor organizations is to provide for full and equitable participation of all workers in defense industries, without discrimination because of race, creed, color, or national origin."[24] Although the FEPC lacked enforcement powers, and racist employers and unions dismissed its

Even in the midst of the critical labor shortage during World War II, Hughes Tool continued its policy of job discrimination by hiring inexperienced white women as machine operators rather than upgrading high seniority black males to these jobs. *Photograph courtesy of the Houston Metropolitan Research Center, Houston Public Library.*

calls to abolish discrimination, black unionists wanted to capitalize on the federal government's recent activism at Hughes Tool. They wanted the federal government to bring its power to bear in their struggle to abolish job discrimination.[25] Despite critical wartime labor shortages, management and the union refused to consider upgrading African Americans to semiskilled machine operator jobs.

Desperately in need of help, Hughes Tool hired large numbers of white women and planned to train them to replace white males serving in the armed forces. Company officials and union leaders never considered promoting black males or hiring black females to fill machine operator or welding jobs. Instead, they hired inexperienced white females rather than taking advantage of Hughes Tool's large pool of experienced black men who would have needed only minimal training to become machine operators and welders, and little supervision once qualified.[26]

Between May, 1942, and September, 1943, the percentage of white women working in the plant increased from 1.4 percent of the workforce to 26.6 percent. They were trained as machine operators in all the machine shop's production departments and as welders in the hydroweld and hard-facing departments; they were only excluded from skilled trades. Hughes Tool assigned draft-deferred, experienced white male machine operators and welders as setup and lead men to help the women perform their duties. By assigning experienced white male employees to predominantly female departments, Hughes Tool managed to keep production flowing.[27] Its policy added a gender dimension to the company's discrimination, and by 1943 Hughes Tool employed a higher percentage of white women than black men.

Ernest Martin, president of CIO's Jim Crow union, Local No. 2457, and fifty other black union members, filed a complaint against Hughes Tool with the FEPC over its discriminatory hiring and upgrading practices.[28] They also filed a complaint against the CIO for enacting a contract that segregated whites into jobs listed as part I and blacks into part II. Part II jobs severely limited African American opportunities and denied them promotions.[29]

The FEPC field examiner W. Don Ellinger met with Ernest Martin, the other complainants, and white CIO staff men in Houston on May 11, 1944. After conferring with the group and examining the CIO's contract with Hughes Tool, he determined that the CIO consented to codifying discrimination at Hughes Tool by agreeing to a contract that segregated jobs by race.[30] Staff men Larry Bench and Martin Burns tried to squash the charges by arguing that Hughes Tool was mostly responsible for job discrimination, not the union. They hoped to con-

TABLE 5 Hughes Tool Employee Data, Main Plant, May, 1942– September, 1943

	Total Employees	White Women (%)	Black Men (%)
May, 1942	3715	53 (1.4)	918 (24.7)
September, 1942	3895	69 (1.8)	880 (22.6)
January, 1943	3846	590 (15.3)	959 (24.9)
May, 1943	4473	1218 (27.2)	997 (22.3)
September, 1943	4860	1,295 (26.6)	1,096 (22.6)

SOURCE: NARASRFW, RCFEP, RG 228, CF 13-BR-34, Form 270.

vince Ernest Martin and the others to drop their charges and avoid a full FEPC investigation. The staff men feared a white exodus from the union if the FEPC pressured the CIO into helping eliminate discrimination.[31] Bench and Burns persuaded Martin and the others to drop their charges by convincing them that the survival of the union was at stake. Martin and many black unionists had long felt that the CIO was the only real union at Hughes Tool and despite its duplicity on race, its racism was nowhere near the level of the Independent Metal Workers Union. They agreed to drop their charges in return for the union taking up the issues with the War Labor Board.[32] The majority of Hughes Tool's African Americans preferred to give the CIO another chance rather than risk destroying the union. The CIO's ploy turned out to be merely a stall, but it worked.[33]

Meanwhile, Hughes Tool's Tom Mobley freely admitted to Will Maslow, the FEPC's regional director of field operations in Dallas, that the company discriminated against blacks. Mobley explained that the working relationship between blacks and whites at Hughes Tool was not primarily a management-labor problem but a social problem. Mobley warned Maslow that any plan promoting racial equality must consider Houston's long-established community thought and practices concerning Jim Crow, and whether integration was really in the best interests of blacks and whites. Poorly planned or impractical integration of white and black employees, he argued, would inevitably result in racial antagonism.[34] The company and union successfully kept racial discrimination in place, but tensions between them erupted in June, 1944, when Hughes Tool disobeyed a direct order by the War Labor Board to implement maintenance of membership.

The CIO's leaders found it nearly impossible to contain rank-and-file anger over the company's disobedience of the board's order. Union member N. H. Shepherd summed up their feelings of frustration when he said, "It [is] unfortunate that the Hughes Tool Company sees fit to operate on the money of the United States Government on war contracts and could not see fit to abide by the laws of the United States." Shepherd and his colleagues demanded that if the War Labor Board was powerless to make Hughes Tool obey, then they would by striking and shutting the plant down. Houston CIO director Frank Hardesty found that "the membership was very disturbed" over Hughes Tool's intransigence and wanted "the officers of the union to do something about it." His plea that the union must keep faith with the NWLB was no longer "a good enough answer." Hardesty and other CIO officials failed to contain the rank and file's anger, and on Thursday June 22, angry CIO members walked off the job.[35]

Desperately trying to regain control, Hardesty convened an emergency meeting at Stonewall Jackson Middle School on June 23 and more than fifteen hundred union members attended. Staff man Martin Burns urged them to go back to work and give the NWLB more time to force Hughes Tool's compliance. Near chaos ensued as passionate firebrands "took the situation into their own hands" and controlled the meeting's agenda. They declared that "their backs were up against the wall" and, amid chants of "no contract, no work," demanded that Hughes Tool obey the War Labor Board order and honor the contract.[36] Speakers warned the union's leadership that their patience had run out; if the federal government would not force Hughes Tool's compliance, then they would shut down the plant. Ignoring calls to return to work by their leaders, picket lines sprang up at all plant gates and urged employees to stay off the job.[37]

Tom Mobley branded the strikers "shirkers" and blamed the union for the walkout. Management offered double time for those reporting to work on Sunday, but by Monday, June 26, approximately three thousand employees had joined the unauthorized strike.[38] Throughout the strike, which lasted from June 23 to June 29, Hughes Tool claimed that only 16 percent of the workforce walked out, while the CIO reported that 60 percent were absent.[39] Union leaders organized a public rally for the evening of June 26 in Sam Houston Coliseum to try to end the work stoppage and publicize the causes of the walkout.

Between thirty-five hundred and four thousand attended the interracial rally. They heard speeches from Frank Hardesty, African American staff man Robert Grovey, and others. All the speakers condemned Hughes Tool's arrogant violation of the law by not obeying the War Labor Board's order. Hardesty told the rally that Hughes Tool must obey government orders just the same as employees. He claimed that Hughes Tool's defiance was part of an overall plan to purge the CIO from Hughes Tool so its IMW ally could regain the bargaining rights.[40]

A significant number of the CIO's nearly eight hundred blacks participated in the strike, and their large presence at the rally showed the depth of their support.[41] The *Houston Post* reported that black CIO staff man Robert Grovey's impassioned speech criticizing Hughes Tool and celebrating the strike's biracial nature received enthusiastic support. He declared, "In the old days every time there was trouble and white men walked off the job the boss would sidle up to the Negro.

If they hang us this time they will have to hang us together."[42] The interracial composition of the meeting showed that in spite of bigotry within the CIO, the seriousness of the dispute had at least temporarily transcended race and galvanized white members into solidarity with their black union brothers.

Management and the white leadership of the Independent Metal Workers Union lashed out, blaming the CIO and the federal government for causing the strike. Tom Mobley branded Hardesty's and Grovey's claims that Hughes Tool provoked the strike as "outright lies."[43] Hughes Tool's executive vice president Noah Dietrich called the CIO's "utter disregard of the no-strike pledge" lawless and irresponsible and in an ironic twist demanded that the War Labor Board force the strikers back to work.[44]

Roy Epperson, IMW Local No. 1 president, promised that his union's membership would continue working "as all right thinking American citizens will do." He impugned the patriotism of CIO members by claiming that "every department is operating through the efforts of the Independent Metal Workers Union and other loyal American citizens who are employed at Hughes Tool" and that the IMW intended to keep production going. Epperson accused the War Labor Board and the CIO of conspiring to destroy his union.[45]

By Wednesday June 28, tempers cooled somewhat and most CIO strikers returned to work with reassurances from the NWLB that it would force Hughes Tool's compliance.[46] But the tenuous peace collapsed almost immediately. Between July and August, 1944, Hughes Tool continued to defy the order implementing maintenance of membership. William Streetman once again questioned that body's legal authority. In a letter to the War Labor Board he scoffed at its authority saying, "We candidly submit to your Board that it cannot make any order which will be binding upon or effective against this company."[47] In a gratuitous slap at its inability to enforce its order, Robert Kelley, one of the company's other attorneys, declared that he "didn't think even the army could enforce maintenance of membership and keep the plant going." Feeling betrayed, angry CIO members girded themselves for another strike.[48]

The board recognized that it had lost control of the situation and it was causing a "substantial interference with the war effort."[49] The NWLB asked President Roosevelt to order the army to seize the plant to keep production going, impose maintenance of membership, and make an example of Hughes Tool for defying the board's authority.

Roosevelt acted quickly, issuing Executive Order 9745-A on September 2, which authorized the army to seize the plant.[50]

The War Department assigned Col. Frank Cawthon to command the army's Hughes Tool operation and directed him to avoid, if possible, using armed troops. Troops proved unnecessary because management assented to a peaceful seizure in order to avoid violence and prevent damage to company property. Hughes Tool's executives also agreed to administer the plant and to continue serving in their regular capacities under army supervision.[51] That did not equate to approval of the army's seizure. Defiant even in defeat, Matt Boehm, Hughes Tool's vice president and general manager, stated that "control of the Hughes Tool Company was not turned over to the War Department voluntarily. The Company will comply . . . but this compliance does not signify any approval of such policy." Noah Dietrich succinctly expressed management's view: "however cordial our personal relations may be [with the army], legally, we regard you as trespassers in our plants."[52]

Colonel Cawthon's orders directed him and his forty-four-member staff to keep production flowing without interruption and to enforce the War Labor Board's order. The army contingent included officers and enlisted men who were specialists in manufacturing techniques, law, labor and public relations, contracts, and stock control. Cawthon reminded all Hughes Tool employees, management and hourly, that it was their "patriotic duty" to keep the main and aircraft strut plants operating. He also urged them to settle their disputes through the NWLB and NLRB and to accept their rulings "whether you agree with them or not" otherwise "our war production will drift into chaos." Cawthon succeeded in keeping the production lines going and in convincing management to recognize the CIO as the employees' bargaining agent.[53]

The Independent Metal Workers Union lashed out at the CIO and the government. Roy Epperson called the army takeover "unwarranted, unjust, and unprovoked." He regarded it as a "slap in face" and "un-American" that the army seized the plant. Epperson declared that the army's "only purpose" was to protect the CIO and "stamp out" the IMW.[54] The union sent terse telegrams to Texas' U.S. senators Tom Connally and W. Lee O'Daniel and to Reps. Albert Thomas and Martin Dies protesting the army takeover.

They asked: "As a member of Congress from our state of Texas what do you propose to do about it?"[55] Connally and Thomas sent bland replies saying they were referring the matter to the NWLB since it was part of the executive branch. Dies was retiring from office and did not bother to respond, but O' Daniel's reply lambasted President Roosevelt and the CIO. A nominal Democrat, O' Daniel led the Texas anti-Roosevelt campaign in the 1944 election, and in his response to the IMW he promised to do everything in his power to eliminate the "domination of American people by labor leader racketeers and bureaucrats . . . and to work forcefully" for a thorough housecleaning in Washington from the White House down. Despite O' Daniel's hyperbole, he did not pursue the matter, nor did Connally, Thomas, or Dies.[56]

Even with the army in control of the plant, Colonel Cawthon was reluctant to enforce maintenance of membership. His greatest fear was that if employees opposed to it were forced to pay union dues they would quit. On the other hand, he recognized that a "substantial number of CIO members were quite insistent upon having union security enforced."[57] With assistance from Lee Pressman, the CIO's general legal counsel, he brokered a compromise solution that created a modified form of maintenance of membership acceptable to the union and management. It established a policy of involuntary dues payment for CIO members; the army disbursing officer assigned to the accounting department would deduct union dues from the first payday of the month.[58] CIO members in good standing would be required to remain members through this involuntary dues payment.[59] With the maintenance of membership issue settled, the CIO's Frank Hardesty turned his attention to the union's promise to push the War Labor Board to eliminate discrimination.

At Hardesty's urging the board directed its arbitrator, Guy Horton, to arrange a hearing with management, CIO, and the army to discuss ways to implement integration of black and white workers and eliminate job discrimination.[60] When Horton convened the meeting on June 18, 1945, he acknowledged that "discriminatory practices do exist which need correction," and he hoped they could eliminate them. He cautioned that integration should " be gradual, starting in certain departments of the plant, and studies be made of jobs where the Negroes could qualify and obtain a rate of pay equal to that paid whites."[61] He also made it clear that the army would take no action on integration without orders from "higher authority," such as the president.[62]

Privately, Horton confided to Colonel Cawthon that using the army to forcibly integrate Hughes Tool would be "embarrassing to the War

Department" since the army was racially segregated.[63] Cawthon feared using force to integrate Hughes Tool because, in his view, it would intensify "racial hatred" among whites and possibly escalate into a race war. He noted in particular that the CIO was bitterly divided over race and that a growing number of white members "were thinking of splitting and joining up with the Independents" in protest against integration.[64]

Speaking for Hughes Tool, William Streetman and Robert Kelley rejected any plan that called for eliminating segregation.[65] They asserted that Hughes Tool's segregation, though discriminatory, had been its labor policy since the company's founding in 1909. According to them, forced integration would "cause a great deal of trouble in the plant and possible rioting."[66] Streetman and Kelley reminded Horton that when the army seized the plant the War Department had acknowledged it could not operate it without management's help. They reminded Horton that management willingly cooperated with the army and kept production going. But if the War Labor Board ordered the army to integrate Hughes Tool the management team would resign, leaving the army to try and run the plant on its own. Both lawyers reassured Horton that the possible resignations were not meant as a threat, but there was no mistaking that it was one.[67] With management, board, and army all opposed to eliminating discrimination, the effort failed. Following its failure on the race issue, the CIO focused its energies on the equally important issue of negotiating a new contract while Hughes Tool was still bound by the War Labor Board order to recognize and bargain with the union. The union had lost considerable white support over its failed attempt to eliminate discrimination, and CIO officials believed that if they won a fairly good contract with significant wage increases it would reenergize disaffected white members.[68]

Throughout June, July, and August, 1945, CIO officials met with management and tried to negotiate a new contract. Though discussions continued all summer, no agreement was reached. With the war coming to an end, the army relinquishing control, and race undermining CIO loyalties, management contented itself with appearing to bargain in good faith while drawing out the negotiations until the army left. Without the War Labor Board and army to restrain it, Hughes Tool looked forward to renewing its battle against the CIO. On August 29, 1945, two weeks after VJ-day, the army relinquished control of Hughes Tool. In his final report to the War Department, Col. Ira Baldinger, who had relieved Col. Frank Cawthon in February, 1945, expressed pessimism over the prospects of postwar labor peace at Hughes Tool. He warned that labor trouble was unavoidable after the army returned control of the plant.[69]

Baldinger's prophecy turned out to be correct, though it took several months before the inevitable clash occurred. Going into the fall of 1945 negotiators from both sides met several times in an effort to hammer out a new contract. Management could not simply ignore the CIO's request for discussions due to its large membership but made it clear that the company would never give in to its demands. Houston's union officials were following a directive handed down by the CIO's national leadership that demanded wage increases in America's largest industries, such as steel and auto, to offset postwar inflation and wage stagnation. The CIO wanted a 25-cents-per-hour raise for all its members in the steel industry. The CIO's United Steelworkers of America represented workers at Hughes Tool.[70] Negotiations stalled when industry leaders flatly refused to consider any pay increase until the government's Office of Price Administration (OPA) eliminated wartime wage and price controls.

Desperate to avoid postwar strikes, President Truman tried to break the deadlock by issuing an executive order abolishing wage and price controls in the steel industry. Truman's order allowed the companies and union some bargaining room, but negotiations once again broke down over wages. The impasse dragged on until January, 1946, at which point Truman offered to act as a mediator and persuaded negotiators from both sides to meet in the White House.[71] Ben Fairless, president of United States Steel and the industry's chief negotiator, consented to an increase of 15 cents an hour and the CIO's president, Philip Murray, countered with an offer to accept 19½ cents. Truman intervened and asked them to accept 18½ cents as a compromise. Murray accepted the offer and Fairless rejected it, making a nationwide steel strike inevitable. Truman's high-level negotiations failed, and on January 21, 1946, approximately 750,000 CIO members struck the nation's basic steel makers, metal fabricating plants, and oil tool industries.[72]

Between September, 1945, and January, 1946, the negotiations between Houston's CIO officials and Hughes Tool followed the same pattern as those at the national level. General manager Ralph Neuhaus, executive vice president Noah Dietrich, and assistant director of industrial relations Jimmy Delmar served as Hughes Tool's chief negotiators and consistently rejected the union's wage demands.[73] They correctly argued that Hughes Tool was a metal fabricating plant and bought semifinished steel products from the country's basic steel industry and the company simply could not afford to peg its wage scale to large national corporations such as United States Steel. Rather than a flat monetary raise, Neuhaus offered a 12½ percent hourly increase. He argued that a larger pay boost was impossible without a compensating rise in the price of the company's products, which was impossible until the OPA lifted price controls from oil drilling equipment (which did not happen until March, 1946). The company's negotiating team blamed what they regarded as the union's unreasonable wage demands and the OPA's price controls for sabotaging negotiations.[74]

Frank Hardesty, who led the CIO's negotiating team, insisted that any wage increase agreed upon between the big steel companies and the CIO must be implemented at Hughes Tool. He rejected management's 12½ percent offer, rightly arguing that a percentage raise discriminated against workers in the lower pay brackets.[75] In particular, a percentage raise would unfairly discriminate against African Americans because they held all the lower pay-bracket jobs. Black members overwhelmingly supported the union's stand on the wage issue.[76]

As negotiations continued Hughes Tool abandoned its percentage raise offer and changed it to 12½ cents per hour with a promise to increase it to 15 cents at an undisclosed date after a new contract was signed. In keeping with the CIO's national demand of 18½ cents, Hardesty rejected the offer. In an effort to keep pressure on management, Hardesty called for a strike vote in November, 1945. The tactic backfired and resulted in weakening the CIO's bargaining leverage.

Employees voted to strike but by a narrow margin, 2,339 in favor to 2,167 against. Another 1,084 eligible voters did not bother to cast ballots. Nearly twice as many voted as actually belonged to the CIO because in National Labor Relations Board–monitored strike votes, all employees in the bargaining unit were eligible to cast ballots. The CIO had the right to a Labor Board–monitored strike vote because of its board certification as the collective bargaining agent. Only 42 percent of the 5,590 eligible voters supported the strike, clearly indicating that implementing an effective walkout would be difficult. Hardesty and other CIO officials downplayed the closeness of the vote by claiming the result was an example of union democracy at work. They also blamed the Independent Metal Workers Union for smearing the CIO over its racial policies and wage demands.[77]

T. B. Everitt, the recently elected president of IMW Local No. 1, skillfully played the race card by issuing an unsubstantiated report that

900 of the 1,100 black voters cast their ballots for the CIO.[78] The IMW had successfully race-baited the CIO since 1941, and Everitt hoped that exploiting racial fears during the postwar turmoil would destroy the CIO. He wanted to frighten whites into thinking that a successful CIO strike with overwhelming black support would bring racial equality to Hughes Tool.[79] Everitt harangued employees about the CIO's Houston leadership having tried, though a vast majority of its white members opposed it, to eliminate the contract's racial segregation and upgrade blacks to parity with whites. He warned that the CIO's attempts to impose racial equality "won't work. . . . [M]ost of the Negroes know it won't work. The white people know it won't work." Everitt concluded that the CIO was inviting "racial friction" and was unfit to "bargain for the employees of Hughes Tool Company."[80]

Everitt also attacked the CIO's intended strike on economic grounds. He announced that the IMW saw no reason to walk out "since the company [had] offered an increase of 12½ cents an hour and [had] agreed to adjust that after a national wage is set."[81] In rhetoric reminiscent of Hughes Tool's defunct company union, Everitt reassured employees of management's sincerity with its latest wage offer and wondered "why in the name of high heaven does our rival union insist on striking?" He warned that the CIO's Hughes Tool "henchmen" were going to shut down the plant for no good reason and urged employees to cross picket lines. Everitt urged employees to help him and the IMW defeat the CIO in its effort to secure an unreasonable wage increase and abolish racial segregation at Hughes Tool. IMW Local No. 1 conducted its own strike vote and its membership voted five to one against a strike.[82] Knowing the depth of black support for a strike, Everitt and the IMW's white officers would not allow the IMW's blacks to vote. But they did succeed in enlisting Richard Guess's help in trying to undermine black CIO support.

Guess's labor activism at Hughes Tool dated back to 1926 when he helped organize the Hughes Tool Colored Club, the firm's black company union. In 1940 he helped organize the IMW's Jim Crow union, Local No. 2, and served as its business agent. One of Hughes Tool's leading black apologists for the company's segregation, he acknowledged that the CIO enjoyed strong black support. Referring to the Labor Board supervised strike vote, he claimed that the nine hundred blacks that voted in favor of the walkout had been duped by slick-talking CIO officials. He claimed they worded the ballot to intentionally confuse black voters. According to Guess, blacks who voted in favor of the strike thought "they were voting for more money and not a strike."[83] The charge was ridiculous since the ballots merely asked whether one approved or disapproved of going on strike.

Using a familiar antiunion argument, Guess also accused Houston CIO director Frank Hardesty of only being "interested in that dollar a month [union dues] so [he] can be sure of [his] big fat salary." Rhetorically Guess asked blacks who was going to pay their rent and buy their groceries if they went on strike while the CIO's leaders lived in luxury. He reminded blacks that the IMW was an independent union and not beholden to the corrupt whims of the "big union [bosses] in Philadelphia, Detroit, or [Houston's] Union National Bank Building." Guess urged them to abandon the CIO and its "spineless and ineffective policies" and asserted that "no body tells us when to work and when not to work."[84] In promoting the IMW, Guess blithely ignored its oppressive racial discrimination as well as the CIO's efforts to end such discrimination.

Despite weak support for a strike, promises by the IMW to cross picket lines, and management's latest wage offer, Hardesty refused to compromise and Hughes Tool's CIO membership joined the national steel strike on January 21, 1946. When the walkout began, animosity between the antagonists had reached a fever pitch generated by the turbulent wartime and postwar labor tensions. It boiled over during the strike and they battled without quarter. The strike proved to be the decisive showdown between Hughes Tool and the IMW, and the CIO. Its aftermath would shape the company's labor and race relations for a generation.

CHAPTER SEVEN

The Independent Metal Workers
Union Era, 1946–1961

THE 1946 STRIKE turned out to be the climactic battle between the CIO, Hughes Tool, and the Independent Metal Workers Union. The CIO's misguided decision to strike in the face of widespread opposition to the walkout, internal racial dissension, management's absolute refusal to accept the union's wage demands, and the IMW's willingness to serve as strikebreakers all coalesced in defeating it. Shortly after the strike the IMW regained the collective bargaining rights, and labor relations at Hughes Tool reverted back to the good-old-boy style of Jim Crow unionism that suited management, white union leaders, and much of the white rank and file. The company regained the upper hand in dealing with a weak independent union that avoided confrontation, toed management's line rather than serving as an aggressive workers' advocate, and accepted racism and job discrimination as part of the natural order of things.

When the strike began on January 21, 1946, Hughes Tool vowed to remain open and continue production. Ralph Neuhaus, Hughes Tool's general manager and vice president, stated in a press release that the company would continue operations as long as possible to protect "the right of employees to work and support their families." He blasted the CIO's walkout as a sympathy strike and criticized it for dragging Hughes Tool's "employees into a fight in which they were not concerned."[1] Neuhaus was referring to the union's demand for an 18½-cents-per-hour increase for all workers in the basic steel making industry. He rejected the demand, arguing that Hughes Tool was a steel fabricator, not a steel producer, and expressed puzzlement over why the union's local leadership failed to accept that difference. The CIO's Frank Hardesty countered that though "Hughes and the other nine [struck] plants are fabricators [that] does not exclude then from the steel industry."[2] Armco Steel's massive mill located on the Houston Ship Channel was the city's only firm that was a basic steel producer and turned raw natural resources into semifinished steel products.

The other nine Houston plants struck by the CIO had made arrangements to shut down operations rather than attempt to operate with an uncertain number of workers.[3] To maintain the peace, the Houston Police and Harris County Sheriff's Department assigned special units to patrol the areas around the struck plants. The CIO concentrated its picketing at Hughes Tool and organized only token picketing at the other struck plants since they had ceased operations.[4] On the first day of the strike, nearly 350 men and women manned the CIO picket lines at Hughes Tool. Approximately 1,000 workers, mostly nonunionists and members of IMW Local No. 1, crossed the lines. The pickets heckled those workers with catcalls and name-calling while police escorted them into the plant, but everything remained peaceful. Veterans who had returned to work after the war engaged in ribald, good-natured teasing and chided each other's strike loyalties.[5]

Determining exactly how many of Hughes Tool's approximately 6,000 employees actually reported to work on that first day and throughout the strike was impossible; management, CIO, and the IMW all offered different totals that supported their position. The cordiality of the strike's first day quickly evaporated. At the end of the first week, derisive cries between strikers and nonstrikers worsened, and law enforcement officers struggled to keep heated verbal exchanges from escalating into violence.[6]

At the end of the strike's first week, police investigated alleged threats made against independent truck drivers who had tried to make deliveries to the company. Four drivers testified before the grand jury that they had been cursed and threatened by strikers in the vicinity of the plant. In addition to the truck drivers who were allegedly threatened, two scabs were reportedly knocked down and beaten on their way home from work by a gang of five strikers.[7]

One of those beaten, A. P. Dare, told police that a week before the strike began one of his assailants had warned him that he better not work if there was a walkout. The other victim, G. A. Krueger, was warned that "[i]f you ever set your foot at the Hughes Tool Company we will get you." Dare and Krueger identified two of the attackers and the police arrested them, but they posted bond and were released. Charles Smith, Houston's assistant CIO director, condemned the attacks and suggested that they happened because of personal differences between those involved and not over Dare and Krueger crossing the picket lines.[8]

According to a Hughes Tool advertisement published in Houston's daily papers, approximately 1,406 employees reported for work on the day the strike started. During the strike's first two weeks management kept production going by putting them all to work on one shift. In a letter dated January 25, 1946, and sent to all employees, Ralph Neuhaus urged them to report back to work. He declared, "Over 1,900 of your fellow employees are now working. Attendance has increased every day of the strike. Your job is ready and so is a wage increase of 15 to 18½ cents an hour." The letter's promise of a raise appeared to have significant effect; by February 2 more than 2,571 people were working, making it necessary to add a second shift.[9]

On February 14 Hughes Tool executive vice president Noah Dietrich reported that 3,511 employees were working. Hughes Tool added a third shift, but Dietrich noted that the company had not yet returned to its "pre-strike status of work" and output. The CIO's Frank Hardesty challenged Dietrich's numbers and asserted that "a lot of office workers and supervisors are on the job" and that union officials counted "at least one-third less cars" in the parking lot after a third shift was added.[10] Though full production had not been restored, it became increasingly clear that the strike was in serious trouble. The company's back-to-work movement gathered momentum for several reasons: the closeness of the strike vote, management's wage counteroffer, and the IMW's effective strikebreaking efforts that included crossing picket lines and Red- and race-baiting the CIO.

After the strike started, Hughes Tool promised an immediate 15 cents per hour wage increase as soon as the company returned to full production on all three shifts.[11] Management also promised to consider increasing that by an additional 3½ cents per hour once the strike was called off.[12] But the company made it clear that it would not give in to the union's wage demand as a condition to end the strike. It would add the additional 3½ cents at its discretion. Noah Dietrich stated in a press release that as soon as full production resumes, "employees will get the same wage increases they would have received if there had been no strike with the exception that the raise would have been granted earlier if the union had not prevented it [by striking]."[13] The company could afford to make the offer because in March the Office of Price Administration was lifting price controls on its products.[14]

Management's strategy was aimed at restoring full production but it also focused on breaking the CIO. The company's offer decisively undermined the CIO's wage demand by matching it. At this point many CIO loyalists questioned the wisdom of continuing the strike and risking the union's survival. If strikers did not immediately return to work they would justifiably be scapegoated for blocking the 15 cents raise and continue to lose their regular earnings in addition to the raise. But CIO International president Murray decreed that no local union could settle for less than the 18½ cents demanded.[15]

Murray's position underscored the CIO's bureaucratic top-down leadership style, which was one of its greatest weaknesses. Rather than being sensitive to and adjusting to local conditions such as the Hughes Tool strike, the union's national leadership was uncompromising over the wage demand even when it threatened the survival of local unions. A lifelong union activist, Murray had suffered through countless defeats in labor disputes prior to the New Deal and he harbored a healthy distrust of management promises. Although the federal government was in the hands of allies of organized labor and the public no longer tolerated companies bludgeoning unions into submission as they had in the past, Murray opposed any concession on the wage issue.[16] The IMW proved extremely effective in exploiting the CIO's autocratic leadership.

T. B. Everitt, president of IMW Local No. 1, lambasted Hughes Tool's CIO locals for obeying the orders of "big union bosses hundreds of miles away" in Pittsburgh and "unfamiliar" with the Houston situation. He urged strikers to exercise "their God-given right of thinking and acting for themselves [by coming] back to work." Everitt trumpeted the IMW's wisdom in voting against the strike and supporting Hughes Tool's wage offer. His biting criticism of the CIO's refusal to allow members to vote on the 15 cents wage offer caused a great deal of dissension within the union's white local.[17] In addition to this, Everitt skillfully exploited the racial issue to deepen the rift between the white and black CIO locals.

Along with A. W. Husted, the secretary of the IMW's white local, Everitt wrote numerous articles in the union's newspaper, the *Independent Journal,* Red- and race-baiting the CIO. They labeled the CIO's calls for racial equality Communistic. In one article Everitt claimed that Ernest Martin, the former president of the CIO's black local, was a "very active member" in the Texas Communist party and accused Martin and the CIO of "spreading the theory of Communism" with its calls for race equality.[18] In another article, Husted charged that Martin, "Czar Frank Hardesty," and their fellow CIO travelers were attempting to "shove Communism down our throats" with their calls for race mixing.[19]

Members of the Texas Communist party unintentionally fed Everitt's and Husted's hysteria by distributing a handbill during the strike that called for racial solidarity. The handbill called on the CIO to abolish its Jim Crow local and end discrimination against Negro workers. It also accused management of encouraging racial divisions so it "could sit back and laugh as [it] raked in profits while the Negro and white worker competed against each other." The notice further stoked IMW frenzy by calling for an immediate end to job and wage discrimination and establishing a biracial CIO local. It also urged workers to support the CIO's strike since it was the only union that "truly represents them in their fight for higher wages."[20]

Though the vast majority of blacks loyally supported the CIO's strike, those in IMW Local No. 2 organized a back-to-work movement similar to Everitt's. In early February, David Butler, its president, and Richard Guess, its business agent, sent a letter to the pastors of Houston's black churches asking them to persuade their congregation members on strike to return to work. They urged the clergymen to announce that the "colored workers [were] being misled" and "double-crossed" by the CIO and warned that if strikers did not return to work they would lose their "good jobs at Hughes Tool." Butler and Guess told pastors that many of the CIO's white members had already betrayed black strikers by returning to work and the strike was doomed. Subtly suggesting that those honoring the walkout faced possible blacklisting, they pleaded with ministers to convince strikers that it would be in their personal interest and "best for the [black] race as a whole" if they went back to work.[21]

Black CIO staff man Forrest Henry responded with a letter of his own in which he defended the union and disputed Butler's and Guess's allegations. He told black pastors that Butler and Guess were part of an "Unholy Alliance" in Houston whose aim was to defeat the CIO at all costs. Henry's letter stated that they were two of a "pitifully few colored men, who for their own personal good, advocate for management" and cautioned that they "mean the Negro race no good." He declared that the CIO's strike was a fight for a higher standard of living for blacks, which would lead to better homes, education, and churches. Henry urged striking congregation members not to return to work until the

CIO staff man Forrest Henry (*with sign*), mans the picket line during the union's 1946 strike against Hughes Tool. *Photograph Courtesy of Wiley Henry, Houston.*

CIO triumphed.[22] In addition to Henry's letter, Frank Hardesty spoke to the black Baptist Minister Union and explained why the union was holding firm in its wage demand. He also asked the clerics for their cooperation and support in bringing the strike to a successful conclusion.[23] Unwavering black support for the walkout enabled it to continue. Even C. W. Rice, editor of the *Houston Negro Labor News* and the CIO's leading black critic, admitted that African American support for the strike was solid in spite of numerous white defections.[24]

The passionate feelings in the black community stirred by the strike served as a backdrop for the worst case of violence during the dispute. On Sunday evening February 17, Richard Guess, longtime Hughes Tool employee and outspoken CIO critic, was murdered while walking home after attending services at Fourth Missionary Baptist Church.[25] Sporadic threats had been made against blacks who crossed the Hughes Tool picket lines, but Guess's murder was the first outright act of violence against an African American. Katherine Guess believed that her husband's murder was linked to his opposition to the CIO's strike. When questioned by police after her husband's murder, she stated that several weeks earlier Olin Dunfred, a black CIO unionist, warned her that her husband was a "marked man" because of his continued work at the company and his outspoken criticism of the CIO. Dunfred also alerted her to threats about their home being blown up.[26] He related his fears to Katherine Guess so she and her husband could take precautions to protect themselves. Despite his good faith effort in alerting the Guess's to the threats on their lives, police arrested Dunfred along with five other black suspects in connection with the murder. After questioning, all were released.[27]

Hughes Tool posted a $2,000 reward for information leading to the arrest of the killer, while black fraternal organizations pledged another $1,000, and the IMW contributed $500. In a rare show of racial sensitivity, T. B. Everitt announced that his union would spend any amount of money necessary to bring Guess's murderer to justice. He implied that the CIO was culpable in Guess's death by noting that "[i]f it should develop that the strike is responsible for the killing it certainly would be a sad commentary that a man cannot work without endangering his life."[28] In the wake of Guess's murder, other blacks came forward and made unsubstantiated claims that black CIO strikers Phillip Tate and Wendell Hawkins had threatened their lives. Police questioned Tate and Hawkins as well as dozens of other CIO members, but no charges were filed. The authorities failed to solve the murder and it was never determined whether the killer was a CIO member, agent provocateur, or someone not associated with the labor dispute.[29]

Funeral services for Richard Guess at Fourth Missionary Baptist Church were presided over by the Reverend E. Stanley Branch. Approximately three thousand mourners paid their respects and bid Guess farewell. Guess had been well known and active in the black community, which accounted for the large turnout. Besides his labor activism, Guess was financial secretary of the Fourth Missionary Baptist Church, served as a director of the Third Ward Civic Club, and occasionally contributed articles to the *Houston Negro Labor News*. Among those who paid him tribute was Lulu White, executive secretary of the Houston NAACP, who promised that her organization would not rest until the guilty person or persons were brought to justice. But the most controversial speaker to deliver a eulogy was Vance Muse, who was the only white person in a sea of black faces.[30] The Reverend Branch allowed Muse, a white supremacist, to give a eulogy.

Muse identified himself as the secretary-treasurer of the Christian American Association; he did not reveal that his organization was committed to white supremacy, the twelve-hour workday, a six-day work week, and less pay for overtime. Muse admitted that he had never met Richard Guess but claimed to be "well acquainted with, and loved and cherished the [anti-CIO] principles for which [Guess] had lived and died."[31] Muse thundered that he and Richard Guess both believed in "the God-given right of every man and women to work regardless of color, creed, or union or nonunion membership." He deemed it an honor to pay Guess a final tribute and credited Guess with inspiring many IMW members to cross the picket lines of the Communist-manipulated CIO.[32] Muse blamed the CIO for Guess's murder and thundered to the mourners "the CIO, Communist Party, and other radical groups got rid of a powerful foe when Richard Guess was murdered in the dark." Muse concluded his tribute in evangelical fervor, declaring, "The bright lights of Heaven were turned on for the Houston Metal Worker so he could pass through the Pearly Gates as did the Carpenter of Galilee who also was crucified for his beliefs."[33] The rousing eulogy for a murdered black unionist by an avowed racist and antiunion zealot brought an immediate and heated response from Carter Wesley publisher of the *Houston Informer.*

Wesley, an outspoken CIO supporter, questioned Muse's motivation for attending the funeral. He editorialized that white people only go to colored funerals when there is a strong personal tie between the living and deceased. Wesley warned that "the presence of Muse gives Negroes something to think about despite their sadness and shock at the death of Richard Guess." Labeling Muse the "high priest" of the antilabor movement, Wesley pointed out that Muse was responsible for the passage of antiunion, right-to-work legislation in several southern states. He concluded by wondering why Vance Muse, the leader of "one of the most prejudiced organizations in the United States should mourn a Negro he had never been introduced to."[34] Wesley's article accurately portrayed Muse and the Christian American Association.

Wesley's arch rival, C. W. Rice, the publisher of the *Houston Negro Labor News,* printed excerpts from Muse's eulogy but offered no explanation for the racist's attendance at the funeral. Nor did Rice comment on the Christian American Association's commitment to racial discrimination. Despite the urging of Muse and Rice, and shock over Guess's murder, most African Americans strikers continued to honor the CIO's picket lines even when their white counterparts abandoned the walkout in ever-increasing numbers.[35]

By the middle of March, the strike had been going on for more than eight weeks. Management reported that more than 4,300 employees had returned to work, but even with so many workers back on the job production was at only 65 percent of capacity. The company held to its promise not to grant the 15-cents-per-hour pay raise until full production resumed on all three shifts.[36] Workers blamed the CIO for holding back production and blocking the pay raise. Many CIO members agreed, and nearly 1,300 members withdrew from the union. Meanwhile, the IMW mounted a highly successful recruiting campaign that netted 1,022 members.[37] Desperate to avoid a complete rout union officials persuaded management to meet with them and discuss ending the strike.

Jimmy Delmar, assistant director of industrial relations, headed management's negotiating team. He enjoyed an immensely powerful position and in essence dictated terms to the CIO's negotiators. Delmar absolutely refused the union's demand for 18½ cents per hour. The company offered 17 cents in return for two major concessions. The union must drop its two unfair labor charges against the company that were pending before the National Labor Relations Board and blocking a new union certification election, and the CIO must consent to a new election within six months after signing the contract.[38] Charles Smith, the union's chief negotiator, received permission from Philip Murray, president of the international CIO, to accept the company's offer. The seventy-seven-day strike ended on April 8, 1946, and the union suffered a crushing defeat. It dropped the charges with the Labor Board, lost the wage issue, and failed to dislodge racial discrimination. CIO loyalists nicknamed the new agreement the "yellow dog contract," because it was clear that management had given the CIO a take-it-or-leave-it choice and the union had no alternative but to accept.[39]

The term "yellow dog contract" was a throwback to the pre–Wagner Act days when employers could legally force employees to sign agreements pledging never to join a union as a condition of employment. The CIO's agreement to hold a union certification election within six months of the signing of the contract was tantamount to a death sentence for the union because its membership had defected in droves to the IMW during the strike.

Management's negotiators also insisted that the new contract must keep Jim Crow in place. CIO officials meekly complied, and the agreement racially segregated job classifications placing whites in classifications titled part I and blacks in part II. Wage scales and promotional ladders remained strictly segregated.[40] This was an especially bitter disappointment for the nearly 600 black CIO unionists who had re-fused to cross the picket line. At the time the contract negotiations were going on, only 300 white unionists were still on strike.[41] The CIO had once again betrayed its most loyal members, Hughes Tool's African Americans. Upon learning of the contract's racial discrimination, C. W. Rice blamed not only white CIO racists but black staff man Robert Grovey, who had acquiesced to the contract's Jim Crowism. Rice declared that the CIO's loyal African Americans had been "given a kick in the britches and thrown to the wolves" by Grovey who was nothing more than a CIO "stooge [and] Uncle Tom."[42]

The IMW's T. B. Everitt immediately petitioned the Labor Board to conduct a union certification election. The union had last filed an election petition in September, 1945, but it was denied because of the CIO's pending unfair labor charges against Hughes Tool. When the CIO dropped the charges as part of its settlement with management, the way was clear for a new election.[43] The Labor Board deemed it essential that an election should take place. It wanted to democratically settle the four-year running battle between the unions that had seen "numerous charges filed before the NLRB, legal action taken in Federal Court, violations of National War Labor Board directives, and seizure of the plant by the Army."[44] The NLRB conducted the election in early August, 1946, and the IMW easily won. It polled 1,865 votes to the CIO's 1,105, while about 810 eligible voters did not cast ballots. The IMW and Hughes Tool negotiated a new contract that went into effect in November, 1946. T. B. Everitt claimed that the agreement restored all the benefits that employees had lost while the CIO was the bargaining agent between 1943 through 1946.[45]

Following the IMW's election victory Carter Wesley editorialized in the *Houston Informer* over why the CIO lost and whether blacks should continue to support the union. Wesley noted during the election that the CIO enjoyed the advantages of incumbency, had maintenance of membership, exacted the largest pay raise ever enjoyed by employees, and still lost the election. He observed that black support for the CIO had wavered very little and blacks had faithfully supported the union despite its Jim Crow segregation. African Americans had accepted the CIO's excuse that a Jim Crow local had been temporarily created because organizing at Hughes Tool was so tough and that eventually it would be abolished. Wesley no longer had any patience for the CIO's broken promise of racial equality.[46]

He urged that before Hughes Tool's blacks put their faith in the CIO again, the union must earn their trust by establishing one integrated local in which blacks enjoyed full equality with whites. In a veiled denunciation of the CIO, Wesley stated, "For the first time since the two unions have been vying out there, the *Informer* takes the position of desisting from criticism of the Independent union. . . . All men who are honest should give the Independent union a fair chance."[47] The CIO had lost the support of Carter Wesley, its most loyal and powerful African American voice for more than a decade.

Hughes Tool's blacks remained committed to the labor movement even though it meant membership in the IMW's segregated local. Black CIO unionists transferred to the IMW, and many who had been officers in the CIO's Jim Crow local won election to the same offices in the black branch of the IMW. They believed that union representation, even by the IMW, gave them a measure of protection from abusive management and a measure of control over their occupational lives.[48] Nonetheless, there were black and white members of the IMW who doubted its effectiveness as an advocate.

Longtime black union activist Columbus Henry believed, as did many others, that the IMW had little influence and its only function was to keep the CIO from returning. Management opposed unions on principle, but if it had to deal with one it preferred the IMW since it was unaffiliated with a large national union and all its members were Hughes Tool employees. Henry's union experience convinced him that management exerted almost total control over the union in contract negotiations, grievance procedures, wage increases, and job classifications. In his view most of the union's officers, black and white, were in the company's back pocket and their main duties were to rubberstamp management policies and serve as cheerleaders to placate restless rank and filers.[49]

For African Americans like Henry the uneven power structure between management and the IMW was skewed even further by racism. He observed that in dealing with management the union's white local had little more power than the Jim Crow local but whatever power the Metal Workers Union had "whites were in the driver's seat." Henry leveled his harshest criticism at those officers in the black local he considered "Uncle Toms," who had "gotten small favors from management . . . and did what was told to them."[50]

Following the 1946 certification election, the Labor Board jointly certified both IMW locals as the collective bargaining agent at Hughes Tool. The IMW's Labor Board certification enabled the union's racially segregated locals to appear to be coequal partners in a unified labor organization, while in practice the certification allowed the white majority to dominate the black members. Technically, according to the NLRB's joint certification of the IMW's two locals, any collective bargaining agreement between the union and Hughes Tool needed the approval of both locals to be valid. But in practice, Local No. 2's minority membership, approximately 25 percent of the union, insured that it could not vote down any contract approved by Local No. 1.[51]

The IMW's constitution and its contracts with Hughes Tool expanded and defined white control over black unionists. It created two segregated locals with Local No. 1 for whites and Local No. 2 for "colored members." The document also established membership requirements and granted each local the authority to handle its own affairs independently. Amending the constitution required that three-fourths of the combined membership from both locals approve proposed amendments. It also enabled Local No. 1 to exploit its numerical superiority, impose racial segregation, control amendments to the constitution, and decide whether or not to include Local No. 2 in contract talks with management.[52]

Contracts negotiated between the IMW and Hughes Tool from 1946 through 1961 perpetuated black subordination. The agreements generally spanned two-year periods and were renegotiated prior to their expiration date. The negotiating procedure called for the officers of each local to prepare proposals in advance of meeting with management. Prior to actual talks with the company, the leadership from both locals would meet in joint session to review the proposals and decide which ones to present during talks with management. After agreeing on specific proposals, the presidents of both locals would then meet with company officials to negotiate the contract. In actuality, Local No. 1's president customarily served as the IMW's only spokesman during the actual talks with Hughes Tool. The process put Local No. 2 at a disadvantage since all proposals prior to contract talks were subject to a vote by the rank and file. This practice carried an implicit threat that any initiatives from the black leadership calling for an end to the Jim Crow status quo could be voted down by the majority white membership. Additionally, the president of Local No. 1 could refuse to accept Local No. 2's proposals, demand revisions that rendered them impotent, or simply refuse to introduce them during the bargaining sessions with management.[53]

The contracts also established a segregated job classification system

TABLE 6 Hughes Tool Company, Labor/Pay Grades and Pay Scales, Effective August 1, 1959

Labor Grade	No. of Pay Grades, White	No. of Pay Grades, Black	Pay Scales
LG 12	6	0	$2.935–3.195
LG 11	5	0	$2.860–3.045
LG 10	4	0	$2.750–2.195
LG 9	4	0	$2.660–2.805
LG 8	4	0	$2.585–2.715
LG 7	6	0	$2.420–2.640
LG 6	4	0	$2.365–2.530
LG 5	1	4	$2.260–2.420
LG 4	1	4	$2.145–2.310
LG 3	0	4	$2.095–2.245
LG 2	0	9	$1.760–2.145
LG 1	0	4	$1.760–1.940

SOURCE: Contract between the Independent Metal Workers Union, Locals 1 and 2, and the Hughes Tool Company, September 15, 1959, NARACP, RNLRB, RG 25, CF 6768–62, "Official Report of Proceedings before the National Labor Relations Board in the Matter of Hughes Tool Company and Independent Metal Workers Union Locals Nos. 1 and 2 and United Steelworkers of America, AFL-CIO," Exhibit GC-2, p. 94.

with twelve hourly labor grades. The classifications were subdivided into two groups with those designated group I being for whites and those in group II reserved for blacks. The grouping system created segregated lines of promotion and demotion that prevented members of group II from being promoted or demoted to jobs in group I.[54] Blacks hired on at the lowest level in labor grade one could not advance higher than grade five, while whites hired on at the highest scale in labor grade five and customarily did not hold any classification lower than that. The highest level in labor grade twelve paid 32 percent more than the highest level available to blacks in labor grade five.

During cutbacks and business downturns, whites received preferential treatment, since the contracts allowed whites facing layoffs in their classification system to bump blacks holding jobs in labor grades four and five who had less seniority. But even during periods of layoffs, whites refused, based on custom and contractual arrangements, to accept jobs in labor grades one, two, and three because those had always been "Negro" jobs. Additionally, the contracts reserved unskilled menial jobs for blacks and specifically excluded them from all occupations that required operating any machinery other than forklift trucks and other material- handling equipment. All skilled trades classifications and apprenticeships for various crafts such as electrician, machinery repairman, and millwright were in group I and reserved for qualified white applicants from within the plant.[55] Contracts between the IMW and Hughes Tool, the union's constitution, management's support of segregation, and the Labor Board's joint certification all contributed to allowing Jim Crow to flourish at the company.

Smothered by the Jim Crow environment that dominated labor relations at Hughes Tool and Houston in general, African American workers had no choice but to accept segregation. Federal agencies offered little hope in reforming the status quo. The NLRB and the federal courts heard cases from black workers in other industries accusing unions of racial discrimination, but neither the Labor Board nor federal judiciary recognized racism within unions as an unfair labor practice subject to punitive action. Between 1945 and 1962, the NLRB and federal courts justified their position by arguing that black workers who voluntarily placed themselves under the bargaining authority of discriminatory white-controlled unions could choose to leave those unions. The NLRB's daily contact with labor problems enabled it to define a union's duty of fair representation. But rather than concerning itself with racial discrimination as well as its normal duties of protecting workers from employer discrimination based on union activity or inactivity, for nearly twenty years following World War II, the NLRB contended that segregated unions, such as the IMW, did not unfairly represent their African American membership. Consequently, the Labor Board continued to jointly certify the IMW's segregated locals and allow them to represent workers in the same bargaining unit.[56]

In addition to race, other issues plagued the IMW and threatened to tear it apart. During the late 1940s and early 1950s, the IMW's white local, Local No. 1, initiated a policy of charging members with delinquent dues a fee to file grievances. It also charged a fee to nonmembers who requested that the union file a grievance on their behalf. Both practices violated the union's Labor Board certification that required it to represent all employees in the bargaining unit regardless of whether they were in good standing with the union or were nonunion.[57] Several disgruntled white members, including grievance man A. L. Curtis, filed unfair labor charges against IMW Local No. 1. In their petition to the Labor Board they demanded that the IMW's certification be revoked for nonrepresentation. The black local, Local No. 2, had never charged fees to process grievances but was included in the Labor Board's decision because it was jointly certified as the collective bargaining agent with Local No. 1.[58]

In a letter to board member Ogden Fields, Curtis declared that the union abused its privileged status as the certified collective bargaining agent by charging employees fifteen dollars to file a grievance and four hundred if the complaint went to arbitration. Curtis battled the IMW's white leadership over the issue but in frustration declared, "there was nothing I could do without the approval of the officers and they're under the thumbs of the Hughes Tool Company." He urged the Labor Board to investigate the case and "do the right thing by the majority of Hughes Tool employees and keep this the good OLD USA."[59]

Ogden Fields looked into the matter, discovered that the abuse was widespread, and was instrumental in convening a Labor Board hearing in February, 1953. Local No. 1 defended its fee system arguing that it was not discriminatory and was merely a way of equitably sharing the costs of representing members whose dues were in arrears and nonmembers who paid no dues. It further defended its action by arguing that members of the International Association of Machinists working at Hughes Tool deluged the IMW with spurious grievances in an effort to drive it into bankruptcy. The Machinists Union dismissed the allegations and argued that the IMW's certification required it to file all grievances without fees, whether for members or not.[60] The charges brought against the IMW were quite serious; they challenged the Labor Board to clearly define a union's obligation to represent employees in the bargaining unit. In particular, could the IMW refuse to represent nonmembers and still retain its Labor Board certification? The board ruled that it could not and ordered the union to end its fee system or lose its certification.

In rendering its decision against the IMW, the Labor Board noted that during its existence it had only heard one other case calling for union decertification for nonrepresentation. In that case it rendered no order because the union voluntarily surrendered its certification. In this case the board ruled that by charging fees to process grievances the IMW "engaged in conduct constituting a clear evasion and abuse of the standard of conduct imposed upon the exclusive representative." It declared that the union's fee system was clearly an unfair labor practice as well as a serious abuse of its privileged position as the collective bargaining agent and "sufficient grounds for the revocation of the [IMW's] certification." Unwilling to lose its Labor Board certification, the IMW abolished its fee system within the ten days stipulated by the order.[61]

In addition to charges of racism and failing to represent employees, the IMW faced another major problem. During the late 1940s and early 1950s a growing number of members lost faith in the union's ability to protect their jobs from outsourcing and new technology. Due to these two factors management reduced its 4,000-member workforce by 1,400 between 1948 and 1949. By 1959 the workforce had shrunk to approximately 2,000.[62] An increasing number of disgruntled employees looked to the United Steelworkers of America or the International Association of Machinists as alternative representatives. Both unions exploited employees' fears of layoff as a means to attract new members, but neither was able to parlay those fears into a movement strong enough to oust the IMW as the certified bargaining agent at Hughes Tool. On three occasions, April, 1950, July, 1959, and September, 1961, the Labor Board conducted union certification elections that pitted the steelworkers, machinists, and the IMW against one another. The IMW won all three elections, but its support shrunk with each one. In July, 1959, for example, the IMW won a runoff against the USWA by a margin of only 29 votes, 1,085 versus 1,056.[63] By 1960 the IMW's hold at Hughes Tool had became precarious.

Substantial voter turnout in the elections and the vigorous competition between unions dramatically demonstrated that unionism was thriving at the company and had become as much a part of its character as the famous drilling bits it manufactured. But for blacks their situation continued to look bleak regardless of what union won the bargaining rights. In the past the Machinists Union had conspicuously denied them membership, and the record of the Steelworkers Union was an appalling string of broken promises to African Americans. Nonetheless, blacks in the IMW's Jim Crow local looked at the union's growing vulnerability with keen interest.

Since its early days the IMW had marginalized African Americans by segregating them in a Jim Crow local and vesting all real power in the white leadership. But during the 1950s and early 1960s, Local No. 2's leadership grew increasingly unwilling to accept the inferior status imposed on them by white union leaders and the company. They had kept abreast of Labor Board decisions and court rulings concerning racial discrimination in organized labor and knew that the struggle to end it would not be easy. As the struggle for bargaining rights at Hughes Tool raged among unions, the past indicated that whoever won would not stand up for racial equality and end job discrimination. Black union activists concluded that they themselves would have to purge Jim Crow from Hughes Tool, but in order to be victorious two things would be necessary: first, the right set of conditions had to be present to mount a challenge to segregation; second, the Labor Board had to recognize racial discrimination as an unfair labor practice.[64] In 1961, deteriorating economic conditions at Hughes Tool and the federal government's increasing commitment to civil rights presented Local No. 2's leadership with an opportunity to challenge Hughes Tool's segregationist tradition.

CHAPTER EIGHT

No Gold Watch for Jim Crow's Retirement

DURING THE LATE 1950S demand for Hughes Tool's drilling products dropped dramatically. According to a monthly company report, the Hughes rig count, which kept track of the number of drilling rigs in operation, between August, 1957, and July, 1958, the number of rigs operating throughout the world dropped from 2,716 to 1,957. In 1957 the company manufactured 2,500 drilling bits a day; in 1959 the number fell to 1,600.[1] In response to the drop-off in its business Hughes Tool reduced its workforce. Between 1959 and 1961 the company eliminated 600 hourly positions and the number of employees stabilized at 2,000, of which 1,600 were whites and 400 were black.[2] Hughes Tool also diversified.

Two of its new ventures included subcontracting machine repair and rebuilding work for government contractors in the space program and supplying specialized products for the Atomic Energy Commission.[3] Hughes Tool's management hoped that securing government contracts would help the company weather the downturn and lead to more work in the future, but federal work presented one major problem: it required that Hughes Tool carry out a policy of nondiscrimination that stemmed from Pres. John F. Kennedy's Executive Order No. 10925 issued in April, 1961. Under the order Hughes Tool could possibly face disqualification from much-needed federal work because of its Jim Crow tradition and willingness to enter into segregated labor agreements with the Independent Metal Workers Union.

Kennedy's order called for an end to racial discrimination in employment and a broadening of opportunities for minorities throughout the country. It called for a program of affirmative action to be carried out by federal departments and agencies under supervision of the newly formed President's Committee of Equal Employment Opportunity (PCEEO). The PCEEO implemented a system to monitor employers' compliance and withhold federal contracts from employers violating the order. Though much ballyhooed as a civil rights breakthrough, in practice the Kennedy Administration subverted Executive Order No. 10925 by including in it a program called "Plans for Progress." [4]

Under Plans for Progress a government contractor could escape PCEEO scrutiny simply by signing a pledge promising to eliminate racial discrimination. Kennedy's order created a Plans for Progress subcommittee of the PCEEO to monitor voluntary compliance. Chaired by Robert Troutman Jr., a political friend and ally of Georgia's two racist U.S. senators William Russell and Herman Talmadge, the subcommittee proved more effective in protecting racial discrimination than in eliminating it. While Troutman successfully reined in the Plans for Progress program, Senators Russell and Talmadge, along with other influential southern members of Congress, guaranteed the failure of the PCEEO by denying it adequate money and staff to investigate discrimination by government contractors. Government contractors soon discovered that they could continue discriminating against blacks with impunity by signing a Plan for Progress.[5]

A year after the order took effect the National Association for the Advancement for Colored People (NAACP) released a highly critical report of Plans for Progress. Herbert Hill the NAACP's labor secretary authored the report and concluded that Kennedy's executive order and Plans for Progress were little more than a public relations exercise aimed at publicizing token civil rights breakthroughs while leaving discrimination in place. He pointed out that Kennedy's order lacked statutory powers and "was impotent when confronted by the powerful financial and political forces in control of industry." This was especially true in the South, where "Negro workers continued to be victims of a tradition of white supremacy which is deeply rooted and gives way but slowly to the forces of social change." Hill blamed weak federal policies, industrial management, and organized labor "for the continued existence of employment discrimination throughout the South."[6]

But Kennedy's executive order did create an atmosphere in which companies became more sensitive about charges of discrimination while still being able to evade mandates to abolish it. The order also made it easier for companies than for labor unions to evade responsibility for discrimination. The Plans for Progress program enabled government contractors to avoid responsibility for job discrimination by merely making a pro forma commitment to eliminate it. On the other hand, if the PCEEO did purse discrimination charges against a government contractor and the company had a collective bargaining agreement that codified racial discrimination, then management could dodge responsibility by blaming the union. Hughes Tool used this strategy during contract talks with the union in the autumn of 1961 after the IMW's black local demanded that discrimination be eliminated from the new contract.

In October and November, 1961, the officers of the white and black locals met several times to draft contract proposals to present management. Local No.2's president, Lorane Ashley, made an unprecedented demand by calling for the IMW to eliminate job discrimination in the new contract. Encouraged by Executive Order No. 10925 and Hughes Tool's desire to secure government contracts, Ashley along with two other officers, Ivory Davis and Columbus Henry, decided that the right set of circumstances were in place to challenge Jim Crow.[7] T. B. Everitt, president of Local No. 1, had been anticipating the demand. Although he denied that blacks at Hughes Tool suffered job discrimination he agreed to consider the demand only after Local No. 2 submitted a formal written proposal outlining a procedure for eliminating it.[8]

On December 14, 1961, Lorane Ashley presented Everitt with the black local's proposal. Without specifically mentioning race, the proposal stated that the current contract blocked "advancement opportunities for all employees" and that the new agreement must eliminate it and "provide greater and more equitable opportunities for all employees."[9] Everitt bristled at the notion that the IMW's contract with Hughes Tool discriminated against blacks, and with support from the union's white leadership refused to include Ashley's demand in the upcoming contract negotiations with management. Everitt did offer to meet with Local No.2's leadership and discuss their differences over job discrimination claims but only after a new contract was signed.[10]

Unbeknownst to officers of the black local, Everitt unofficially met with Jimmy Delmar, Hughes Tool's director of industrial relations, gave him a copy of Local No. 2's demand, and warned him that a confrontation was brewing between the IMW's two locals over discrimination.[11] In a calculated move to allow the company to deny culpability for discrimination, Delmar made it clear to Everitt that the racial dispute between the two locals was their own business. Delmar backed up the company's position by asserting that the basis for discrimination

Officers of the Hughes Tool Company's Independent Metal Workers Union, Local No. 2, ca. 1959–62. *Left to right:* Lorane Ashley, president; Charles Benson, vice president; Pinkston Bell, secretary; Ivory Davis, treasurer. *Photograph courtesy of Ivory Davis, Houston.*

in the contract was rooted in the IMW's constitution and by-laws, and therefore it was the union's responsibility to abolish them.[12] He shocked Local No. 1's president and the company's other white unionists by blaming the union for the company's discrimination.[13] In one deft stroke Hughes Tool abandoned its longtime segregationist allies.

Eventually Hughes Tool signed a memorandum under the Plans for Progress pledging to eliminate discrimination. But job discrimination did not end. With little fear of oversight from the PCEEO, Hughes Tool kept segregation and job discrimination in place to reassure white employees that the company had not abandoned its tradition of racism.[14] Despite securing government contracts and its pledge to eliminate discrimination, the company continued to maintain the position that any plan promoting racial equality must consider Houston's long-established community thought and practices concerning Jim Crow, and whether integration was really in the best interests of blacks and whites. Company officials had argued in the past that poorly planned or impractical integration of white and black employees would inevitably result in racial antagonism. During World War II William Streetman, the company's attorney, had helped block an integration plan by warning that it would "cause a great deal of trouble in the plant and possible rioting." [15] Steeped in the same racism as its white employees, management had grudgingly abandoned its public support of its racist contract with the IMW but continued to support a delaying action against integrating its workforce. On the other hand the IMW's white local did not renounce its support for the discriminatory contract. Consequently, during contract negotiations in 1961 the focus for the company's racism shifted to the union.

T. B. Everitt and Lorane Ashley met with Jimmy Delmar and other Hughes Tool officials on December 18, 1961, to sign a new contract. The major provisions of the agreement included across the board wage increases and expansion of the apprenticeship program by including three more trades.[16] Everitt served as the IMW's sole spokesman during the meeting but signed the contract as representative of Local No. 1. Ashley refused to sign the new agreement. Supported by Ivory Davis and Columbus Henry, he withheld Local No. 2's approval because Local No. 1 refused to include a clause calling for the elimination of discrimination based on race, creed, or color.[17] This marked the first time in Hughes Tool's history that a Jim Crow labor organization had refused to rubber-stamp a racist contract, but the company and Local No. 1 put the contract into effect without Local No. 2's approval. Nonetheless, Local No. 2's stand raised two critical legal questions concerning the IMW's role as the collective bargaining agent at Hughes Tool. One involved the Labor Board's joint certification of the IMW's two locals; the other, the union's obligation under its certification to fairly represent all employees in the bargaining unit.

The Labor Board had jointly recertified the IMW's two locals in October, 1961, and the certification prohibited either local from enacting a separate agreement with management.[18] The new contract, signed only by Local No. 1, violated the provisions of the IMW's certification and was grounds for punitive action by the Labor Board. Local No. 2 had exercised its power under the IMW's certification by refusing to sign the new contract. Shortly after the new contract was signed, the black leadership formulated a plan to pressure the Labor Board into helping them eliminate racial discrimination by forcing the union to honor its duty of fair representation.

Members of Local No. 2's governing council and officers, ca. 1959–62. *Clockwise from left:* Pinkston Bell, Charles Benson, Ivory Davis, Raymond Laboe, unidentified member, unidentified member, Harold Foster, Garfield Barnett, F. White, U. H. Brown, William Neely, Columbus Henry, J. Wynn, A. J. Godwin, and Lorane Ashley. *Photograph courtesy of Ivory Davis, Houston.*

On February 15, 1962, Hughes Tool posted a bid announcing that the company was accepting applications for the newly created tool and die maker apprenticeship. Ivory Davis bid on the job even though the 1961 contract denied blacks admission into apprenticeship programs.[19] The following week the company posted the list of workers chosen for the apprenticeship and, as expected, Davis's name did not appear. Davis, Columbus Henry, and Lorane Ashley met with management to discuss Davis's rejection in light of Hughes Tool's pledge to integrate its workforce. Management explained that Davis could bid on the apprenticeship, but that Hughes Tool was bound to honor its contract obligations with the IMW that limited apprenticeships to white employees.[20] Dissatisfied with Hughes Tool's response, Davis filed a grievance. Since Local No. 2 was not under contract with Hughes Tool and technically could not file a grievance on his behalf, Davis took the heretofore unprecedented, unheard of step of asking the white local to represent him and file the grievance.

The black leadership knew that the IMW's Labor Board certification required Local No. 1 to file the grievance, even though doing so would violate its racially segregated contract with Hughes Tool. Ashley, Davis, and Henry knew that the white leadership would never represent a black member, but it had never been their intention to have Local No. 1 win Davis's grievance. As part of their strategy to abolish Jim Crow at Hughes Tool, they anticipated that the white local would refuse to process the grievance—and that represented the linchpin of their plan. Local No. 1's refusal would give them the opportunity to file an unfair labor charge against Local No. 1 with the Labor Board and force an official investigation into the union's racial discrimination and non-representation of black workers.[21] With the support of Ashley and Henry, Davis wrote to Everitt on April 17, 1962, and asked him for representation in the apprenticeship dispute.[22]

Davis waited more than a month for Everitt to respond to his grievance and when it became clear that an answer was not forthcoming, Local No. 2 lodged a formal complaint against the white local with the Labor Board's Houston office on May 23, 1962. The complaint accused Local No. 1 of violating Davis's rights under the National Labor Relations Act by refusing to file a grievance on his behalf. The Labor Board's regional director notified Hughes Tool and Local No. 1 of the charge, reviewed it, and assigned a Labor Board agent to investigate the complaint.[23]

The investigation lasted until August, and the agent assigned to the case determined that Davis's complaint had merit. The report concluded that the Labor Board should conduct a formal hearing in order to determine if the white local had broken the law and abused its certification. The Labor Board's regional director affirmed the report's findings and scheduled a hearing for October 3, 1962, at the Federal Building in Houston.[24]

Local No. 1's attorney, Tom Davis, responded to the Labor Board's report on September 12, 1962. He defended Local No.1's refusal to process Ivory Davis's grievance and denied any wrongdoing. Davis's brief argued that based on the union's constitution and by-laws Ivory Davis's grievance was the responsibility of the black local. And in an effort to shift blame to the company, he pointed out that in the past Hughes Tool had insisted that Local No. 1 handle grievances for whites and Local No. 2 those for blacks. The brief's last point stated that the black leadership had rejected a contract amendment proposed by Local No. 1 that would attempt to create equal opportunities in the plant. The arguments in Tom Davis's brief were unsuccessful in persuading the regional director to drop the complaint against Local No. 1.[25]

Local No. 2 also took action during the period leading up to the hearing. In September, the black leadership asked the NAACP to represent Local No. 2 and act as its attorney in the case. Since the black local could not afford legal representation, the NAACP readily agreed to take the case.[26] The NAACP had been aware of the Hughes Tool situation for more than four years but had been unable to act because prior to this no black employee had been willing to step forward and file an unfair labor charge against the union or the company. The NAACP's awareness of the discrimination at Hughes Tool came from an unlikely source.

In 1957 the general vice president of the International Association of Machinists contacted Herbert Hill, the NAACP's labor secretary, and alerted him to the overt Jim Crow segregation at Hughes Tool. The Machinists' official provided Hill with a list of names, addresses, and telephone numbers of the black local's officers.[27] The Machinists Union had worked all through the 1950s to unseat the IMW at Hughes Tool and apparently felt that making the NAACP aware of the discrimination at the company would help its cause. This was ludicrous since the Machinists Union was as discriminatory as the IMW, but the issue that riveted Hill's attention was that the IMW had a Jim Crow local.

The IMW's overt discrimination and Jim Crow local increased the odds that the NAACP could successfully argue before the Labor Board that racial discrimination by unions was an unfair labor practice. Unions such as the Machinists, though discriminatory, accepted blacks and whites into the same locals making it harder to make a case against them. But the IMW's segregated locals "constituted a clear and unambiguous example of unfair representation." Hill had grasped this in 1957 but without anyone at Hughes Tool willing to come forth and file charges he could do nothing.[28] Now the situation had changed dramatically because Ivory Davis stepped forward and was determined to see the case through. Hill and the NAACP's general counsel, Robert Carter, marshaled their forces for a decisive battle at Hughes Tool. Carter worked out of the civil rights group's New York office and persuaded the Labor Board to postpone the hearing so he could prepare his case.[29] The board granted his request and postponed the hearing until November 7, 1962. Ivory Davis, Columbus Henry, and Lorane Ashley could not have wished for a more determined advocate than Carter.

Robert Carter joined the legal staff of the NAACP in 1944 after being admitted to the New York State Bar. He served his apprenticeship as a civil rights lawyer under the tutelage of eventual Supreme Court

Robert Carter, general counsel for the NAACP, represented Local No. 2 and Ivory Davis before the National Labor Relations Board. *From the photograph collection of the Library of Congress.*

justice Thurgood Marshall. The NAACP's leadership demonstrated their confidence in Carter by appointing him the organization's general counsel in 1956. While serving under Marshall, and after becoming general counsel, Carter devoted a great deal of effort in the fight for school desegregation. In the early 1960s he redirected that energy at racial discrimination in unions. Carter's decision to wage a legal battle against discrimination in labor unions horrified some in the labor movement. Speaking of Carter's decision one colleague remarked, "The hue and cry against the NAACP went off in every direction and soon zeroed in on Carter." [30]

Telephone calls from "bigwigs," advice from government officials, and numerous official and semiofficial delegations pressured Carter to back off. They all conveyed a similar message: "legal action against labor unions is wrong, not politic, won't work, is illegal, and will harm the NAACP." They all underestimated Carter's resolve and sense of justice. Carter was not the sort of person who went along to get along. He refused to adapt himself and his views to what was popular or politically safe.[31]

After researching the case, Carter concluded that the only way to guarantee that blacks received equal opportunity at Hughes Tool was for the Labor Board to rescind the IMW's certification. Decertification by the Labor Board was the severest punishment the board could mete out to a union. Unions holding board certification enjoyed important legal protections. They included requiring management to recognize a certified union as the collective bargaining agent for its employees and to negotiate in good faith with union representatives. Moreover, during the life of a contract a certified union was protected from competing unions trying to raid its membership. On the other hand, uncertified unions enjoyed no such safeguards.

Carter decided on decertification based on the IMW's tradition of discrimination and its long record of black inequality. He theorized that the Labor Board could force the IMW, under threat of decertification, to handle Ivory Davis's grievance, but after entering the apprenticeship white coworkers could easily have him disqualified by insisting that Davis could not perform the duties he was assigned. Carter wanted to protect Davis from that kind of retribution, but more importantly he wanted to use the case to establish a precedent whereby in the future, qualified blacks seeking whites-only jobs did not have to fight their cases individually. If the Labor Board merely forced the IMW to process Davis's grievance and left the union in place, all blacks seeking whites-only jobs would face the same daunting process that confronted Ivory Davis. Carter concluded that the only way to prevent that, and to guarantee equal opportunity for black workers in the future, was to persuade the Labor Board to revoke the IMW's certification.[32] Convincing the board to decertify the IMW because it racially discriminated against Ivory Davis would establish a legal precedent that the board could use in the future to outlaw racial discrimination throughout organized labor. Carter felt confident that the NAACP could win the case. On October 24, 1962, Carter submitted a brief requesting that the Labor Board decertify the IMW as the collective bargaining agent at Hughes Tool.[33]

In an attempt to avoid a Labor Board hearing and possible decertification, Tom Davis advised Everitt that a merger of the two locals might persuade the Labor Board that a good faith effort had been made to end discrimination and eliminate the need for a public hearing. Davis's plan called for disbanding Local No. 2, opening up membership in Local No. 1 to blacks, and amending the IMW's constitution and by-laws to include a pro forma commitment to eliminate discrimination based on race, color, or creed. [34] The white IMW desperately wanted to avoid a possible Labor Board mandate forcing desegregation. Tom Davis asked the board for another postponement of the hearing so the leadership and attorneys of both locals could meet and negotiate a merger agreement that would resolve the charges against Local No. 1. The Labor Board looked favorably on the proposal and agreed to postpone the hearing until December 11, 1962. Clifford Potter, the Labor Board's regional director in Houston, urged the NAACP's Robert Carter and the IMW's black leaders to accept the white local's merger proposal.[35]

Carter and the black leadership, however, opposed the merger because it did not spell out in precise detail how the consolidated IMW would carry out its obligation of fair representation, eliminate separate lines of promotion, and facilitate black entry into training programs. Carter and his supporters intended to use Local No. 2's leverage to block the proposal. The Labor Board's joint certification empowered Local No. 2 to reject the proposed merger in the same way that Local No. 2 blocked ratification of the 1961 contract.[36] Thus Jim Crow's "separate but equal doctrine" came back to haunt Local No. 1, since the board's certification empowered Local No. 2 to veto any merger offer from the white local that fell short of full racial equality.

During November, 1962, the white leaders and their attorney pressed for a meeting between the officers of both locals.[37] Robert Carter met with the Lorane Ashley, Columbus Henry, and Ivory Davis in mid-November, 1962, and cautioned them not to accept any provisions outlined in the merger proposal without specific guarantees for equal job opportunities and the elimination of existing discrimination in the plant.[38] Their counterparts, Local No. 1's president T. B. Everitt and attorney Tom Davis, expressed their desire for a quick merger, but Carter mistrusted their motives. Like many whites at Hughes Tool,

they relied on a convoluted logic that blamed blacks for the IMW's segregation. Everitt and Tom Davis echoed a widely held white belief that
when the union was first organized in 1941, the blacks not the whites,
had insisted on segregated locals. It was said that blacks felt that such
an arrangement was necessary to protect their interests and give them
full voice in managing their affairs in the IMW.[39] This argument was
fallacious for two reasons. Local No. 2 emanated from the Hughes Tool
Colored Club, which was steeped in the company's segregationist tradition. Second, Houston's historic, oppressive Jim Crow tradition pre-
cluded widespread white support for integration and racial equality
in the IMW. Blacks had never demanded that they be segregated and
relegated to an inferior status in the IMW or at Hughes Tool; it was imposed on them by a tradition of white supremacy.[40]

Moreover, Carter was well aware that blacks suffered similar and
often worse discrimination in integrated unions. The NAACP attorney
speculated that the consolidation of the two locals was a ruse to create
a seemingly integrated union, which would actually purge blacks from
leadership positions and make the IMW's discrimination worse.[41] Carter feared that the merger would abrogate the need for a hearing and
would allow the IMW's racism to escape Labor Board scrutiny. Carter insisted that a hearing was vital if the black leaders hoped to decertify the IMW and then persuade the Labor Board to issue a binding proclamation that outlawed racial discrimination in any union that
represented workers at Hughes Tool.[42] Carter advised the black leaders
to avoid meeting with representatives from Local No. 1, but the white
leaders pressed hard, and, against Carter's advice, Lorane Ashley agreed
to a meeting between the officers of both locals.[43]

On November 13, 1962, Ashley, Davis, and Henry met with Everitt
and the other white officers of Local No. 1. During the meeting, they
prevented the white leadership from disbanding Local No. 2 and forming one local by insisting that a biracial committee be organized and
meet at a later date to draft wording changes in the union's constitution
and by-laws concerning a merger. Afterward the revised documents
would be presented to the rank and file of each local for approval.[44]
Davis, Henry, and Ashley agreed to meet with the committee's white
representatives on November 26.

On the twenty-sixth they met with the seven members of Local
No. 1's governing council. During the meeting the committee revised
the constitution and by-laws by deleting the designation "colored" for
black employees, but the white committeemen refused to include a

declaration banning discrimination based on race, color, or creed that had been proposed by Ashley, Davis, and Henry.[45] The white negotiators voted the proposal down and made a vague promise to include one in future contracts negotiated with Hughes Tool. The meeting reached an impasse when Ashley, Davis, and Henry informed the others that any further movement on the merger would have to wait until Robert Carter and Local No. 2's membership examined the revisions and offered their opinions. Before the committee met, Carter had instructed them not to agree to any proposals by the white committee members, especially any merger scheme.[46]

Following the committee meeting, T. B. Everitt and Tom Davis singled out Local No. 2's president Lorane Ashley and increased their pressure on him to adopt the amended constitution, merge the locals, and drop the charges pending against Local No. 1. Pressure also came from another source, and it bore the stamp of official sanction: Clifford Potter, the Labor Board's regional director in Houston. In a telephone conversation with Ashley, Potter told him that the black local should accept the white local's merger offer, drop the unfair labor charge against the white local, and direct Robert Carter to withdraw the motion to decertify the IMW.[47]

In correspondence to other Labor Board officials, Potter blamed Robert Carter for unnecessarily dragging the case out and blocking the merger effort. He asserted that "so long as Carter is retained as counsel by Local 2 the merger of Locals 1 and 2 will not be accomplished without a decision by the Board."[48] Columbus Henry and Ivory Davis distrusted Potter and resented his pressuring Ashley. They regarded Potter's push to merge the unions and drop the charges as an effort to save the IMW and Hughes Tool from forced integration.

Both men considered Potter "in the pocket of Houston's big business," and more than willing to leave Jim Crow in place. Davis and Henry believed that Potter played a major role in expunging the original unfair labor charges against Hughes Tool. Initially the complaint alleged that the company and Local No. 1 conspired to deny Davis an apprenticeship. But when the Labor Board levied its unfair labor charge it was only against Local No. 1. As far as Davis and Henry were concerned, Potter was responsible for the company's escaping culpability for job discrimination.[49]

But Potter and the union's white leadership softened up Ashley. He lost his nerve and now proved willing to resolve the dispute by merging the two locals and dropping the charges before the Labor Board.[50]

Without Davis or Henry's approval, Ashley notified Carter by telegram that "Local Number 1 had shown a sincere desire to meet our demands without going through a hearing . . . [and] I must say that they are now displaying a spirit of sincerity."[51] Ashley's apparent willingness to accept their offer and drop the charges angered Carter. He fired off a heated reply reminding Ashley that "we had all agreed you would not agree or consent to anything until you had an opportunity to study the proposals and consult with me." Carter cautioned Ashley that a merger with a new labor agreement that "merely states in general terms that you are going to negotiate a contract free of discrimination will get you nowhere."[52]

Venting his frustration, Carter rebuked Ashley by telling him that the Hughes Tool case was of national importance and a victory would end job discrimination in organized labor. If they failed, "it is going to be the fault of the Negro union leaders [in Local No.2], and no one else if this is not settled satisfactorily."[53] With his characteristic candor Columbus Henry noted that "the company could always count on Uncle Tom's like Ashley."[54] He never forgave Ashley for his "effort to sell us down the river."[55] Ivory Davis and Henry managed to block Ashley's efforts to forge a merger, but the rift ended the men's working relationship. Afterward Ashley changed sides and worked with T. B. Everitt in trying to merge the two locals.[56]

On December 11, 1962, Labor Board trial examiner Frederick Reel opened the hearing and took testimony for two days. Both Galveston attorney Arthur Safos, the Labor Board's general counsel, who presented Ivory Davis's charges to the trial examiner, and Robert Carter built their cases against Local No. 1 on two issues: the IMW's duty to fairly represent all employees in the bargaining unit at Hughes Tool and the union's racial discrimination, which prevented it from fulfilling that duty. Witnesses called during the hearing included Ivory Davis, Lorane Ashley, Columbus Henry, T. B. Everitt, R. G. Neel, secretary of the white local, and J. P. Thompson, Hughes Tool's superintendent of manufacturing.[57]

Carter's witnesses, Davis, Ashley, and Henry, testified that the IMW's segregation created an unequal, race-based job classification and promotional system that discriminated against black employees in the bargaining unit. Their testimony and their responses to Tom Davis's cross-examinations made it clear that Local No. 1, despite the Labor Board's joint certification of both locals, dominated the IMW and used its power to subordinate the black membership. Carter argued against the white local's merger plan by warning that the IMW's tradition of inequality would carry over into the consolidated union even if the Labor Board issued an order banning racial discrimination. Carter remained staunchly committed to decertifying the IMW as the only solution to breaking down the color barrier at Hughes Tool.[58]

Tom Davis, who had served as the IMW's attorney since its creation in 1940, did not dispute Local No. 1's history of segregation or dominance over the IMW. Davis and the witnesses he called, Everitt, Neel, and Thompson all defended Local No. 1 by testifying that when the IMW was organized in 1940, blacks demanded that the union be segregated and insisted that segregationist clauses be included in the union's constitution, by-laws, and contracts, therefore black-approved union statutes, not race, influenced Everitt's refusal to process Ivory Davis's grievance.[59] Second, he argued that "it was not the intention of Congress when enacting the National Labor Relations Act to make racial discrimination a violation of the Act." He correctly pointed out that for twenty-eight years the Labor Board had "continuously certified unions with separate locals based on race" and had refused to recognize racial discrimination as an unfair labor practice. At Hughes Tool he pleaded that "the contract and other [union] documents reflect that the segregated jobs at Hughes are clearly not the *animus* of white racists who control or dictate anymore than the Board was when it certified segregation."[60] Third, Davis argued vigorously throughout the hearing that the white leadership's merger proposal demonstrated a good faith effort on their part to eliminate Jim Crow. Though Local No. 2 spurned the offer, white officials remained willing to desegregate the IMW using their plan.[61] Davis blamed the trouble at Hughes Tool on Robert Carter and accused him of jumping "on the bandwagon and joining the anti-racial discrimination parade."[62]

The trial examiner Frederick Reel played a critical role in the proceedings. The Labor Board in Washington had empowered him to conduct the hearing, gather testimony and evidence, and use the data to determine if the IMW had violated the law by refusing to represent Ivory Davis. If Reel determined that it did, he was required to recommend appropriate punitive action against the union. During the two days of testimony, Reel queried Tom Davis, Robert Carter, and Arthur Safos at length concerning the IMW's joint certification as the collective bargaining agent. Reel also wanted their interpretation of Local No. 1's obligation under that certification to fairly represent all employees in the bargaining unit regardless of union membership or race.

Trial Examiner Reel took particular interest in Tom Davis's admission that race had not influenced Everitt's refusal to process Ivory Davis's grievance as well as Everitt's unwavering testimony that Ivory's skin color had nothing to do with the complaint.[63]

Everitt stated in his testimony that "the color of Davis's skin did not affect any decision in rejecting or not processing his grievance." He sought cover in the contract by asserting that Ivory Davis attempted to bid on a job that "the contract didn't provide that he was entitled to." He also tried to infer that whites were subjected to the same contract restrictions as blacks by pointing out that "[i]n Local No. 2 they have certain jobs that the colored people are entitled to, that the white people are not entitled to, and vice versa."[64] Everitt offered no explanation as to why all the lowest paying and most menial jobs were reserved for blacks or why whites had never agitated for inclusion into these dead-end positions.

Reel dismissed the merger issue since the current charges would have to be resolved before the Labor Board could consider a merger of the IMW's two locals. Reel concluded the hearing on December 13, 1962, and afterward instructed the attorneys representing the parties in the case to submit their briefs to him in Washington, D.C., by January 14, 1963. Reel's conclusions based on the evidence gathered, briefs received, and his own research into the legalities of the case would all influence his recommendation to the Labor Board in Washington, D.C., and the future of the IMW at Hughes Tool.[65]

Frederick Reel presented his report to the board in Washington, D.C., on February 28, 1963. He determined that Local No. 1 had violated its certification by discriminating against Ivory Davis and that it had been bound to process Davis's grievance regardless of his race. When it failed to do so, the union violated its obligation to fairly represent all employees in the bargaining unit. Reel recommended that the Labor Board rescind the IMW's certification because the union "discriminated on the basis of race in determining eligibility for full and equal membership, and segregated [its] members on the basis of race." He also suggested that in the future, any union seeking to become the bargaining representative at Hughes Tool be required to post notices throughout the plant that it would not ratify any contract that discriminated against employees because of race.[66]

Robert Carter hailed the report although he cautioned that "an intermediate report is merely a recommendation which the Board may adopt or reject." He thought the board would accept Reel's report because President Kennedy had just taken two affirmative steps to abolishing discrimination in organized labor. He had ordered the U.S. Justice Department to intervene in racial discrimination cases pending before the Labor Board and had ordered the board to take action to end racial discrimination in labor unions.[67]

Local No. 1 could avoid decertification by simply complying with the intermediate report. Tom Davis and T. B. Everitt reintroduced the merger issue as a means of complying with the order. Clifford Potter supported their effort and wanted a local solution without a Labor Board order. They clung to the hope that they could maintain local control over the case, settle it in their favor, and leave Jim Crow in place. But the merger issue, the status of the IMW's contract with Hughes Tool, and indecision by the Labor Board itself all worked to slow down the wheels of justice. The Labor Board's decision on the intermediate report would not be rendered for seventeen months.

One reason the Labor Board in Washington, D.C., withheld its decision on the intermediate report was due to disagreement over whether a merger had indeed occurred. The controversy swirled around the fact that in November, 1962, the IMW's two locals had drafted a new constitution to replace one drawn up in 1957 that specifically created two locals, one for blacks and one for whites. The new constitution supposedly reflected a merger of the IMW's two locals and established one local designated Local No. 1.[68] The new constitution's solution to eliminating discrimination was to simply delete specific language relegating blacks to Local No. 2 and whites to Local No. 1. Everitt and the white leadership maintained their staunch opposition to a clause specifically banning racial discrimination. Lorane Ashley approved the document but Ivory Davis and Columbus Henry regarded it as a public relations exercise that made it appear as if discrimination were eliminated while in actuality it dissolved Local No. 2, denied blacks power in the merged local, and kept job discrimination in place.

Both locals conducted a ratification vote and Local No. 1's membership voted in favor. Local No. 2 agreed to adopt the new constitution but only after Robert Carter had approved it. Carter made it clear that he would not approve it in its original form. He demanded that the constitution specifically lay out methods, means, assurances, and guarantees that segregation would be eliminated. He also asserted that he would not consider approving the new constitution or authorizing such action by Local No. 2 until the Labor Board had issued its decision on Frederick Reels's intermediate report.[69] Without Local No. 2's approval, the new constitution could not go into effect. In one last desperate effort to force a merger T. B. Everitt orchestrated a referendum vote in late 1963. According to the union's existing by-laws approval of three-quarters of the rank and file was necessary to amend the constitution. But the effort backfired.

Only 930 members voted out of a membership of 2,000. Of that number 927 were white and 3 were black. In all, 855 votes were cast in favor with 75 against. Columbus Henry, who by this time had replaced Lorane Ashley as president of Local No. 2, urged members of the black local to boycott the election, and his efforts succeeded. Only 3 blacks broke ranks and voted, while more than 300 members of Local No. 2 did not vote. In a letter to Robert Carter, Henry praised Local No. 2's solidarity by saying, "Our people exhibited excellent manners and stayed away from the polls, we had only three members of our local vote, I am really proud of 'us.'" Thanks to Carter's guidance and the determination and leadership of Columbus Henry, Local No. 2 successfully resisted every effort by the white local to effect a merger.[70]

The merger issue also became entangled in an effort to determine the status of the contract signed between Hughes Tool and Local No. 1 in December, 1961. Technically, there was no labor agreement between Hughes Tool and the IMW, since Local No. 2 had refused to sign the 1961 contract. Moreover, since the IMW still held the collective bargaining rights at Hughes Tool, it was required to be under contract with the company or face Labor Board charges of dealing in bad faith with management.

Hughes Tool expressed a willingness to amend its contract with the IMW to eliminate discrimination based on race, creed, color, or national origin. In January, 1963, Columbus Henry and T. B. Everitt met with Jimmy Delmar and amended the contract accordingly. Everitt signed the contract as president of Local No. 1 and, acting on Robert Carter's advice, Henry signed as president of Local No. 2. Henry emphasized to Everitt and Delmar that his signing the agreement in no way reflected a merger of the IMW's two locals or constituted an admission that discrimination had been eliminated at Hughes Tool. Delmar signed as an imperative to keep the company operating and shield it from charges of unfair labor practices and discrimination. But Delmar and management agreed with Tom Davis's and T. B. Everitt's assertion that the amended contract rendered the Labor Board case against the IMW moot since the contract "is completely free of discrimination."[71] Carter rejected their view and sharply challenged their assertion that the amended contract eliminated discrimination at Hughes Tool.

In a statement to the trial examiner concerning the amended contract, Carter drew a parallel between *Brown v. Board of Education* and the Hughes Tool case. He pointed out that while the *Brown v. Board of Education* case was pending before the U.S. Supreme Court, the school board of Topeka, Kansas, ordered the reorganization of the school system to eliminate all racial discrimination. During their oral arguments before the Supreme Court, attorneys for the Topeka School Board brought this to the justices' attention and argued that this rendered the case moot. The justices dismissed the argument by noting that racial discrimination was systemic in many of the nation's school districts and only an affirmative decision by them could end it.[72] Carter drew a powerful parallel between the two cases.

At Hughes Tool the discriminatory contracts between the company and the IMW were only one indication of the racial discrimination cited in the charges against the union. Adopting the amended contract would not, even during the contract's duration, protect blacks from future discrimination. After the contract expired, blacks would be in the same position as before, particularly in the event that Hughes Tool no longer had government contracts. Carter stated that a local remedy for past wrongs was not enough, just as it had not been enough in *Brown v. Board of Education*. Carter stood by his position that government work or an amended labor agreement would not eliminate job discrimination at Hughes Tool. Only a decision by the Labor Board outlawing discrimination in labor unions could prevent such abuse in the future.[73]

Blacks at Hughes Tool had found that promises of racial equality from the union's white leadership could not be trusted. The amended contract bore this out. Despite the agreement's integrationist intent, after its ratification the company imposed new restrictions on blacks seeking whites-only jobs, which effectively kept Jim Crow in place. One regulation required all blacks, but not whites, seeking apprenticeships to take an aptitude test. Moreover, as late as October, 1964, several months after President Johnson signed the Civil Rights Act, Hughes Tool still maintained racially segregated restrooms, dining areas, and drinking fountains.[74]

Another factor that delayed a decision was the Labor Board's reluctance to render a ruling on such a sensitive political issue. In the past the board had refused to recognize racial discrimination by unions as an unfair labor practice, but it was now under orders from President Kennedy to do just that. The political fallout from the board's reversing its tradition on racial discrimination threatened to spark a firestorm of protest from organized labor.

The numerically strong and politically powerful United Steelworkers of America wanted the case settled without a Labor Board decision. If the board accepted the intermediate report then discriminatory unions like the Steelworkers could face the same fate as the IMW. Prior to the Hughes Tool case, the NAACP had represented black unionists belonging to Steelworkers Local 2401 at Atlantic Steel in Atlanta, Georgia, in a very similar case and lost. The Steelworkers successfully resisted NAACP efforts by keeping the black protest confined within the union and satisfying the Labor Board that discrimination had been eliminated, the same tactic being attempted by the IMW at Hughes Tool.[75]

Another political issue emerging from the case was its potential to negatively affect a civil rights bill working its way through Congress in early 1964. One of the bill's major provisions called for the creation of a permanent Equal Employment Opportunity Commission (EEOC). In the U.S. Department of Justice a division of opinion developed over whether a Labor Board ruling outlawing racial discrimination in the Hughes Tool case would lessen the chances of including a permanent EEOC in the bill. If the Labor Board ruled against the IMW, congressional opponents of the EEOC would have ammunition to support their contention that the EEOC was unnecessary and might even prompt proponents to rethink their support for creation of another federal bureaucracy. The chance to finally establish a potentially powerful federal agency to fight job discrimination would be lost. The responsibility for eliminating job discrimination would then fall to the Labor Board and federal courts, two agencies that in the past had failed miserably at that task.[76]

In a move aimed to force the Labor Board to make a decision, both Robert Carter and Tom Davis filed exceptions to the intermediate report, which afforded them the opportunity to argue their cases before the five-member board in Washington, D.C. Robert Carter filed his in April, 1963, and Tom Davis filed in May, 1963. Their efforts were of no avail and a decision was not forthcoming. The antagonists suspected that unspecified parties were exerting political pressure on the board in an effort to sabotage their respective cases.[77]

Frank McCulloch, the board's chairman, reassured them that he was aware of their desire for a speedy decision. But he cautioned them that the "thorny issues" involved in this case "are extraordinarily complex . . . and that any decision may have far-reaching consequences in the collective bargaining field." The thorniest issue of course was whether McCulloch and the other board members were willing to break with twenty-eight years of labor law and declare racial discrimination by unions illegal. They preferred a "voluntary agreement of [the] parties to resolve their problems" rather than a ruling in the case. This was the primary reason why Clifford Potter, the board's regional director in Houston, had pushed for a merger of the IMW's two locals.[78]

In September, 1963, Potter increased his pressure on Robert Carter and Local No. 2's president, Columbus Henry, to drop the charges. In August, Hughes Tool accepted Ivory Davis into the machinery repairmen apprenticeship. As far as Potter and T. B. Everitt were concerned the basis for the complaint was moot after Davis entered the training program. Carter voiced his "absolute opposition" to dropping the charge.[79] Henry rebuked Everitt's entreaties by pointing out that "Ivory Davis being awarded an apprenticeship, in your opinion seem[s] to make all things right, but there are other [black] employees than Mr. Davis to consider." In an early 1964 letter to Ogden Fields, the secretary of the Labor Board, Henry reiterated Local No. 2's steadfast "intentions to hold our separate locals until the NLRB rules in the case," and his belief that "Local No. 1 [has] forfeited any consideration as representative for employees at Hughes Tool."[80] With Henry and the black rank and file's unwavering support, Carter demanded that the board hear oral arguments from both parties or render its decision without delay.

Tom Davis and T. B Everitt wanted to argue their case before the Labor Board as well. They wanted the charge dismissed based on (1) the new contract that had, at least in their minds, eliminated discrimination, (2) Ivory Davis's having been accepted into an apprenticeship program, and (3) one other black's having upgraded into a whites-only job.[81] The Labor Board's hesitancy in rendering a decision or allowing the parties to argue their case in Washington, D.C., infuriated Everitt. He blamed political chicanery for the delay. Everitt contacted two Houston congressmen and U.S. senator John Tower demanding that they launch an immediate investigation into the Labor Board's handling of the case.

Everitt praised Clifford Potter's efforts in trying to persuade Robert Carter and Local No. 2 to accept a merger and a negotiated settlement without a board decision. But he regarded Potter and the Houston regional board as "mere puppets of the National Board" in Washington, D.C., and believed that the IMW was being used "as a political football by the top echelons of the [Kennedy] administration to promote and create a Fair Employment Practice Committee, not by law but by arming the board with usurped authority to police every labor contract in the country." He warned Reps. Albert Thomas and Bob Casey and Senator Tower that "this political pussyfooting around has stripped the union of its usefulness as a bargaining agent," and he wanted them to take action against the Labor Board on Local No. 1's behalf.[82] All three forwarded Everitt's concerns to the Labor Board.

Ogden Fields responded to their inquiries by pointing out that the board was "actively engaged in processing [the] case for a decision." Fields expressed regret over the time "a case of this complexity and significance requires," but reassured them that a decision would be forthcoming after the "case receives the analysis and consideration commensurate with the importance of the issues involved."[83] Apparently satisfied with Fields's explanation, the congressmen and senator took no further action on Everitt's demand. The board finally handed down its decision on July 1, 1964, twenty-six months after Local No. 2 filed its charges.

In a unanimous decision, the Labor Board decertified the IMW as the collective bargaining agent at Hughes Tool. The five-member board affirmed Frederick Reel's findings that Local No. 1 had violated its duty of fair representation when it refused to process Ivory Davis's grievance. Board members Boyd Leedom, Gerald Brown, and Howard Jenkins concurred with Reel's conclusion that Local No. 1's action was racially motivated, but the chairman Frank McCulloch and member John Fanning dissented on the race issue. Nonetheless, the majority agreed that racism was the basis of Davis's unfair treatment and established a precedent whereby unions enjoying the protections of Labor Board certification could no longer discriminate on the basis of race. For the first time in its history, the board ruled that racial discrimination by labor unions was an unfair labor practice prohibited by the National Labor Relations Act. The Labor Board's decision was of great significance not only because it purged Jim Crow unionism from Hughes Tool but also because it established a legal precedent whereby unions that hold board certification must eliminate racial discrimination and provide equal representation or face punitive action from the NLRB.[84]

The civil rights movement enjoyed another satisfying triumph two days later when Pres. Lyndon Johnson signed the Civil Rights Act of 1964 into law. Included among its eleven sections was Title 7 that prohibited discrimination in employment because of race, color, religion, sex, or national origin, and created a permanent Equal Employment Opportunity Commission charged with investigating complaints. But the enactment of the Civil Rights Act of 1964 fell short of expectations in its usefulness in fighting employment discrimination. Congressional opponents of the act, who regarded racial discrimination as random incidents of prejudice rather than a systemic problem in American culture, successfully blocked giving the EEOC statutory power to issue cease-and-desist orders or take injunctive action against employers and unions that discriminated. The denial of cease-and-desist and injunctive powers to the EEOC was the political price paid to end a filibuster against the bill. Congressional compromises on the enforcement provisions of Title 7 relegated the EEOC to merely a conciliatory body. These compromises prevented it from making a meaningful attack on institutional discrimination.[85]

While the EEOC lacked enforcement powers, the National Labor Relations Act empowered the Labor Board to issue cease-and-desist orders and mandatory injunctions against unions. After the Hughes Tool case, racial discrimination by unions constituted an unfair labor practice that could be restrained through the board's injunctive powers. Another powerful precedent set by the Hughes Tool decision was that in a case where an employer conspired with a board-certified union in racial discrimination the employer would also be subject to cease-and-desist orders.

Back at Hughes Tool, T. B. Everitt responded to the Labor Board's decision by saying that the IMW had been unfairly cast as a "bunch of racists" and was made the "scapegoat" in the drive to integrate Hughes Tool and undo the company's history of discrimination. From the beginning, he blamed the NAACP for causing the rift between Locals Nos. 1 and 2 by insisting that decertification, not merger, was the only way to purge the IMW of discrimination.[86] The Labor Board's ruling did not disband the IMW or prevent it from trying to recertify itself through another election. Indeed, the board had postponed a certification election requested by the United Steelworkers of America until it had announced the decision in the case.

Following the announcement, Local No. 1 also petitioned for a new election, and Everitt confidently predicted that the IMW would once again defeat its traditional opponent. The Labor Board scheduled an election for August 4, 1964, and the Steelworkers defeated the IMW by a very thin margin of 69 votes. The IMW polled 917 votes to the Steelworkers' 986.[87]

Extracting racial justice at Hughes Tool ultimately required agitation and determination by individual black workers such as Ivory Davis and Columbus Henry who were willing to stay the course. Unwavering in their determination to purge Jim Crow from Hughes Tool, their struggle resulted in an unprecedented civil rights victory that also represented a milestone in the American labor movement. In the years that followed, organized labor was forced to abandon its color barriers and to provide African American workers the full benefits of trade unionism.

THE JULY, 1964, NLRB DECISION was more than a triumph for unionism and civil rights at Hughes Tool. It became a rallying point for equality in the workplace nationwide. The struggle had begun in December, 1918, when the company's white machinists, patternmakers, and blacksmiths joined a citywide strike by the Houston Labor Council against the city's largest manufacturers. Hughes Tool's managers played a key role in defeating that strike and the company justly earned a reputation as a tough antiunion employer. Nevertheless, fifty-six years later black workers won racial and economic justice, and the successful unionization of the company in the 1930s and 1940s, a united effort of allied African American and white workers, challenges the notion that Houston was a backwater in the struggle for labor and civil rights.

Acting in unison, the labor and civil rights movements in Houston empowered workers at Hughes. That empowerment ultimately paved the way for the NLRB's landmark 1964 decision, bringing an end to segregation in organized labor. Much has been written about the roles of the state, race, and unions in labor relations and their inability to overcome organized labor's traditional discrimination and segregation.[1] The intersection of the civil rights and labor movements at the Hughes Tool Company set in motion the events that helped cause that to change. This book advances our knowledge of the roles played by the state, race, and unions in American labor relations. Moreover, there are no comparable studies of labor in Texas and it fills a significant gap in our historical knowledge of the Lone Star State that the scholar F. Ray Marshall lamented more than three decades ago.[2] Workers in Houston, Texas, actively engaged in the struggle for the basic right to join a union and then triumphantly broke down organized labor's racial barriers. Scholars have previously chronicled Houston's rich civil rights history, which resulted in desegregation victories of national importance.[3] This study brings in the long neglected role of labor.

Houston civil rights activists, in alliance with the NAACP and the federal government, broke down discrimination in Texas voting rights and higher education. Twenty-one years before the passage of the Voting Rights Act of 1965 they played a major role in convincing the Supreme Court to strike down the discriminatory all-white primary that barred African Americans from voting in Texas' Democratic primary elections. The whites-only Democratic primary disfranchised blacks because Texas was a one-party state at the time, and the winner of the Democratic primary uniformly won the general election. In *Smith v Allwright,* the Supreme Court determined that barring blacks from the Democratic primary effectively denied them voting rights for state and federal elections.[4] Following this success, black Houstonians attacked racial barriers in higher education.

Four years before the landmark 1954 Supreme Court decision in *Brown v Board of Education,* Houstonians took the lead integrating the University of Texas. At the urging of Houston civil rights activists, Heman Sweatt, a Houston post office worker and college graduate, applied for admission to the University of Texas Law School. University of Texas president Theophilus Painter rejected Sweat's application and for the next four years the NAACP fought for racial equality on Sweatt's behalf.

Texas state leaders tried to undermine the suit by establishing a segregated Jim Crow law school in the basement of the state capitol. The NAACP argued before the Supreme Court that in comparison to the University of Texas' highly regarded law school, the one to which Sweatt was relegated offered an inferior education and did not meet the legal requirements of "separate but equal." The Court agreed, ordered the University of Texas law school integrated, and demanded Sweatt's admission. In his seminal study of desegregation of higher education in Texas, African American scholar Amilcar Shabazz definitively concluded that "Texas, of all the southern states, recommends itself for special study because with *Sweatt v Painter* it gave the nation the landmark case that launched the dismantling of racial discrimination in higher education."[5] The similarities and ramifications between the Supreme Court's decision in the *Sweatt* case and the NLRB's 1964 decision at Hughes Tool are striking and bear witness to the critically important contribution made by black Houstonians to purge the country of the scourge of racial segregation.

Between 1960 and 1962, black student activists from Houston's Texas Southern University launched a drive to desegregate the city's public places. White elites feared that a student-led sit-in movement sweeping the nation in the early 1960s, might well trigger vicious, violent white backlash. This would come at a moment when negative publicity would be particularly troublesome; luring companies and professional sports teams to the area was a priority.[6] By this time, believing that desegregation was inevitable because of the growing national support for civil rights, and seeking to prevent what they considered subversive organizations like the NAACP and the Student Nonviolent Coordinating Committee (SNCC) from taking a leadership role in the process, they enlisted the help of Houston's black elites.

Houston's black aristocracy, like most advantaged people regardless of race, was conservative and not necessarily sympathetic to the goals, much less the methods, of the national leadership of the NAACP or SNCC, and white elites regarded the cooperation of their black counterparts as essential to suppress black students. In a biracial effort, local movers and shakers of every hue successfully distracted students with a mix of paternalism, cajolery, threats, and a divide-and-conquer strategy. Houston quietly integrated the city's hotels, restaurants, and movie houses by 1962. The idealistic quest for racial and social justice that motivated activists to abolish the all-white Democratic primary and integrate the University of Texas Law School contrasts strikingly with the discretely patrician experience of desegregating Houston's public accommodations. Shared concerns, economic self-interest, and fears of negative publicity commanded the public accommodations battle in Houston.

These examples of Houstonians' struggles to dismantle segregation, regardless of motivation, demonstrate the city's significant role in the civil rights movement, but they also overshadow the critically important role played by Houston's working class. This book about Hughes Tool Company's labor history illuminates that contribution. Race and labor events at the Hughes Tool Company importantly link the struggles for workers' rights, civil rights, and economic justice. Workers at Hughes Tool ultimately concluded that the quest for racial equality remained unfulfilled unless it ended job discrimination and secured economic justice in the workplace. Black union activists at

Columbus Henry (*left*) and Ivory Davis in 1994, thirty years after the Labor Board's landmark decision in the Hughes Tool Case. *Photograph from author's collection.*

Hughes asserted that voting rights, access to higher education, and the integration of Houston's public places were hollow victories without eliminating the job discrimination and wage inequality that blocked their upward socioeconomic mobility. Years after his victory in the NLRB's Hughes Tool case, Ivory Davis reflected, "What good was it for my daughter to be able to go to college with whites if I couldn't move up to a job that would pay for it. . . . I couldn't worry about going shopping downtown if I didn't have a job that paid me enough to buy those things." Davis, Columbus Henry, and other black activists identified unions as a catalyst in the overall struggle.[7] As far as Davis and Henry were concerned, unions, though a partner in discrimination with management, served as a training ground for blacks willing to assert their labor rights under federal law and defeat job discrimination.

As seen at Hughes Tool, organized labor faced great difficulties establishing and maintaining unions, but unions helped bring the company's workers into the city's civil rights and labor arenas on a potent and long-term basis. Unions paid off for workers at Hughes Tool. Finally, workers had stable wage rates, promotional and demotional job ladders, pensions, fringe benefits, and active participation in shop floor governance. The militancy of workers at Hughes Tool, initially stimulated by hard times in the 1930s, finally won them economic justice and recognition of their human dignity. A powerful wave of unionization engulfed the company as reflected in J. P. Thompson's testimony at a Labor Board hearing conducted in Houston in July, 1939, when he remarked, "All the talk out there at the plant, at the time, was unionism, has been ever since."[8] Union recognition, forced on management by a combination of worker activism, passage of the National Labor Relations Act, the National Labor Relations Board, wartime policies, and National War Labor Board demands empowered Hughes's workers.

On the other hand, unionization also showed the limitations of organized labor in ending job site discrimination. Leaders of the CIO might well promote racial equality in their organizing campaigns, but faced with the massive, entrenched racism of the white rank and file, ideals often gave way to Jim Crow realities. The important collective bargaining and contract achievements of the CIO and its rival, the Independent Metal Workers Union, did improve the economic conditions of blacks but only marginally in comparison to whites. Unions most served African Americans when they showed courage sufficient to couple federally guaranteed union rights with enlightened commitment to human dignity. Only then did American unions live up to their collective obligations.

In assessing the labor history of the Hughes Tool Company it is clear that the employees themselves played the most important role in bringing economic and racial justice to the company. Federal law empowered them to organize, but it was their own initiative and determination to take advantage of these protections that enabled their success. Union and civil rights activists at Hughes Tool were ordinary people of extraordinary courage willing to take enormous risks by standing up for their beliefs and defending what they thought was right. In pursuit of their American dream, advocating nothing more than common fairness in the workplace, they faced dismissal, systematic threats, intimidation, and ostracism from fellow employees. Undaunted by these obstacles the workers at Houston's Hughes Tool Company remained loyal to their beliefs, shirked no duties, and many times over earned their honored place in America's labor history.

ABBREVIATIONS

CF	Case File
HMRC	Houston Metropolitan Research Center
HTC	Hughes Tool Collection
IMWU	Independent Metal Workers Union
NAACP	National Association for the Advancement of Colored People
NARACP	National Archives and Records Administration, College Park
NARASRFW	National Archives and Records Administration, Southwest Region, Fort Worth
NARAW	National Archives and Records Administration, Washington, D.C.
NLRB	National Labor Relations Board
NWLB	National War Labor Board
RCFEP	Records of the Committee on Fair Employment Practices
RFMCS	Records of the Federal Mediation and Conciliation Service
RG	Record Group
RNLRB	Records of the National Labor Relations Board
RNWLB	Records of the National War Labor Board (WW I)
RPMG	Records of the Provost Marshall General

INTRODUCTION

1. National Association for the Advancement of Colored People, Records, Manuscript Division, Library of Congress, Group III, Box A 188, Robert Car-

ter to Branch Presidents, August 31, 1964; Group V, Box 2309, "NAACP Hails NLRB's Anti-Bias Decision," NAACP news release, July 2, 1964, hereafter cited as NAACP with reference to specific documents. National Labor Relations Board, *Decisions and Orders of the National Labor Relations Board,* 147:1578, hereafter cited as NLRB, *Decisions.*

2. Herbert Hill, *Black Labor and the American Legal System,* 93–169; H. Hill, "The Racial Practices of Organized Labor," 286–357; Robert L. Carter and Maria L. Marcus, "Trade Union Practices and the Law," 380–400; H. Hill, "Racism within Organized Labor," 109–18.

3. Alan Draper, *Conflict of Interests: Organized Labor and the Civil Rights Movement in the South,* 14–16.

4. Ibid., 14–15; as quoted in Draper, *Conflict of Interests,* 23.

5. H. Hill, "The Problem of Race in American Labor History," 190; H. Hill, "Race and the Steelworkers Union" 2; H. Hill, "Myth-Making as Labor History."

6. H. Hill, "Race and the United Steelworkers Union," 1–69; H. Hill, "Lichtenstein's Fictions," 82–107; H. Hill, "Lichtenstein's Fictions Revisited:," 148–63; H. Hill, "The AFL-CIO and the Black Workers:," 1–80; H. Hill, "Race and Ethnicity in Organized Labor," 5–50. In response, labor historians Nelson Lichtenstein, David Brody, and Eric Arnesen have weighed in against Hill's interpretations. See Nelson Lichtenstein, "Walter Reuther in Black and White," 133–47; David Brody, "Hill Discounts Larger Context," 38–41; Eric Arnesen, "Up from Exclusion," 146–74.

7. Daniel Letwin, *The Challenge of Interracial Unionism: Alabama Coal Miners, 1878–1921,* 3, 6; Brian Kelly, *Race, Class, and Power in the Alabama Coalfields, 1908–1921;* Joe William Trotter Jr., *Coal, Class, and Color: Blacks in Southern West Virginia, 1915–1932;* Alan Dawley and Joe William Trotter Jr., "Race and Class," 486–94; Trotter, "African-American Workers: New Directions in U.S. Labor Historiography," 495–523.

8. Bruce Nelson, *Divided We Stand: American Workers and the Struggle for Black Equality,* xxii; B. Nelson, "Class, Race, and Democracy," 368.

9. B. Nelson, "The CIO Meant One Thing for the Whites and Another Thing for Us," 119; Ivory Davis, interviewed by author, Houston, Tex., May 1, 1997.

10. B. Nelson, "CIO Meant One Thing for the Whites," 135; Herbert Hill, interviewed by author, August 25, 1999.

11. Robert H. Zieger, *American Workers, American Unions,* 197.

12 Joe Feagin, *Free Enterprise City: Houston in Political-Economic Perspective,* 58–59; Joseph A. Pratt, *The Growth of a Refining Region;* David, McComb, *Houston: The Bayou City.*

13. F. Ray Marshall, "Some Reflections on Labor History," 140. Professor Marshall was an early pioneer in studying the intersection of the civil rights and labor movements. See Marshall, *The Negro and Organized Labor;* Mar-

shall, "Union Racial Problems in the South," 117–28; Marshall, "Unions and the Negro Community," 179–202; Marshall and Vernon M. Briggs Jr., *The Negro and Apprenticeship.*

14. George Norris Green, "Discord in Dallas: Auto Workers, City Fathers, and the Ford Motor Company, 1937–1941," 20–33; Rhinehart, "A Lesson in Unity: The Houston Municipal Workers Strike of 1946," 137–53; Rick Halpern, "Interracial Unionism in the Southwest: Fort Worth's Packinghouse Workers, 1937–1954," 158–82; Ernest Obadele-Starks, *Black Unionism in the Industrial South;* Obadele-Starks, "Black Labor, the Black Middle Class, and Organized Protest along the Upper Texas Gulf Coast, 1883–1945"; Obadele-Starks, "Black Texans and Theater Craft Unionism: The Struggle for Racial Equality"; James V. Reese, "The Early History of Labor Organizations in Texas, 1838–1976," 1–20; Reese, "The Evolution of an Early Texas Union," 158–85; George T. Morgan, Jr., "No Compromise—No Recognition," 193–204; Morgan, "The Gospel of Wealth Goes South," 186–97; Robert E. Ziegler, "The Limits of Power," 71–90; James C. Maroney, "Labor's Struggle for Acceptance:," 5–24.

15. Zieger, *The CIO, 1935–1955,* 22–41, 83–85.

16. Halbert Mabry, interviewed by author, October 26, 1993; C. D. Wilson, interviewed by author, Houston, Tex., November 30, 1993; Allison Alton, interviewed by author, Houston, Tex., December 1, 1993; "CIO Men Claim Pressure Used at Hughes Tool Plant," *Houston Post,* July 21, 1939; "Red Charge Is Denied by CIO Worker," *Houston Chronicle,* July 21, 1939.

CHAPTER 1

1. Don E. Carleton, *Red Scare!* 6–7; McComb, *Houston,* 12–14, 16–37, 91; Don E. Carleton and Thomas H. Kreneck, *Houston: Back Where We Started,* 2–5; Pratt, *Growth of a Refining Region,* 15–23, 27–28.

2. Harold L. Platt, "Houston at the Crossroads," 51–61; McComb, *Houston,* 98–113; Pratt, *Growth of a Refining Region,* 19–23, 53–56; Joseph Stephen Cullinan Papers, MSS 69, Houston Metropolitan Research Center, Houston Public Library, Will Hogg to Mrs. William Sharp et al., December 18, 1912; Will Hogg to Mrs. William Sharp and Mr. James Cullinan, November 8, 1913; Howard Hughes to Mrs. William Sharp et al., November 11, 1913, hereafter cited as Cullinan Papers; Carleton and Kreneck, *Houston,* 5–6; Charles R. Hamilton, "Images of an Industry," 45–54; Peter Harry Brown and Pat H. Broeske, *Howard Hughes: The Untold Story,* 28–31, 126–31.

3. Reese, "The Worker in Texas, 1821–1876," 233–35; Reese, "Early History of Labor Organizations," 7–9.

4. Reese, "Early History of Labor Organizations," 6.

5. Ziegler, "The Workingman in Houston," 77–79.

6. Ibid., 74–79, 141–43.

7. Howard Beeth and Cary D. Wintz, eds., *Black Dixie,* 15–19; Writers' Program of the Works Progress Administration in the State of Texas, *Houston,* 38; Kenneth W. Wheeler, *To Wear a City's Crown,* 107–10; James M. SoRelle, "The Darker Side of Heaven," 5–6.

8. Beeth and Wintz, *Black Dixie,* 24.

9. SoRelle, "Darker Side of Heaven," 17–18; McComb, *Houston,* 157–66; Randolph B. Campbell, *Gone to Texas: A History of the Lone Star State,* 270–89.

10. McComb, *Houston,* 157–66; Ziegler, "Workingman," 84–85; SoRelle, "Darker Side of Heaven," 35–36.

11. McComb, *Houston,* 35–37.

12. Reese, "Early History of Labor Organizations," 13.

13. Foster Rhea Dulles and Melvyn Dubovsky, *Labor in America: A History,* 90–96; David Montgomery, *Beyond Equality: Labor and the Radical Republicans, 1862–1872,* 225.

14. Reese, "Early History of Labor Organizations," 12–13.

15. *Houston Weekly Telegraph,* September 5, 1867; Reese, "Early History of Labor Organizations," 255–56.

16. Melvyn Dubovsky and Warren Van Tyne, eds., *Labor Leaders in America,* 45; Leon Fink, *Workingmen's Democracy: The Knights of Labor and American Politics,* 7.

17. Dubovsky and Van Tyne, *Labor Leaders in America,* 45.

18. Fink, *Workingman's Democracy,* xiii, 7.

19. Ziegler, "Workingman," 39, 46–47, 94, 82, 80–81.

20. SoRelle, "Darker Side of Heaven," 35–36.

21. Dulles and Dubovsky, *Labor in America,* 132–34.

22. Ruth Allen, *Chapters in the History of Organized Labor in Texas,* 21–25; Dulles, *Labor in America,* 137; Ziegler, "Workingman," 134, 138, 266.

23. Ziegler, "Workingman," 74.

24. Mullennix, "History of the Texas State Federation of Labor," 7–8; 12–72, Ziegler, "Workingman,"141; Maroney, "Labor's Struggle," 8.

25. Ziegler, "Workingman," 148–49; Maroney, "Labor's Struggle," 5–6, 13.

26. Max Andrew president of the Texas State Federation of Labor as quoted in the Texas State Federation of Labor, *Convention Proceedings* (1905), 48; *Galveston Daily News,* June 13, February 26, 1878; Ziegler, "Workingman," 9–10, 77–78; Maroney, "Organized Labor in Texas," 135; Robert Calvert and Arnoldo De León, *History of Texas,* 110; John Bodnar, *The Transplanted: A History of Immigrants in Urban America,* 105–107.

27. Mullennix, "History of the Texas State Federation of Labor," 12–72.

28. Ibid.; John R. Commons et al., *History of Labour in the United States, 1896–1932,* 3:517.

29. Texas State Federation of Labor, *Convention Proceedings* (1905), 48. The

Texas State Federation of Labor was formed at the beginning of the twentieth century as Texas urban areas entered into the early stages of industrialization. In his work on Texas labor, history professor Jim Maroney observed that as Texas industries developed employers entered into trade associations to protect their interests and minimize labor costs and these employer combinations helped spark Texas workers to form the Texas State Federation of Labor so they could protect themselves form the power of concentrated capital. See Maroney "Labor's Struggle," 5.

30. Quote is from Jesse O. Thomas, *A Study of the Social Welfare Status of the Negroes in Houston, Texas* (Houston, 1929), 13–14; see also James M. So-Relle, "An De Po Cullud Man Is in De Wus Fix uv Awl," 16–17.

31. Texas State Federation of Labor, *Convention Proceedings* (1905), 48; Mullennix, "Texas Federation of Labor," 145–48; Ziegler, "Workingman," 150–51; Maroney, "Labor's Struggle," 5.

32. Olson and Howard, "Armed Elites," 55; Bruce Olson, "The Houston Light Guards:," 126–28, 133–37; Robert Fisher, "Where Seldom Is Heard a Discouraging Word," 79.

33. Olson, "Houston Light Guards," 126.

34. Ziegler, "Workingman," 124–27; Olson and Howard, "Armed Elites," 52–54.

35. Arnoldo De León, *They Called Them Greasers*, ix-xii.

36. De León, *Ethnicity in the Sunbelt*, 6–9; McComb, *Houston*, 157–66.

37. Olson and Howard, "Armed Elites," 56–57; Ziegler, "Limits of Power," 205–11; Morgan, "No Compromise," 196–97; *Houston Daily Post*, March 20, 21, 1898.

38. George T. Morgan, "The Gospel of Wealth," 186–88.

39. Olson and Howard, "Armed Elites," 56–57; Ziegler, " Limits of Power," 73–78; Ziegler, "Workingman," 205–11; Morgan, "No Compromise," 196–97; *Houston Daily Post*, March 20, 21, 1898. The quote is from the *Houston Daily Post*, March 19, 1898.

40. Ziegler, "Workingman," 208–10; Olson and Howard, "Armed Elites," 58.

41. Olson and Howard, "Armed Elites," 59–60; Ziegler, "Limits of Power," 76–77.

42. As quoted in Dulles and Dubovsky, *Labor in America*, 186; Allen M. Wakestein, "The Origins of the Open Shop Movement," 460–61.

43. As quoted in Commons et al., *History of Labour in the United States*, 131.

44. Ziegler, "Limits of Power," 86; Jay Littman Todes, "Organized Employer Opposition to Unionism in Texas, 1900–1930," 36–46; Maroney, "Labor's Struggle," 10–13. Whether the Houston Citizens' Alliance predated the strike or was formed after the strike began is not clear. Reading the sources, especially Jay Littman Todes's account of the strike, one can reasonably conclude

that Houston employers had organized themselves before the strike and Mc-
Gregor was designated their front man to lead their campaign to rid the city
of unions.

45. Ziegler, "Limits of Power," 82–83; Stephen H. Norwood, *Strikebreaking
and Intimidation*, 38.

46. Norwood, *Strikebreaking and Intimidation*, 36–39.

47. Todes, "Organized Employer Opposition," 36–41, 79–87.

48. Ibid., 38–39; Maroney, "Labor's Struggle," 12; Maroney, "Organized
Labor," 109.

49. Ziegler, "Limits of Power," 88–89.

50. Todes, "Organized Employer Opposition," 38–39; Maroney, "Labor's
Struggle," 12; Ziegler, "Limits of Power," 88.

51. Ziegler, "Workingman,"221–24.

52. "A Federal Injunction: Temporary Writ Issued against Six Unions by
Judge Waller Burns," *Houston Daily Post,* October 6, 1911.

53. As quoted in Commons et al., *History of Labour,* 370; Maroney, "Organized Labor," 136–39; Ziegler, "Workingman," 229–30.

54. Ziegler, "Workingman," 229–30; Maroney, "Organized Labor," 138–39;
Commons et al., *History of Labour,* 370–71.

55. "A Federal Injunction," *Houston Daily Post;* Ziegler, "Workingman,"
229–30.; Maroney, "Labor's Struggle," 15.

56. Maroney, "Labor's Struggle," 15; Commons et al., *History of Labour,*
370–71.

57. Maroney, "Organized Labor," 230–32.

58. Wilson, interviewed by author, November 30, 1993; Mabry, interviewed
by author, October 26, 1993; George McMahon, interviewed by author,
April 17, 1997.

CHAPTER 2

1. Daniel Yergin, *The Prize,* 85–87.

2. Pratt, *Growth of a Refining Region,* 3; Yergin, *The Prize:,* 85–87; Oral History of Texas Oil Industry, Center for American History, University of Texas
at Austin, Granville A. Humason interviewed by William Owens, July 7, 1953;
John Keats, *Howard Hughes,* 4; *Hughes News,* 9.

3. *Hughes News,* 6.

4. James A. Clark and Michel T. Halbouty, *Spindletop,* 153–54, 188, 197–
98; Walter Rundell Jr, *Early Texas Oil: A Photographic,* 25–26, 65–66; John O.
King, *Joseph Stephen Cullinan: A Study in the Texas Petroleum Industry.* Master driller Walter Sharp drilled exploratory wells at Spindletop in 1893 and 1897
without finding oil. Within days of the January 10, 1901 Spindletop strike,
Sharp hurried to the area and secured leases on thousands of acres. In 1902,

Sharp, along with James Cullinan, James Stephen Hogg, John Gates, Arnold Schlaet, and James Roche formed the Texas Company and chartered it for $3,000,000. Cullinan, who had made a fortune in the Corsicana Oil Field during the 1890s provided needed capital for the venture, Sharp contributed leases and drilling expertise, former Texas governor James Hogg political connections, Gates and Roche provided real estate expertise, and Schlaet brought capital.

5. Oral History of Texas Oil Industry, Humason interviewed by Owens, July 7, 1953; Charlie Lane interviewed by W. A. Owens, May 1, 1956, 1–5.

6. *Hughes News*, 6; Rundell, *Early Texas Oil*, 81; Clark and Halbouty, *Spindletop*, 197; Keats, *Howard Hughes*, 5–6.

7. Oral History of Texas Oil Industry, Lane interviewed by Owens, May 1, 1956, 7–11; Clark and Halbouty, *Spindletop*, 153–54, 188, 197–98.

8. Hughes Tool Collection, RG 1005, HMRC; Hamilton, "Images of an Industry," 45–54; Oral History of Texas Oil Industry, Lane interviewed by Owens, May 1, 1956, 7–9.

9. Cullinan Papers, MSS 69, Will Hogg to Mrs. William Sharp et al., December 18, 1912; Will Hogg to Mrs. William Sharp and Mr. James Cullinan, November 8, 1913; Howard Hughes to Mrs. William Sharp and Mr. James Cullinan, November 11, 1913; "Funeral for Hughes Will Be Wednesday," *Houston Chronicle*, January 15, 1924, p. 1; Keats, *Howard Hughes*, 112–13.

10. Hogg to Sharp et al., December 18, 1912.

11. Hughes earned his reputation for financial irresponsibility in various Louisiana and Texas oil fields. Ed Prather, another business associate of Hughes, Sharp, and James Cullinan sold his shares of the original Sharp-Hughes Tool Company because of Hughes's questionable business practices. Hughes did appreciate the financial importance of proprietary ownership of his patents and because of this, and in spite of his lack of financial sense, he eventually became fabulously wealthy. See Oral History of Texas Oil Industry, Lane interviewed by Owens, May 1, 1956, 31–35; Clark and Halbouty, *Spindletop*, 196–97 and Keats, *Howard Hughes*, 5–11.

12. Pratt, *Growth of a Refining Region*, 55–56; Robert Maxwell, "Texas Economic Growth, 1890 to World War II," 183–206.

13. Bruce Andre Beauboeuf, "World War I and Houston's Emergence as an Industrial City," 358; McComb, *Houston*, 116–17; Pratt, *Growth of a Refining Region*, 54–56; Maxwell, "Texas Economic Growth," 206–24.

14. Feagin, *Free Enterprise City*, 58–59, 76–80; Pratt, *Growth of a Refining Region*, 161–62.

15. Cullinan Papers, Howard Hughes to Joseph Cullinan, October 27, May 7, 1913; Cullinan Papers, Sales Report, Sharp-Hughes Tool Company, December 1, 1914. Each employee received a five-dollar Christmas bonus in 1913 and again in 1914.

16. Clark and Halbouty, *Spindletop*, 196–97; Oral History of Texas Oil In-

dustry, Lane interviewed by Owens, May 1, 1956, 30 –35; Keats, *Howard Hughes*, 4 –11; Rundell, *Early Texas Oil*, 81.

17. HTC, RG 1005, Louie Enz interviewed by Mary Lyens, T. E. Parish, and Jim Clark, January 16, 1968; Oral History of Texas Oil Industry, Lane interviewed by Owens, May 1, 1956, 8 –9; *Directory of City of Houston, 1910 –1911*, 192; Cullinan Papers, MSS 69, Howard Hughes to David Brown, January 20, 1913; *Hughes News*, 5 –6.

18. Hamilton, "Images of an Industry," 49 –50; *Directory of City of Houston, 1913*, 747; Cullinan Papers, MSS 69, Howard Hughes to David Brown, January 20, 1913; *Hughes News*, 5 –6.

19. HTC, RG 1005, Enz interviewed by Lyens, Parish, and Clark, January 16, 1968; "Safety News: Phil Page," *Hughes News* 1947.

20. "Safety News: Phil Page" *Hughes News*, 1947; HTC, RG 1005, Enz interviewed by Lyens, Parish, and Clark, January 16, 1968. Hughes had a sterner side with his employees. The shop on 2nd and Girard was situated next to Buffalo Bayou. When employees ruined parts during machining they simply threw them in the bayou to hide their mistake. One day Howard Hughes Sr. walked along the stream during low water and found a great deal of scarp. He called Superintendent Barr on the carpet over it. Trouble, like water flows downhill, and after Hughes finished with Barr, Barr chewed out the employees. More than fifty years later Louie Enz recalled Barr's dressing down by saying merely, "Oh boy!"

21. Richard Hack, *Hughes: The Private Diaries, Memos, and Letters*, 29; Brown and Broeske, *Howard Hughes*, 11. I cite these two popular biographies of Howard Hughes Jr. only briefly and with great caution. Their accuracy is suspect. Both books have extensive works cited sections, but there are no footnotes or endnotes citing sources in the text, making the books mostly worthless as history since one cannot easily go back and check the accuracy of the citations and assertions.

22. Department of Labor, *Monthly Labor Review* 7 (July, 1918): 88; "Facts and Figures," *Houston Labor Journal*, January 25, 1919, p. 1; "Do You Want to Put Houston Off the Map as an Industrial City?" *Houston Post*, January 22, 1919, p. 8. During World War One Hughes Tool instituted a nine-hour day, six-day work week.

23. National Archives and Records Administration, Washington, D.C., Records of the National War Labor Board (WW I), RG 2, *Administrative History of the National War Labor Board*, pp. vii–xii, hereafter cited as NARAW, RNWLB, RG 2, with reference to specific documents; Joseph A. McCartin, *Labor's Great War*, 90 –93. The three-member NWLB included representatives of business, labor, and the public. It had two critical weaknesses: it had no legal authority or coercive powers, and it depended on the voluntary cooperation of labor and management to honor its decisions. In the case of a strike or a lockout, it dispatched one employer representative and one labor repre-

sentative to gather facts, hold hearings, and present evidence to the NWLB for a decision. Only in cases where both sides jointly agreed to submit to the NWLB's decision did the force of law come into play. Either party could appeal the board's decision to the courts to obtain compliance on the ground that noncompliance constituted a breach of contract. In all other cases, the NWLB published its findings in the hopes that public opinion and patriotic feeling would force acceptance of the board's recommended resolutions in disputes.

24. McCartin, *Labor's Great War*, 179–80, 191; "Do You Want Houston Put Off the Map?" Houston Post, January 22, 1919, p. 8; "Strike Situation as It Really Is!" *Houston Post*, February 28, 1919, p. 10; "The Strike Situation," *Houston Chronicle*, February 26, 1919, p. 12; "Outraged by Radicalism," *Houston Labor Journal*, March 1, 1919, p. 1.

25. In 1917 there were 4,450 strikes and lockouts. See Bureau of Labor Statistics, *Strikes in the United States, 1880–1936*, 35.

26. "Do You Want Houston Put Off the Map?" *Houston Post*, January 22, 1919, 8.

27. NARAW, RNWLB, RG 2, Houston Metal Trades Council to W. Jett Lauck, telegram, December 10, 1918; HTC, RG 1005, Enz interviewed by Lyens, Parish, and Clark, January 16, 1968.

28. "Manufacturers Confer with U.S. Conciliator on Metal Workers Strike," *Houston Post*, February 14, 1919, p. 7.

29. NARAW, RNWLB, RG 2, RGB to W. E. Carroll, February 10, 1919; "Labor Council to Decide on General Strike," *Houston Chronicle*, February 8, 1919, p. 9.

30. "Mechanical Trades Strike," *Houston Labor Journal*, December 21, 1918, p. 2; "Machinists Strike Here: Many Plants Tied Up," *Houston Chronicle*, December, 18, 1918, p. 13; HTC, RG 1005, Enz interviewed by Lyens, Parish, and Clark, January 16, 1968.

31. "Mechanical Trades Strike," *Houston Labor Journal*, December 21, 1918, p. 2.

32. "Mayor Will Bar All Strikebreakers," *Houston Post*, January 19, 1919, p. 3.

33. "Will Find Jobs for Discharged Soldiers Here: Chamber of Commerce to Co-Operate with Other Agencies in Placing Men in Touch with Employers," *Houston Chronicle*, January 24, 1919, p. 12; "Houston Industries Would Employ 142: Business Men Respond Readily to Call for Positions," *Houston Post*, January 24, 1919, p. 6.

34. Quote is from "The Strike Situation," *Houston Chronicle*, February 26, 1919, p. 12; see also "Strikebreak'rs [*sic*] Stranded Here, Report to City," *Houston Chronicle*, February 10, 1919, p. 1; "Metal Operators Deny Misleading Imported Workmen," *Houston Post*, February 11, 1919, p. 3.

35. "Strikebreak'rs [*sic*] Stranded Here Report to City," *Houston Chronicle*, February 10, 1919, p. 1; "Lucey Offers to Send Imported Workers Home,"

Houston Chronicle, February 11, 1919, p. 17; "Outside Metal Workers Given Tickets Home," *Houston Chronicle,* February 14, 1919, p. 8; "Machinists from Pittsburgh Say They Are Willing to Make Affidavits of Misrepresentation," *Houston Chronicle,* February 15, 1919, p. 8; "Metal Operators Deny Misleading Imported Workmen," *Houston Post,* February 11, 1919, p. 3; "Metal Workers to Sign Affidavits Labor Man States," *Houston Post,* February 14, 1919; "Machinists Given Fare to Positions," *Houston Post,* February 15, 1919, p. 10.

36. "Strikebreak'rs [*sic*] Stranded Here Report to City," *Houston Chronicle,* February 10, 1919.

37. NARAW, RNWLB, RG 2, W. E. Carroll to W. Jett Lauck, February 1, 1919. The Houston Labor Council had changed its name to the Houston Labor and Trades Council by this time. "Labor Council to Decide On General Strike," *Houston Post,* February 8, 1919, p. 9; "Metal Trades Strike Special Order for Next Meeting of Labor Council with Men Standing Firm on Demands," *Houston Labor Journal,* February 15, 1919, p. 1.

38. "Strike Proposal Comes Up Tonight," *Houston Post,* February 18, 1919, p. 4.

39. Quote is from "Sympathy Strike Plan Voted Down: Labor Council Representing 42 Unions Oppose General Walkout," *Houston Post,* February 19, 1919, p. 1; "Trades Council Votes against General Strike: Does Not Wish to Work Hardship Upon People of City but Expresses Sympathy with Metal Trades," *Houston Chronicle,* February 19, 1919, p. 1.

40. Quote is from "Congratulations to Organized Labor," *Houston Chronicle* February 20, 1919, p. 4; see also "The Sympathy Strike Abandoned," *Houston Post,* February 20, 1919, p. 6; *Houston Labor Journal* "Unions Are Responding to Call for Assessment to Help Strikers' in Metal Industry Win Their Strike," February 1, 1919, p. 1.

41. "City Will Protect Strikers' Pickets and Nonunion Men," *Houston Post,* March 7, 1919, p. 1; "Grand Jury and City Take Hand in Strike Here," *Houston Chronicle,* March 6, 1919, p. 13; "Strike Goes On in Quiet Way, Baker Reports," *Houston Chronicle,* March 8, 1919, p. 1.

42. "City Will Protect Strikers," *Houston Post;* "Grand Jury and City Take Hand," *Houston Chronicle;* "Strike Goes On," *Houston Chronicle.*

43. "Business Men to Confer on Strike Trouble," *Houston Chronicle,* March 9, 1919, p. 3; "Houston Business Men to Meet with Metal Trades Men," *Houston Post,* March 9, 1919, p. 1; "Strike in Houston Metal Industry Ended by a Citizens' Committee Suggested by Workers Involved," *Houston Labor Journal,* March 15, 1919. A sampling of the committee included banker and committee chairman John T. Scott, clergymen Rev. William States Jacob of the First Presbyterian Church, the Rev. Father Walsh, public school superintendent Professor P. W. Horn, the undertaker Sid Westheimer, and the developer Denton Cooley.

44. "Plant Owners to Meet Mediators to Discuss Strike," *Houston Post,* March 10, 1919.

45. "Committee Says Strikers Should Return to Work: Plant Owners to Take Back Former Employees at the Old Wage Scale," *Houston Post,* March 11, 1919, p. 1.

46. "Committee Says Strikers Should Return to Work," *Houston Post;* "Plant Owners to Meet," *Houston Post,* March 10, 1919.

47. "Metal Trades Strike Is Off by Agreement," *Houston Chronicle,* March 11, 1919, p. 1; "Strike in Houston Metal Industry Ended by a Citizens' Committee by Workers Involved," *Houston Labor Journal,* March 15, 1919; "Old Wage Accepted by Metal Workers," *Houston Post,* March 12, 1919, p. 9.

48. Feagin, *Free Enterprise City,* 106–48.

49. "Committee Says Strikers Should Return to Work," *Houston Post,* March 11, 1919, p. 1.

50. HTC, RG 1005, Enz interviewed by Lyens, Parish, and Clark, January 16, 1968; National Archives and Records Administration, Southwest Region, Fort Worth, Records of the National War Labor Board, RG 202, Case No. 111-2083-D, "Intermediate Report: In The Matter of Hughes Tool Company and Steel Workers Organizing Committee Lodge No. 1742 and Employees Welfare Organization of Hughes Tool Company, and H.T.C. Club of Hughes Tool Company, Parties to the Contract," pp. 4–7, hereafter cited as NARASRFW, RNWLB, RG 202, with reference to specific documents.

51. For a discussion of this event see chapter 1, pp. 000–000.

52. Wakestein, "Origins of the Open-Shop Movement," 460–61, 464; Todes, "Organized Employer Opposition," 19–49; Mullennix, "History of the Texas State Federation of Labor," 243–52; Maroney, "Labor's Struggle," 12–13; David Brody, "The Rise and Decline of Welfare Capitalism," 148–49, 157; McCartin, *Labor's Great War,* 213–20.

53. Brody, "Rise and Decline of Welfare Capitalism," 154–55.

54. Daniel Nelson, "The Company Union Movement, 1900–1937: A Re-examination," 155–59; Brody, "Rise and Decline of Welfare Capitalism," 155–59; McCartin, *Labor's Great War,* 164, 216–17; the quote is from McCartin, 164.

55. McCartin, *Labor's Great War,* 164, 216–17; Brody, "Rise and Decline of Welfare Capitalism," 158–59; D. Nelson, "Company Union Movement," 335–37; D. Nelson, *Managers and Workers,* 140.

56. NARASRFW, RNWLB, RG 202, CF 111-2083-D, "Intermediate Report," pp. 4–7.

57. National Archives and Records Administration, College Park, Md., Records of the National Labor Relations Board, RG 25, Case File 1661, "Official Report of the Proceedings before the National Labor Relations Board: In the Matter of Hughes Tool Company and Steel Workers Organizing Committee, Lodge 1742, Employees Welfare Organization of Hughes Tool Company

and H.T.C. Club of Hughes Tool Company," pp. 28–30, hereafter cited as NARACP, RNLRB, RG 25, with reference to specific documents.

58. "Strike Is Off," *Houston Chronicle;* "Strikers Should Return to Work," *Houston Post;* HTC, RG 1005, People File.

59. Independent Metal Workers Collection, RG R-1, HMRC, *Summary of Agreement Arrived at by the Hughes Tool Company and Its Hourly Employees, October 1, 1937;* HTC, RG 1005, Enz interviewed by Lyens, Parish, and Clark, January 16, 1968; NARASRFW, RNWLB, RG 202, CF 111-2083-D, "Intermediate Report," p. 4; "AFL Wins at Hughes Tool Company: Preference for Bona Fide Labor Union," *Houston Labor Messenger,* April 27, 1934, p. 1; "Hughes Tool Refuses to Abide by Result of Election," *Houston Labor Messenger,* May 4, 1934, p. 2

60. Independent Metal Workers Collection, RG R-1, HMRC, *Summary of Agreement.*

61. SoRelle, "Darker Side of Heaven," 152–53; Maroney, "Organized Labor," 177–81; Robert Eli Teel, "Discrimination against Negro Workers in Texas," 27–28. Two black locals of the International Longshoremen's Association had been established by the end of World War One, Local 872, organized in 1914 and Local 1271, organized in 1919. The white and black locals of the ILA split available work on a fifty-fifty basis.

62. NARASRFW, RNWLB, RG 202, CF 111-2083-D, "Intermediate Report," p. 4; "Brief History of Colored Independent Union of Hughes Tool Company," *Houston Negro Labor News,* January 18, 1938, p. 5; "Hughes Tool Workers Say They Are Satisfied," *Houston Negro Labor News,* March 30, 1940, p. 5.

63. NARACP, RNLRB, RG 25, CF 1661, pp. 1394–1400.

64. Carter Wesley, "Colored Workers Courted," *Houston Informer,* August 23, 1941, p. 1; Allison Alton, interviewed by author, December 1, 1993; Ivory Davis and Columbus Henry, interviewed by author, May 3, 1994; Lonnie Rhone, interviewed by author, November 5, 1998; John Gray, interviewed by author, November 19, 1998.

65. NARACP, RNLRB, RG 25, CF 1661, pp. 1360–1453; Hobart Taylor, "C. W. Rice, Labor Leader," 25–38, 48–52.

66. Taylor, "C. W. Rice," 35; "SoRelle, "Darker Side of Heaven," 154–56; Columbus Henry, interviewed by author, January 11, 1994. Blacks sympathetic to organized labor accused Rice of charging excessive fees to workers seeking jobs through his agency and believed that Rice's hostility toward organized labor stemmed from viewing it as a competitor to his lucrative job placement business. They believed that the only black person Rice cared about was himself. Henry interview, January 11, 1994; Taylor, "C. W. Rice," 36, 48–52.

67. Taylor, "C. W. Rice," 34.

68. *Hughes News,* 22–24; NARACP, RNLRB, RG 25, CF 3066, "Official Report of Proceedings before the National Labor Relations Board: In the Matter of Hughes Tool Company and Independent Metal Workers Union, Locals

Nos. 1 and 2," pp. 112–14; Patrick Nicholson, *Mr. Jim: The Biography of James Smither Abercrombie*, 232–35.

69. HTC, RG 1005, Enz interviewed by Lyens, Parish, and Clark, January 16, 1968; NARACP, RNLRB, RG 25, CF 1661, p. 26.

70. "Howard R. Hughes, Noted Business Leader, Dies While at Work in Office," *Houston Post*, January 15, 1924.

71. "Kuldell Reveals His Resignation as Head of Hughes Tool Firm," *Houston Chronicle*, July 17, 1939, p. 1; "Col. [*sic*] Retires as Hughes Chief," *Houston Post*, July 18, 1939, p. 1; NARACP, RNLRB, RG 25, CF 1661, p. 18–26; Robert Kuldell, interviewed by author, July 27, 1999.

72. Howard Hughes Sr. to R. C. Kuldell, telegram, January 5, 1919, copy in author's possession, Hughes to Kuldell, November 21, 1919; Childs to R. C. Kuldell, January 6, 1920; Hughes to Kuldell, December 28, 1920, copy in author's possession; Kuldell, interviewed by author, July 27, 1999.

73. *Forbes*, "The Top Salaries of American Business,"March 15, 1934, 14; "Stanley Brown, Replacing Kuldell at Hughes Tool, Rose from Firm's Ranks," *Houston Chronicle*, July 18, 1939, p. 2.

74. Kuldell, interviewed by author, July 27, 1999.

75. Davis, interviewed by author, May 1, 1997; Kuldell, interviewed by author, July 27, 1999.

76. Kuldell to Hughes, September 20, 1972; NARACP, RNLRB, RG 25, CF 3066, "Official Report," pp. 346–54.

77. NARASRFW, RNWLB, RG 202, CF 111-2083-D, "Intermediate Report," pp. 6–7.

78. The annual cost of Hughes Tool's welfare benefits in the late 1920s and early 1930s amounted to approximately $5,800. See, NARASRFW, RNWLB, RG 202, CF 111-2083-D, "Intermediate Report," p. 7.

CHAPTER 3

1. NARACP, RNLRB, RG 25, CF 1661, pp. 26–27; "To The Machine Shop Workers Employed at Hughes Tool Company, Attention," *Houston Labor Messenger*, November 17, 1933, p. 1; Mabry, interviewed by author, October 26, 1993; Marsha Gaunt Berryman, "Houston and the Early Depression," 84; E. Thomas Lovell, "Houston's Reaction to the New Deal, 1932–1936," 129–30.

2. NARACP, RNLRB, RG 25, CF 1661, pp. 26–27; *Houston Labor Messenger*, November 17, 1933; Brody, "Rise and Decline of Welfare Capitalism," 158–64; H. M. Gitelman, "Welfare Capitalism Reconsidered," *Labor History* 33 (Winter 1992), 22–31.

3. Quote is from NARACP, RNLRB, RG 25, CF 1661, p. 756; SoRelle, "'An De Po Cullud Man," 16–17.

4. Lovell, "Houston's Reaction to the New Deal," 33–46; Berryman, "Houston and the Early Depression," 84–85; Yergin, *The Prize*, 248–59; Pratt, *Growth of a Refining Region*, 191–94, 212.

5. Yergin, *The Prize*, 250–51; American Petroleum Institute, *Facts and Figures, 1950*, 130.

6. William Edward Montgomery, "The Depression in Houston during the Hoover Era, 1929–1932," 117–21; Randy J. Sparks, "Heavenly Houston or Hellish Houston?" 355.

7. Houston Chamber of Commerce, *Annual Report, 1932*, 7; Berryman, "Houston and the Early Depression," 17–20; W. Montgomery, "The Depression in Houston," 121; H. Weber Page, *Houston and Harris County Facts*, 463.

8. NARACP, RNLRB, RG 25, CF 1661, pp. 26–28; "Union Leader Fires Charges at Kuldell," *Houston Chronicle*, February 10, 1934, p. 1; "Notice to All Hughes Tool Company Employees," *Houston Labor Messenger*, November 17, 1933, p. 1.

9. William Leuchtenberg, *The Perils of Prosperity, 1914–1932*, 247; Berryman, "Houston and the Early Depression," 28–29; Lovell, "Houston's Reaction to the New Deal," 115–16.

10. Roger Biles, *A New Deal for the American People*, 29; Anthony Badger, *The New Deal: The Depression Years, 1933–1940*, 7; Lovell, "Houston's Reaction to the New Deal," 5–12.

11. Arthur Schlesinger, *The Coming of the New Deal*, 96–102, 144–49; William E. Leuchtenberg *Franklin D. Roosevelt and the New Deal, 1932–1940*, 57–58; James D. Rose, *Duquesne and the Rise of the Steel Unionism*, 66–67.

12. Schlesinger, *The Coming of the New Deal*, 146–49; Gary Dean Best, *Pride Prejudice, and Politics*, 40–41, 60–61.

13. Schlesinger, *The Coming of the New Deal*, Badger, *The New Deal*, 120, 126–27.

14. NARACP, RNLRB, RG 25, CF 1661, pp. 253–65, 660–68, 679–86; NARACP, RNLRB, RG 25, CF 3066, "Official Report," pp. 345–64; "Two Sides to Question Say Hughes Workers," *Houston Labor Messenger*, August 18, 1933, p. 1.

15. NARACP, RNLRB, RG 25, CF 3066, "Official Report," Exhibits B-6B; Zieger, *The CIO*, 29; Irving Bernstein, *Turbulent Years, 1933–1941*, 685–86. The AFL's recruiting campaign at Hughes Tool was patterned after the federation's national strategy to break with tradition and promote industrial unionism in rubber, auto, steel, electrical, and other mass producing industries.

16. "Labor Board Asked to Probe Fake Union at Hughes Tool," *Houston Labor Messenger*, April 6, 1934, p. 1; "Coercion at Hughes Tool Reported in Hughes Bulletin," *Houston Labor Messenger*, February 2, 1934, p. 1; NLRB, *Decisions*, 33:1092.

17. Beeth and Wintz, *Black Dixie*, 92; Herbert Northrup, *Organized Labor*

and the Negro, 5–6; Horace Cayton and George Mitchell, *Black Workers and the New Unions*, vi.

18. "Houston Answers the Call," *Houston* 4 (August, 1933): 3–5; Maroney, "Organized Labor," 209–15; Krenek, "Jake Wolters," 101–10.

19. "Two Sides to Every Question Say Hughes Workers," *Houston Labor Messenger*, August 18, 1933, p. 1.

20. "Union Leader Fires Charges at Kuldell," *Houston Chronicle*, February 10, 1934, p. 1; "Notice to All Hughes Tool Company Employees," *Houston Labor Messenger*, November 17, 1933, p. 1.

21. "Two Sides to Every Question Say Hughes Workers," *Houston Labor Messenger*, August 18, 1933; Mabry, interviewed by author, October 26, 1993; Arthur Hensley, interviewed by author, July 27, 1994.

22. "Hughes Says Plant Has No Labor Dispute," *Houston Chronicle*, November 15, 1933, p. 3; "Hughes Tool Workers to Vote on Industrial Freedom," *Houston Labor Messenger*, November 6, 1933, p. 6; "Hughes Tool Violates Agreement with Labor Board," *Houston Labor Messenger*, March 30, 1934, p. 1.

23. Kuldell quote in "Tool Company Workers Will Name Leaders," *Houston Post*, November 16, 1933, p. 7; Carroll quote in "Union Leader Fires Charges at Kuldell," *Houston Chronicle*, February 10, 1934.

24. NARACP, RNLRB, RG 25, CF 1661, pp. 188–89, 685, 922, 1363; American Petroleum Institute, *Facts and Figures, 1950*, 130.

25. "NRA Labor Aid Is Ordered to Houston," *Houston Post*, November 15, 1933, p. 10.

26. NARASRFW, RNWLB, RG 202, CF 111-2083-D, "Intermediate Report," p. 4.

27. NLRB, *Decisions*, 27: 843; NARACP, RNLRB, RG 25, CF 1661, Exhibit B-2, pp. 45–59; NARASRFW, RNWLB, RG 202, CF 111-2083-D, "Intermediate Report," pp. 3–4.

28. "Board Prepares to Conduct New Ballot at Plant," *Houston Labor Messenger*, March 2, 1934, p. 1.

29. NARACP, RNLRB, RG 25, CF 1661, pp. 45–51; "NRA Labor Aid Is Ordered to Houston," *Houston Post*, November 15, 1933, p. 10.

30. "Board Prepares to Conduct New Election," *Houston Labor Messenger* March 2, 1934, p. 1; NARACP, RNLRB, RG 25, CF 1661, pp. 45–52.

31. "Supervisor for Hughes Tool Co. Election on Way," *Houston Chronicle*, November 14, 1933, p. 8; "Hughes Tool Co. Election Date Has Not Been Set," *Houston Chronicle*, November 28, 1933, p. 2; "NRA Labor Aid Is Ordered to Houston," *Houston Post*, November 15, 1933, p. 10.

32. "NRA Labor Aid Is Ordered to Houston," *Houston Post*, November 15, 1933, p. 10.

33. D. Nelson, "Company Union Movement," 30–31.

34. American Iron and Steel Institute, *Collective Bargaining in the Steel Industry*, 4.

35. Zieger, *The CIO*, 56–57.

36. NARASRFW, RNWLB, RG 202, CF 111-2083-D, "Intermediate Report," pp. 4–5; NARACP, RNLRB, RG 25, CF 1661, pp. 299–300.

37. NARASRFW, RNWLB, RG 202, CF 111-2083-D, "Intermediate Report," pp. 4–5; "E.W.O. Observes Its Fifth Anniversary as Bona-Fide Union," *Houston Labor Journal*, December 16, 1938, p. 2; E. M. Ramsey, "Labor Act Amendments in Interest of Equality by Ramsey," *Houston Labor Journal*, December 16, 1938, p. 1; "Aims, Objects of Independents Fill Needs of Workers," *Houston Labor Journal*, October 7, 1938.

38. NARACP, RNLRB, RG 25, CF 1661, pp. 315–19, Exhibit B-39.

39. NLRB, *Decisions*, 27: 841; NARACP, RNLRB, RG 25, CF 1661, pp. 34–35.

40. NARACP, RNLRB, RG 25, CF 1661, pp. 300–28, Exhibit B-15.

41. Botson, "Jim Crow," 103–106; Cayton and Mitchell, *Black Workers and the New Unions*, x; Northrup, *Organized Labor and the Negro*, 5.

42. "Hughes Tool Workers Are Ready to Vote Next Week," *Houston Labor Messenger*, November 24, 1933, p. 1; NARACP, RNLRB, RG 25, CF 1661, pp. 319–26, Exhibit B-40.

43. Rohlf was given the nickname "Daddy Rohlf" early in his Hughes Tool career. Many employees did not know that his name was John. Davis, interviewed by author, August 21, 1998. NARACP, RNLRB, RG 25, CF 1661, pp. 335–38, Exhibit B-41; NARASRFW, RNWLB, RG 202, CF 111-2083-D, "Intermediate Report," pp. 5–6; NLRB, *Decisions*, 27: 841–42.

44. NARACP, RNLRB, RG 25, CF 1661, pp. 324–40; NARASRFW, RNWLB, RG 202, CF 111-2083-D, "Intermediate Report," pp. 5–6.

45. NARASRFW, RNWLB, RG 202, CF 111-2083-D, "Intermediate Report," pp. 5–6, 666–68, 2042–50.

46. Ibid., pp. 5–6.

47. "Right of Workers to Organize to be Tested at Hughes Tool: Balloting Will be Done under NRA Supervision," *Houston Labor Messenger*, November 3, 1933, p. 1; "Lord and Master," *Houston Labor Messenger*, February 2, 1934, p. 1.

48. "Notice to All Hughes Tool Company Employees," *Houston Labor Messenger*, November 17, 1933, p. 1.

49. NARACP, RNLRB, RG 25, CF 1661, Exhibit B-2; NARASRFW, RNWLB, RG 202, CF 111-2083-D, "Intermediate Report," pp. 6–7; NLRB, *Decisions*, 27: 843–44.

50. NARACP, RNLRB, RG 25, CF 1661, Exhibit B-2; NARASRFW, RNWLB, RG 202, CF 111-2083-D, "Intermediate Report," p. 7.

51. NARACP, RNLRB, RG 25, CF 1661, Exhibit B-3.

52. 67. "Notice to All Hughes Tool Company Employees," *Houston Labor Messenger*, November 17, 1933.

53. NARASRFW, RNWLB, RG 202, CF 111-2083-D, "Intermediate Report," p. 7; "Company Union Wins Election at Hughes Tool," *Houston Labor Messenger,* December 8, 1933, p. 1.

54. Mabry, interviewed by author, October 26, 1993; Wayne Dearman, interviewed by author, August 1, 1994; *Houston Chronicle,* February 10, 1934; *Houston Labor Messenger,* December 8, 1933.

55. "New Election Ordered at Hughes Tool," *Houston Labor Messenger,* February 9, 1934, p. 1; "Board Prepares to Conduct New Ballot at Plant," *Houston Labor Messenger,* March 2, 1934, p. 1.

56. "Company Union Wins Election at Hughes Tool," *Houston Labor Messenger,* December 8, 1933.

57. NARACP, RNLRB, RG 25, CF 1661, pp. 347–50.

58. Ibid., pp. 193–97, 355–80.

59. Ibid., EWO/HTC Exhibit-2, pp. 169–72; NARACP, RNLRB, RG 25, CF 1661, Exhibit B-17, 441–42.

60. Ibid., Exhibit B-9, 85–87, 441–42. The EWO's constitution granted membership to general foremen, foremen, and assistant foremen. See NARACP, RNLRB, RG 25, CF 1661, Exhibit B-17; *Houston Labor Messenger,* November 24, 1933.

61. NLRB, *Decisions,* 27: 851; NARASRFW, RNWLB, RG 202, CF 111-2083-D, "Intermediate Report," p. 8.

62. Philip Taft, *Organizing Dixie:,* 81–85; Robert J. Norrell, "Caste in Steel,": Jim Crow Careers in Birmingham, Alabama," 677; NARASRFW, RNWLB, RG 202, CF 111-2083-D, "Intermediate Report," p. 8.

63. "Independent Union at Hughes Tool Still Bargaining Agency, Workers not Disturbed over NLRB Ruling," *Houston Negro Labor News,* April 13, 1940, p. 1; "Over 3,000 Attend Labor Leader's Funeral," *Houston Labor Messenger,* March 2, 1946, p. 1.

64. "R. H. Guess Says Informer Editor Unfair, Misrepresented Facts in NLRB Ruling," *Houston Negro Labor News,* March 2, 1940, p. 1.

65. Davis and Henry, interviewed by author, May 3, 1994; "Fallacies in the Argument," *Houston Informer,* May 27, 1939, p. 2; Carter Wesley, "Examiner Calls HTC Co. Union," *Houston Informer,* February 24, 1940, p. 1.

66. Botson, "Jim Crow," 110–14.

67. NARACP, RNLRB, RG 25, CF 1661, pp. 1366–76; NARASRFW, RNWLB, RG 202, CF 111-2083-D, "Intermediate Report," pp. 9–10; NLRB, *Decisions,* 27: 852–53.

68. Davis and Henry, interviewed by author, May 3, 1994; Rhone, interviewed by author, November 5, 1998; Gray, interviewed by author, November 19, 1998; Taylor, "C. W. Rice," 38–48; C. W. Rice and *Negro Labor News* Collection, HMRC, MSS 242, "Worth Considering: Employment and Reference Bureau of Texas Business and Laboring Men's Association," hereafter cited as Rice Collection with reference to specific documents.

69. Taylor, "C. W. Rice," 36, 48–52; Henry, interviewed by author, January 11, 1994.

70. NARACP, RNLRB, RG 25, CF 1661, pp. 78–82, Exhibit B-7; NLRB, *Decisions*, 27: 845.

71. NARACP, RNLRB, RG 25, CF 1661, pp. 82–83, 1715–19, Exhibits B-8, R-80; "Coercion at Hughes Tool Reported in Hughes Bulletin," *Houston Labor Messenger*, February 2, 1934, p. 1.

72. "New Election Ordered at Hughes Tool," *Houston Labor Messenger*, February 9, 1934, p. 1; "Labor Board Asked to Probe Fake Union at Hughes Tool," *Houston Labor Messenger*, April 6, 1934, p. 1; NLRB, *Decisions*, 27: 844.

73. "Union Leader Fires Charges at Kuldell," *Houston Chronicle*, February 10, 1934.

74. "Welfare Organization Denies Charges," *Houston Labor Journal*, April 6, 1934, p. 1.

75. "Hughes Tool $5,000 Raise Fails to Materialize," *Houston Labor Messenger*, April 13, 1934, p. 1; "Coercion at Hughes Tool Reported in Hughes Bulletin," *Houston Labor Messenger*, February 2, 1934.

76. "Hughes Tool Raise Blocked by Outsiders," *Houston Labor Messenger*, April 20, 1934, p. 1.

77. NLRB, *Decisions*, 27: 843; "Hughes Tool Company Refuses to Abide by Result of Election." *Houston Labor Messenger*, p. 1; "AFL Is Given Recognition as Bargaining Agency at Tool Company," *Houston Labor Messenger*, September 28, 1934, p. 1.

78. Schlesinger, *The Coming of the New Deal*, 147–49; Biles, *A New Deal for the American People*, 84–89, 157–59; Badger, *The New Deal*, 126–28; "Proposed Capital-Labor Truce Should Welcome Sound Philosophy of Employee Representation Plans," *Iron Age*, October 11, 1934, 39–41.

79. "AFL Is Given Recognition as Bargaining Agency at Tool Company," *Houston Labor Messenger*, September 28, 1934.

80. Ibid.

81. NARACP, RNLRB, RG 25, CF 1661, pp. 1715–19, Exhibit B-8, B-80; "AFL Is Given Recognition as Bargaining Agency at Hughes Tool Co.," *Houston Labor Messenger*, September 28, 1934, p. 1.

82. NARACP, RNLRB, RG 25, CF 3066, "Official Report," pp. 36–63, Exhibit, B-6B, B-6C; NLRB, *Decisions*, 33:1092.

83. Quote is from Wilson; Mabry, interviewed by author, October 26, 1993; Wilson, interviewed by author, November 30, 1993.

84. NLRB, *Decisions*, 27: 845–47; NARASRFW, RNWLB, RG 202, CF 111-2083-D, "Intermediate Report," p. 13; NARACP, RNLRB, RG 25, CF 1661, pp. 1152–67, 1215–24.

1. Sumner H. Slichter, *Union Policies and Industrial Management* (Washington D. C.: Brookings Institution, 1941), 1; Joseph McCartin, "An American Feeling," 70–77.

2. Schlesinger, *The Coming of the New Deal*, 150–51, 396–405; Milton Derber and Edwin Young, *Labor and the New Deal* (Madison: University of Wisconsin Press, 1957), 128; Roger Biles, *A New Deal for the American People* (Dekalb: Northern Illinois University Press, 1991), 89.

3. Schlesinger, *The Coming of the New Deal*, 150–51, 396–405; Harvard Sitkoff, *The Depression Decade*, 52; I. Bernstein, *The Turbulent Years*, 349.

4. H. Hill, *Black Labor and the American Legal System*, 100–106; William Harris, *The Harder We Run*, 110; Carter and Marcus, "Trade Union Practices and the Law," 385–86; Leon Keyserling as quoted in Sitkoff, *The Depression Decade*, 52; Kenneth M. Casebeer, "Clashing Views of the Wagner Act: Leon Keyserling's Files," 49–50.

5. H. Hill, *Black Labor*, 100–106; Harris, *The Harder We Run*, 110; Carter and Marcus, "Trade Union Practices and the Law," 385–86.

6. Automobile Manufacturers Association circular as quoted in Casebeer, "Clashing Views," 51, 52–54; I. Bernstein, *The Turbulent Years*, 337–39.

7. Schlesinger, *The Coming of the New Deal*, 406, 486–88; I. Bernstein, *The Turbulent Years*, 450; Reed as quoted in George Wolfskill, *The Revolt of the Conservatives*, 72.

8. NLRB, *Decisions*, 27: 847; NARASRFW, RNWLB, RG 202, CF 111-2083-D, "Intermediate Report," p. 15; NARACP, RNLRB, RG 25, CF 1661, pp. 141–48, Exhibits B-33.

9. NARACP, RNLRB, RG 25, CF 1661, Exhibit B-31.

10. NARASRFW, RNWLB, RG 202, CF 111-2083-D, "Intermediate Report," pp. 10–13; NARACP, RNLRB, RG 25, CF 1661, pp. 1350–51.

11. NARACP, RNLRB, RG 25, "Official Report," CF 3066, 84; Henry, interviewed by author, August 5, 1994; Alton, interviewed by author, December 1, 1993.

12. NARASRFW, RNWLB, RG 202, CF 111-2083-D, "Intermediate Report," p. 12.

13. NARACP, RNLRB, RG 25, CF 1661, pp. 175–76, 914–16, Exhibit EWO/HTC-3; Mabry, interviewed by author, October 16, 1993.

14. NARACP, RNLRB, RG 25, CF 1661, pp. 694–714; NARASRFW, RNWLB, RG 202, CF 111-2083-D, "Intermediate Report," p. 13; Mabry, interviewed by author, October 16, 1993; Harry Callender, interviewed by author, July 21, 1994.

15. NLRB, *Decisions*, 27: 847; NARASRFW, RNWLB, RG 202, CF 111-2083-D, "Intermediate Report," pp. 13–14.

16. NARACP, RNLRB, RG 25, CF 1661, p. 537; "C.I.O. Men Claim Pressure Used at Hughes Tool Plant," *Houston Post,* July 21, 1939, p. 1, sec. 2.

17. NARACP, RNLRB, RG 25, CF 1661, p. 553, 564–65; NLRB, *Decisions,* 27:848.

18. NARACP, RNLRB, RG 25, CF 1661, pp. 542–43.

19. Ibid., pp. 150–53, 678–93, 1715–19, Exhibit R-78.

20. Ibid; "Wage, Hour Law Favored by Kuldell," *Houston Chronicle,* June 5, 1937, p. 1; "Witness says E.W.O. Denied Aid by Firm," *Houston Chronicle,* July 19, 1939, p. 1; "Red Charge Is Denied by C.I.O. Worker," *Houston Chronicle,* July 21, 1939, p. 8; "Washington News," *Iron Age,* June 10, 1937., 62–63. Between June 2 and June 5, 1937, Colonel Kuldell testified before the LaFollette Committee and admitted to using detective agencies to spy on his employees.

21. NARACP, RNLRB, RG 25, CF 1661, pp. 678–93; *Houston Chronicle,* July 21, 1939; *Houston Post,* July 19, 1939.

22. NARACP, RNLRB, RG 25, CF 1661, pp. 688, 1522–24, Exhibits R-38, R-39.

23. NARASRFW, RNWLB, RG 202, CF 111-2083-D, "Intermediate Report," pp. 15–16; NARACP, RNLRB, RG 25, CF 1661, pp. 854–55; Nelson Lichtenstein, *Labor's War at Home,* 3–5; I. Bernstein, *The Turbulent Years,* 768–74.

24. Zieger, *The CIO,* 17–21; Schlesinger, *The Coming of the New Deal,* 408–409.

25. Michael Goldfield, "Race and the CIO," 7–8; Sitkoff, *The Depression Decade,* 180–83. The history of John L. Lewis's commitment to interracial unionism has come under biting criticism by Herbert Hill. The UMW's vaunted racial egalitarianism was adopted for practical matters such as eliminating blacks as strikebreakers rather than a desire by white miners to include blacks in the union. The CIO's racial history parallels the UMW's. See H. Hill, "Myth-Making,"132–95.

26. Zieger, *The CIO,* 84; Davis, interviewed by author, May 1, 1997.

27. I. Bernstein, *The Turbulent Years,* 432–98; Walter Galenson, *The CIO Challenge to the AFL: A History of the American Labor Movement, 1933–1941* (Cambridge: Harvard University Press, 1960), 75–122. Hughes Tool employees used the acronym CIO rather than SWOC, so I will do the same. In 1942 the SWOC changed its name to the United Steelworkers of America (USWA) but Hughes Tool workers continued to call it the CIO. Robert Zieger also found this to be the case with steelworkers in the northern steel towns, "SWOC was a direct arm of the CIO, and the steelworkers referred to themselves as members of the CIO, not SWOC." See Zieger, *The CIO,* 61.

28. Alton, interviewed by author, December 1, 1993; Dearman, interviewed by author, August 1, 1994; Gray, interviewed by author, November 19, 1998; Henry, interviewed by author, August 5, 1994; David McDonald Papers, Historical Collections and Labor Archives, Pennsylvania State University, Frank

Hardesty to David McDonald, October 8, 1945, hereafter cited as McDonald Papers; NLRB, *Decisions*, 33:1092.

29. McDonald Papers, Frank Hardesty to David McDonald, September 8, 1942, and David McDonald to Frank Hardesty September 12, 1942; "N.A.A.C.P. Conducts Labor Forum," *Houston Informer*, May 29, 1937, p. 1.

30. "N.A.A.C.P. Conducts Labor Forum," *Houston Informer*, May 29, 1937, p. 1.

31. "Leader Warns Workers to Shy Both Unions," *Houston Informer*, July 14, 1937, p. 9.

32. Taylor, "C. W. Rice," 38–42. The Houston locals of both the International Longshoreman's Association and the International Brotherhood of Teamsters, Chauffeurs, Stablemen, and Helpers had negotiated agreements with employers that took jobs away from their black members in order to give them to whites.

33. Ibid., 38–40.

34. NARACP, RNLRB, RG 25, CF 1661, pp. 246–49, 388–96, 401–404, 1311–15, Exhibit B-37; NARASRFW, RNWLB, RG 202, CF 111-2083-D, "Intermediate Report," p. 17; National War Labor Board, *War Labor Report: Reports of Decisions and Orders*, 16:123–34; Henrietta M. Larson and Kenneth Wiggins Porter, *History of Humble Oil and Refining Company*, 373–75.

35. NLRB, *War Labor Report*, 16:125–34.

36. NARACP, RNLRB, RG 25, CF 1661, pp. 1313–14.

37. NLRB, *Decisions*, 27: 855; NARACP, RNLRB, RG 25, CF 1661, pp. 94–101, 396–99, Exhibits B-11, B-12, B-13; Wilson, interviewed by author, November 30, 1993; Mabry, interviewed by author, October 26, 1993; Dearman, interviewed by author, August 1, 1994; Botson, "Jim Crow," 113–14.

38. V. Bernstein, "The Antilabor Front," 334.

39. Southern Conference for Human Welfare Papers, Robert W. Woodruff Library, Atlanta University Center, *Southern Patriot* 2 (December, 1944): 1–8; I. Bernstein, *The Turbulent Years*, 334–36; George Norris Green, *The Establishment in Texas Politics*, 61–68; Stetson Kennedy, *Southern Exposure*, 84.

40. NARACP, RNLRB, RG 25, CF 1661, pp. 246–249, 404, Exhibit B-37; NARASRFW, RNWLB, RG 202, CF 111-2083-D, "Intermediate Report," p. 17.

41. NARACP, RNLRB, RG 25, CF 1661.

42. NARASRFW, RNWLB, RG 202, CF 111-2083-D, "Intermediate Report," pp. 16–18; NARACP, RNLRB, RG 25, CF 1661, pp. 116–53, Exhibits B-4, B-15, B-21, B-22, B-23, B-23A, B-24, B-25, B-26, B-49, EWO/HTC-5. The quasi contract titled *Summary of Agreement Arrived at by the Hughes Tool Company and Its Employees, October 1, 1937*, was an eleven-page booklet; see Exhibit B-15.

43. NARACP, RNLRB, RG 25, CF 1661, Exhibits B-4, B-23A, B-23B; NLRB, *Decisions*, 27: 850.

44. NARACP, RNLRB, RG 25, CF 1661, pp. 1005–40, Exhibit B-49.

45. NARACP, RNLRB, RG 25, CF 1661, Exhibit B-15.

46. NARACP, RNLRB, RG 25, CF 1661, p. 914.

47. NARASRFW, RNWLB, RG 202, CF 111-2083-D, "Intermediate Report," pp. 17–18; NARACP, RNLRB, RG 25, CF 1661, pp. 101–103, 245–46, Exhibits B-14, B-36.

48. NARACP, RNLRB, RG 25, CF 1661, Exhibit B-15.

49. Mabry, interviewed by author, October 16, 1993; Callender, interviewed by author, July 21, 1994; Wilson, interviewed by author, November 30, 1993; NLRB, *War Labor Report,* 16:112–48.

50. Employees referred to Rohlf by his nickname and few knew that John was his first name. Davis, interviewed by author, August 21, 1998. NARASRFW, RNWLB, RG 202, CF 111-2083-D, "Intermediate Report," p. 18; NARACP, RNLRB, RG 25, CF 1661, pp. 522–24, Exhibit B-52.

51. NARACP, RNLRB, RG 25, CF 1661, p. 775.

52. Ibid., pp. 772–75, 1614–15, 523.

53. Setup men held low level management positions even though they were hourly paid employees. They are significant to the Hughes Tool case because management used its front line shop floor supervisors, in particular setup men and foremen, to implement its reign of intimidation against the CIO. NARACP, RNLRB, RG 25, CF 1661, pp. 606–609, 622–23.

54. NLRB, *Decisions,* 27: 855; NARACP, RNLRB, RG 25, CF 1661, pp. 609, 611–13.

55. NLRB, *Decisions,* 27:856.

56. NARACP, RNLRB, RG 25, CF 1661, pp. 610–14.

57. Employees called Hogan "Hy" rather than Henry, as did Hogan himself. Hy, an intentional misspelling of "high," referred to Hogan's reputation as a high and mighty tyrant over the machine shop. Hogan reveled in his nickname. Wilson, interviewed by author, December 30, 1994, November 30, 1993.

58. Mabry, interviewed by author, October 26, 1993, Wilson, interviewed by author, November 30, 1993; Dearman, interviewed by author, August 1, 1944; NARACP, RNLRB, RG 25, CF 1661, pp. 767–77; Lichtenstein, *Labor's War at Home,* 14. Nelson Lichtenstein made this point for steelworkers in the basic steel industry during and after the Little Steel strike. Interviews with Hughes Tool CIO stewards show that they encountered the same reluctance to pay union dues and resorted to similar ploys to collect dues.

59. David McDonald, *Union Man,* 90–98.

60. NARASRFW, RNWLB, RG 202, CF 111-2083-D, "Intermediate Report," p. 20.

61. Officials in CIO Local No. 1742 often held one or more leadership positions in the union. For example, J. T. Barnett served as shop steward and financial secretary, J. B. Harris was also the local's vice president, and J. C. Caffal and W. M. Hicks served as shop stewards and grievance men. See, NARACP, RNLRB, RG 25, CF 1661, pp. 724–25, 756–57, 773–75.

62. NARACP, RNLRB, RG 25, CF 1661, pp. 735–36.

63. Ibid., pp. 561–65; "C.I.O. Men Claim Pressure Used at Hughes Tool Plant, *Houston Post,* July 21, 1939, p. 1; "Red Charge Is Denied by C.I.O. Worker," *Houston Chronicle,* July 21, 1939, p. 8.

64. Lichtenstein, *Labor's War at Home,* 18–19; McElvaine, *The Great Depression,* 298–300; Leuchtenberg, *Roosevelt and the New Deal,* 243–51; I. Bernstein, *The Turbulent Years,* 452. The SWOC laid off 250 field organizers and the remaining 183 were put on nineteen-days-a-month pay.

65. NARACP, RNLRB, RG 25, CF 3066, "Hearing on Objections," pp. 263–76. Drilling activity fell from 31,622 oil and gas wells in 1937 down to 26,297 in 1939, a drop of 5,325 total wells. See American Petroleum Institute, *Petroleum Facts and Figures,* 9th ed. (New York: American Petroleum Institute, 1950), 130.

66. NARACP, RNLRB, RG 25, CF 1661, pp. 1241–46, 1251–57, 1263–65, 1306–1309, Exhibit EWO/HTC-46; "Organizers of Union at Tool Firm Say Company Had No Hand in Procedure," *Houston Post,* July 25, 1939, p. 7.

67. NARACP, RNLRB, RG 25, CF 1661, pp. 2001–2009, Exhibit B-1A; "Col. Kuldell Retires as Hughes Chief," *Houston Post,* July 18, 1939, p. 1; "Kuldell Reveals His Resignation as Head of Hughes Tool Firm," *Houston Chronicle,* July 17, 1939, p. 1; Mabry, interviewed by author, October 26, 1993; Wilson, interviewed by author, November 30, 1993.

68. NARACP, RNLRB, RG 25, CF 1661, pp. 2001–2009; Wilson, interviewed by author, November 30, 1994.

69. Michael Botson, "Organized Labor at the Hughes Tool Company," 72–73; NLRB, *Decisions,* 33:1092; NARACP, RNLRB, RG 25, CF 3066, "Hearing on Objections," pp. 263–76.

70. NARACP, RNLRB, RG 25, CF 3066, "Hearing on Objections," p. 7, Exhibit B-1A.

71. Galenson, *The CIO Challenge to the AFL,* 112–13; Zieger, *The CIO,* 121–33; Lichtenstein, *Labor's War at Home,* 33–34.

72. NLRB, *Decisions,* 27: 837–36; NARASRFW, RNWLB, RG 202, CF 111-2083-D, "Intermediate Report," pp. 1–2.

73. NARACP, RNLRB, RG 25, CF 1661, p. 7, Exhibit B-1A; "Kuldell Reveals His Resignation," *Houston Chronicle,* p. 1; "Stanley P. Brown Takes the Helm at Tool Company," *Houston Post,* July 18, 1939.

74. NARACP, RNLRB, RG 25, CF 1661,"Appeals Hearing, Official Report of Proceedings before the National Labor Relations Board In the Matter of Hughes Tool Company and Steel Workers Organizing Committee, Lodge No. 1742 and Employees Welfare Organization of Hughes Tool Company and H.T.C. Club of Hughes Tool Company," pp. 13-15; *Houston Chronicle,* July 17, 1939; *Houston Post,* July 18, 1939.

It seems that Kuldell retired for three reasons. One was the continuing difficulty he had in quelling the labor disturbances that rocked Hughes Tool beginning in 1933. Second was Kuldell's alienation from Howard Hughes Jr.

because of Hughes's increasing reliance on Noah Dietrich to mange the company. An intense personal and professional rivalry developed between Kuldell, the engineer who built the company into a juggernaut in the 1920s and 1930s, and Dietrich the accountant. Howard Hughes depended on the profits generated by his company to satisfy his lavish passions and he depended on Dietrich's accounting skills to pay the bills. Kuldell constantly worried that Hughes would bankrupt the company whereas Dietrich was willing to pacify Hughes regardless of the financial risks. Dietrich's triumph in the struggle with Kuldell for Hughes's attention disillusioned Kuldell. Third, Kuldell became weary of having to fill in for Howard Hughes in Houston's elite society. Kuldell believed that Hughes should have involved himself in society and interacted with the city's elite as part of his responsibilities as the owner of Hughes Tool Company. It troubled Kuldell's sense of propriety and ran counter to his sense of noblesse oblige that Hughes ignored his philanthropic and social responsibilities and preferred a flamboyant California life style. Robert Kuldell, interviewed by author, July 27, 1999.

75. NARACP, RNLRB, RG 25, CF 1661, pp. 849–52, 885–87, 1180–95, 1338–42, 1386–91, 2007–2008.

76. NARASRFW, RNWLB, RG 202, CF 111-2083-D, "Intermediate Report," pp. 18–19; NARACP, RNLRB, RG 25, CF 1661, p. 1540.

77. NARACP, RNLRB, RG 25, CF 1661, pp. 1706–25, Exhibits B-15, R-97, R-98, R-99.

78. NARASRFW, RNWLB, RG 202, CF 111-2083-D, "Intermediate Report," p. 16.

79 NLRB, *Decisions*, 27: 848–49.

80. NARACP, RNLRB, RG 25, CF 1661, pp. 1215–24, Exhibit B-6.

81. Ibid., pp. 1217, 1220–22; NARASRFW, RNWLB, RG 202, CF 111-2083-D, "Intermediate Report," pp. 14–15; NLRB, *Decisions*, 27: 848–49.

82. NARACP, RNLRB, RG 25, CF 1661, pp. 1037–50, 1216–23, Exhibit B-60; "Organizers of Union at Tool Firm Say Company Had No Hand in Procedure," *Houston Post*, July 25, 1939, p. 7.

83. NARACP, RNLRB, RG 25, CF 1661, 1215–24.

84. I. Bernstein, *The Turbulent Years*, 646–63.

85. Galenson, *The CIO Challenge to the AFL*, 612–15.

86. "N.L.R.B. Called Grand Jury, Judge, Jury, and Appellate Court by EWO Attorney," *Houston Post*, Jul 26, 1939 sec. 2, p. 1.

87. NARACP, RNLRB, RG 25, CF 1661, p. 855.

88. I. Bernstein, *The Turbulent Years*, 648; Lichtenstein, *Labor's War at Home*, 33–34; "Labor Unrest Casts Shadow over Steel Institute Meeting," *Iron Age*, June 3, 1937, 32–33.

89. NARACP, RNLRB, RG 25, CF 1661, pp. 852–63, 1056–63.

90. Ibid., pp. 1322–348, 1384–92, Exhibits EWO/HTC-52, EWO/HTC-54.

91. Ibid., pp. 1060–63, 1329–32, 853–54.

92. Ibid., pp. 2062–63.

93. NARASRFW, RNWLB, RG 202, "Intermediate Report," CF 111-2083-D, pp. 24–27; I. Bernstein, *The Turbulent Years,* 650.

94. NARASRFW, RNWLB, RG 202, "Intermediate Report," CF 111-2083-D, p. 26.

95. NARACP, RNLRB, RG 25, CF 1661, "Appeals Hearing," pp. 2–8, 13–14.

96. Ibid., 13.

97. "Hughes Tool Union Refuses to Act on N.L.R.B. Report," *Houston Post,* February 25, 1940, p. 1; "Workers of Tool Firm Here Plan to Continue Union," *Houston Chronicle,* February 25, 1940, p. 25.

98. I. Bernstein, *The Turbulent Years,* 646–52.

99. Larson and Porter, *History of Humble Oil,* 373–75; NLRB, *War Labor Report,* 16:116–45; Joseph Pratt, "The Oil Workers International Unions' Organization of the Upper Texas Gulf Coast," 27–30.

100. NARACP, RNLRB, RG 25, CF 1661, pp. 384–96.

101. Ibid., CF 3066, "Hearing on Objections," Exhibit B-5; NARACP, RNLRB, RG 25, CF 1661, Exhibit B-15.

102. NLRB, *Decisions,* 27: 862–63.

103. NARACP, RNLRB, RG 25, CF 3066, "Hearing on Objections," pp. 129–34, Exhibit B-5.

104. "Examiner Calls HTC Co. Union," *Houston Informer,* February 24, 1940, p. 1.

105. NLRB, *Decisions,* 33:1092.

106. NARACP, RNLRB, RG 25, CF 1661, "Appeals Hearing," p. 13.

CHAPTER 5

I thank Louis Marchiafava, editor of the *Houston Review,* for allowing me to reproduce parts of this chapter that previously appeared as an article in that journal.

1. NARACP, RNLRB, RG 25, CF 402–46, "Official Report of Proceedings before the National Labor Relations Board in the Matter of Hughes Tool Company and Independent Metal Workers Union, Locals Nos. 1 and 2, Affiliated with Confederated Unions of America," pp. 6–48.

2. Howard Curtiss Papers, Historical Collections and Labor Archives, Pennsylvania State University, Independent Metal Workers Union, handbill, cited hereafter as Curtiss Papers.

3. Ibid.; NARACP, RNLRB, RG 25, CF 406-42, Exhibit I-7.

4. NARACP, RNLRB, RG 25, CF 402–46, Constitution of Independent Metal Workers Union, Exhibit P-3.

5. NARACP, RNLRB, RG 25, CF 3066, "Official Report," p. 304.

6. Ibid., pp. 304–306; Carter Wesley, "Form Local of M.W.U.," *Houston Informer,* November 19, 1940, p. 1; NLRB, *Decisions,* 33:1092–96.

7. NARACP, RNLRB, RG 25, CF 1661, pp. 1322–48, 1384–92, Exhibits EWO/HTC-52, EWO/HTC-54.

8. NARACP, RNLRB, RG 25, CF 6768-62, "Official Report of Proceedings before the National Labor Relations Board in the Matter of Hughes Tool Company and Independent Metal Workers Union Locals Nos. 1 and 2 and United Steelworkers of America, AFL-CIO," pp. 45–62, 72–82, 91–96, Exhibits P-1, P-4, P-5.

9. NARACP, RNLRB, RG 25, CF 1661, pp. 1168–78.

10. Ibid., CF 6768-62, "Official Report," pp. 45–62, 72–82, 91–96.

11. Ibid., pp. 129–33, 33–36, 256–58; Davis and Henry, interviewed by author, May 3, 1994.

12. NLRB, *Decisions,* 27: 840.

13. NARACP, RNLRB, RG 25, CF 3066, "Official Report," p. 114.

14. Botson, "Jim Crow," 104–105; Davis, interviewed by author, May 1, 1997; Gray, interviewed by author, November 19, 1998; Henry, interviewed by author, August 5, 1994.

15. NARACP, RNLRB, RG 25, CF 3066, "Official Report," pp. 255, 248–57, Exhibit B-5.

16. Ibid., p. 254.

17. Ibid., pp. 65–66, 80–81, 199–207, Exhibit B-5; Davis and Henry, interviewed by author, May 3, 1994.

18. NARACP, RNLRB, RG 25, CF 3066, "Official Report," pp. 80–89.

19. Ibid., CF 3066, "Hearing on Objections," pp. 5–6.

20. NARASRFW, RNWLB, RG 202, CF 111-2083-D, "Hearing before War Labor Board, in Re: Hughes Tool Company, Houston, Texas," pp. 15, 132.

21. *Houston Informer,* November 16, 1940; *Greater Houston (Texas) City Directory,* 45:535. Local No. 1 elected Henry Foster president, Richard Thompson vice president, Wilson Harrison secretary, and Jackson Pruett treasurer. Local No. 1 opened an office at 6513 Harrisburg, across the street from the plant. Local No. 2 elected B. J Lewis president, S. B. Grant vice president, R. M. Grant secretary, and Lee Henderson treasurer. The black local opened an office at 3704 Dowling Street, in Houston's African American Third Ward.

22. NARASRFW, RNWLB, RG 202, CF 111-2083-D, "Hearing," RG 202, p. 134.

23. Alton, interviewed by author, December 1, 1993; Henry, interviewed by author, January 11, 1994; Mabry, interviewed by author, October 26, 1993; Wilson, interviewed by author, November 30, 1993; NARACP, RNLRB, RG 25, CF 3066, "Hearing on Objections," pp. 22–28, 64.

24. NARACP, RNLRB, RG 25, CF 1661,"Appeals Hearing," pp. 2–8.

25. Ibid., pp. 1322–48, 1384–92, Exhibits EWO/HTC-52, EWO/HTC-54.

26. Ibid., CF 3066, "Hearing on Objections," pp. 64–70; NARACP, RNLRB, RG 25, CF 9630, "Official Report of Proceedings before the National Labor Relations Board in the Matter of Hughes Tool Company and United Steel Workers of America Locals Numbers 1742 and 2457," Exhibit R-7D.

27. NARACP, RNLRB, RG 25, CF 9630, "Official Report of Proceedings." pp. 66–68.

28. Ibid., pp. 70–74.

29. "Guess Runs into Hole, Gives Out of Answers in Tiff," *Houston Informer,* March 16, 1940, sec. 2, p. 1; "H.T.C. Factions Hurl Charges; C.I.O. May Ask Grand Jury Probe," *Houston Informer,* April 20, 1940, p. 1.

30. "R. H. Guess Says Informer Editor Unfair, Misrepresented the Facts in NLRB Ruling," *Houston Negro Labor News,* March 2, 1940, p. 1.

31. "Hughes Tool Workers Say They Are Satisfied," *Houston Negro Labor News,* March 30, 1940, p. 1.

32. "It Is No Disgrace for Negroes to Speak Kindly of Outstanding or Big White People Who Are Helping the Race," *Houston Negro Labor News,* December 26, 1942, p. 1.

33. C. W. Rice, "As I See It," *Houston Negro Labor News,* December 26, 1942, p. 1.

34. "Rice Urges CIO and AFL Leaders to Back Wagner Labor Act Amendment to remove Color Bar from Unionism," *Houston Negro Labor News,* July 22, 1939, p. 1.

35. Rice, "As I See It," *Houston Negro Labor News,* November 29, 1941, p. 1.

36. "Grovey Is New Third Ward Civic Club Head," *Houston Informer,* October 14, 1939; "Grovey Tells Why He Supports CIO-SWOC in Hughes Plant," *Houston Informer,* October 11, 1941; McDonald Papers, Frank Hardesty to David McDonald, September 4, 1942.

37. "Our Policy on Labor," *Houston Informer,* March 9, 1940, p. 1.

38. "Guess and Grovey Crash at Hughes Tool Labor Meeting," *Houston Informer,* August 31, 1941.

39. R. R. Grovey, "R. R. Grovey Issues Burning Challenge to Debate C. W. Rice," *Houston Informer,* August 16, 1941, p. 1.

40. NARACP, RNLRB, RG 25,CF 3066, Paul Gardner and Woody Clayton to E. M. Martin, April 26, 1941, Exhibit PU-1.

41. Ibid., CF 402-46, T. B. Everitt, "Real Facts Regarding the Racial Issue," *Independent Journal: Official Organ of the Independent Metal Workers Union,* December 17, 1945, p. 1, Exhibit I-16.

42. NLRB, *Decisions,* 33:1092; NARACP, RNLRB, RG 25, CF 3066, "Official Report," Exhibit B-1B.

43. NLRB, *Decisions,* 33:1092–93.

44. NARACP, RNLRB, RG 25, CF 3066, "Official Report," pp. 9–12.

45. NLRB, *Decisions,* 33:1092–93.

46. NARACP, RNLRB, RG 25, CF 3066, "Official Report," pp. 32,44, Exhibit B-4.

47. Ibid., pp. 200–201.

48. Ibid., pp. 80–86, 199–263, 135.

49. Ibid., 135; Davis and Henry, interviewed by author, May 3, 1994.

50. NLRB, *Decisions,* 33:1096–1101; NLRB, *Decisions,* 36: 904–905.

51. C. W. Rice, "White Unionists Trying to Scare Colored Hughes Tool Workers into Joining the CIO," *Houston Negro Labor News,* January 9, 1943, p. 1.

52. *Houston Negro Labor News,* July 22, 1939, p. 1; Dulles and Dubovsky, *Labor in America,* 259–60, 278–88, 297–98.

53. "Geo. O. Duncan Defends Rice at Grovey Meeting," *Houston Negro Labor News,* March 2, 1940, p. 1.

54. Carter Wesley, "Colored Workers Courted," *Houston Informer,* August 23, 1941, p. 1.

55. Carter Wesley, "Our Policy on Labor," *Houston Informer,* March 9, 1940, p. 1.

56. "Grovey Tells Why He Supports CIO-SWOC in Hughes Plant," *Houston Informer,* October 11, 1941, p. 5.

57. NARACP, RNLRB, RG 25, CF 3066, "Official Report," pp. 35, 29–43; "NLRB Takes Statements in Hughes Election," *Houston Informer,* October 18, 1941, pp. 1, 50, 87.

58. NLRB, *Decisions,* 36: 905.

59. Ibid., 904–905.

60. "Hughes Tool Workers," *Houston Informer,* July 11, 1942, p. 1.

61. "Grovey Tells Why He Supports CIO-SWOC in Hughes Plant," *Houston Informer,* October 11, 1941.

62. Botson, "Jim Crow," 114–15; Alton, interviewed by author, December 1, 1993; Henry, interviewed by author, January 11, 1994.

63. R. R. Grovey, "Hughes Tool Co. from the Ringside," *Houston Informer,* May 16, 1942, p. 1.

64. "Hughes Tool Workers," *Houston Informer,* July 11, 1942, p. 1.

65. "CIO Requests an Election at Hughes Tool Company," *Houston Informer,* July 18, 1942, p. 1.

66. NARACP, RNLRB, RG 25, CF 3066, "Hearing on Objections," pp. 22–28, 83–91; Carter Wesley, "Duncan, Martin Join; Organization of All Workers Underway," *Houston Informer,* May 1, 1941, p. 1; "Martin Gives Lie to Rice Statements; Call Parley," *Houston Informer,* June 14, p. 1;.

67. "CIO Requests an Election at Hughes Tool Company," *Houston Informer,* July 18, 1942, p. 1.

68. NARACP, RNLRB, RG 25, CF 3066, "Official Report," Exhibit B-1B; National Archives and Records Administration, College Park, Md., Records of

the Federal Mediation and Conciliation Service, RG 280, Case File 465-240, "Preliminary Report," hereafter cited as NARACP, RFMCS, RG 280, with reference to specific documents.

69. NARACP, RNLRB, RG 25, CF 6288, "Official Report of Proceedings before the National Labor Relations Board in the Matter of Hughes Tool Company (Dickson Gun Plant) and the United Steelworkers of America Locals 1742 and 2457," pp. 9, 34–39.

70. Ibid., CF 3066, "Official Report," pp. 72–75; Dearman, interviewed by author, August 1, 1994; Mabry, interviewed by author, October 26, 1993; Wilson, interviewed by author, November 30, 1993; "Unionization of Southwest Now Probable," *Steel Labor,* December 19, 1941, p. 8.

71. NARACP, RFMCS, RG 280, CF 209-2783, Exhibit B-5, pp. 7, 1–12; the quote is found on p. 7.

72. NLRB, *Decisions,* 45: 823.

73. Chris Dixie, interviewed by author, November 30, 1998.

74. NLRB, *Decisions,* 45: 822–25.

75. "CIO Scores a Major Triumph at Houston Plant," *Houston Informer,* December 19, 1942, p. 1.

76. C. W. Rice, "Who Was Repudiated at Hughes Tool?" *Houston Negro Labor News,* December 26, 1942, p. 1; *Houston Negro Labor News,* January 2, 1943, p. 1; Carter Wesley, "Independents and Rice Repudiated by Hughes Workers," *Houston Informer,* December 19, 1942, p. 1.

77. "CIO Committee of 12 Is Appointed, 6 White, 6 Colored," *Houston Informer,* December 19, 1942, p. 1.

78. R. R. Grovey, "Negro Workers Benefitted by Hughes -CIO Deal," *Houston Informer,* April 10, 1943, p. 1; NARACP, RNLRB, RG 25, CF 6288, "Official Report of Proceedings," Exhibit Pet. 2.

79. "Rice Controlled Union Cost Workers $147,000 Last Year," *Houston Informer,* April 17, 1943, p. 1.

80. NARACP, RNLRB, RG 25, CF 6288, "Official Report of Proceedings," Exhibit Pet. 2; NARACP, RNLRB, RG 25, CF 3066, "Official Report," Exhibit B-5; NARACP, RFMCS, RG 280, CF 209-2783.

81. National Archives and Records, Southwest Region, Fort Worth Records of the Committee on Fair Employment Practices, 1941–1946, RG 228, Case File 13-BR-34, W. Don Ellinger to Will Maslow, Report, November 7, 1944, hereafter cited as NARASRFW, RCFEP, RG 228, with reference to specific documents; National Archives and Records, College Park, Md., Records of the Provost Marshall General, RG 389, Case File 3-38, "History of the Army Operation of the Hughes Tool Company, Houston Texas, September 6, 1944–August 29, 1945, under Executive Order No. 9457-A," Exhibit H, hereafter cited as NARACP, RPMG, RG 389, with reference to specific documents.

82. NLRB, *War Labor Report,* 11: 477–94.

83. Lichtenstein, *Labor's War at Home,* 78–81; Joel Seidman, *American La-*

bor from Defense to Reconversion, 91–108. During the First World War the NWLB exacted a no-strike pledge from labor in return for collective bargaining and the right to organize without management retribution and provided temporary protection for workers against being coerced into company unions, yellow-dog contracts, and discharge for union membership. The Wagner Act outlawed company unions, yellow-dog contracts, discharging for union membership, and protected the right to organize and bargain collectively. World War II's NWLB offered workers union security through maintenance of membership in return for a no-strike pledge.

84. Lichtenstein, *Labor's War at Home*, 78–81; Joel Seidman, *American Labor from Defense to Reconversion*, 91–108.

85. NARASRFW, RNWLB, RG 202, CF 111-2083-D, William Streetman to William H. Davis, May 27, 1943.

CHAPTER 6

1. Zieger, *American Workers*, 92–93. I rely heavily on Zieger's description of maintenance of membership, the no-strike pledge, and their ramifications; his is a clear and concise explanation.

2. NARASRFW, RNWLB, RG 202, CF 111-2083-D, Martin Burns to Leonard Berliner, December 8, 1944, Floyd McGowan to Leonard Berliner, March 18, 1944, W. M. Streetman to William H. Davis, May 27, 1943; NARASRFW, RNWLB, RG 202, CF 111-2083-D, "Hearing," pp. 188–97; Zieger, *American Workers*, 92–93.

3. Seidman, *American Labor*, 131–51; Nelson Lichtenstein, *Labor's War at Home*, 178–82, 186–88, 201–202.

4. NARACP, RPMG, RG 389, CF 3-38, Fred Vinson to Franklin Roosevelt, memorandum, August 29, 1944, Fred Vinson to William Davis, August 26, 1944.

5. NARASRFW, RNWLB, RG 202, CF 111-2083-D, "Hearing," p. 25; NLRB, *War Labor Report*, 11: 482; NARACP, RFMCS, RG 280, CF 300-5223, "Preliminary Report, April 12, 1943," "Final Progress Report June 4, 1943."

6. NARASRFW, RNWLB, RG 202, CF 111-2083-D, "Hearing," pp. 188–97; "CIO Scores Major Triumph at Houston Plant," *Houston Informer*, December 19, 1942, p. 1.

7. NARASRFW, RNWLB, RG 202, CF 111-2083-D, "Hearing," Exhibit A, Streetman to Davis, May 27, 1943; Noah Dietrich to Leonard Berliner, April 4, 1944.

8. NARASRFW, RNWLB, RG 202, CF 111-2083-D, "Hearing," pp. 11–18.

9. NLRB, *War Labor Report*, 11: 488–89; NARACP, RNLRB, RG 25, CF 9630, "Official Report of Proceedings."

10. NLRB, *War Labor Report*, 11: 488.

11. Ibid., pp. 41–44.

12 NARASRFW, RNWLB, RG 202, CF 111-2083-D, "Minutes of the Meeting of the Eighth Regional War Labor Board, August 3, 4, and 5, 1943, Records of the Office of the Board."

13. NARASRFW, RNWLB, RG 202, CF 111-2083-D, Floyd McGowan to Leonard Berliner, memorandum, March 18, 1944; "Minutes."

14. Ibid., "Minutes."

15. Ibid., Floyd McGowan to Leonard Berliner, memorandum, March 18, 1944.

16. Ibid., Noah Dietrich to Leonard Berliner, April 4, 1944. Dietrich's denial of any collusion between Hughes Tool and Mosher Steel is suspect when considering the antiunion history of both companies. Mosher Steel led Texas' open-shop campaign in the 1920s. See Todes, "Organized Employer Opposition," 68–73; Thomas B. Brewer, "State Anti-Labor Legislation: Texas-A Case Study," 63–64.

17. NARACP, RPMG, RG 389, CF 3-38, John S. Myers to Office of the Provost Marshall General, memorandum, September 2, 1944; NARASRFW, RNWLB, RG 202, CF 111-2083-D, Floyd McGowan to Leonard Berliner, telegram, March 14, 1944.

18. NARASRFW, RNWLB, RG 202, CF 111-2083-D, Martin Burns to Leonard Berliner, December 8, 1944.

19. NARACP, RPMG, RG 389, CF 3-38, Fred Vinson to Franklin Roosevelt, memorandum, August 29, 1944, Robert Patterson to William Davis, November 27, 1944, George Taylor to Franklin Roosevelt, August 29, 1944; NARASRFW, RNWLB, RG 202, CF 111-2083-D, Samuel Hill to Jesse Freidan, July 27, 1944.

20. NARACP, RPMG, RG 389, CF 3-38, John Myers to Provost Marshall General, memorandum, September 23, 1944, Patterson to Davis, November 27, 1944.

21. NARASRFW, RNWLB, RG 202, CF 111-2083-D, William Davis to Albert Thomas, September 19, 1944; NARACP, RPMG, RG 389, CF 3-38, Tab C; NARACP, RNLRB, RG 25, CF 9630, Exhibit B-5, pp. 663–69; Curtiss Papers, Martin Burns interview by Alice Hoffman, November 9, 1976, pp. 18–20.

22. NARACP, RFMCS, RG 280, CF 442-292, Commissioner Hubbard to Mr. Williams, memorandum, February 24, 1944; NARACP, RFMCS, RG 280, CF 442-2238, "Progress Report, August 11, 1944"; NARASRFW, RNWLB, RG 202, CF 111-2083-D, Floyd McGowan to Theodore Kheel, memorandum, March 28, 1944, Clifford Potter to Wales Madden, memorandum, August 23, 1944.

23. Merl E. Reed, *Seedtime for the Modern Civil Rights Movement: The President's Committee on Fair Employment Practice, 1941–1946*, 15. See Emilio Zamora, "The Failed Promise of Wartime Opportunity for Mexicans in the Texas Oil Industry," 323–50, for a study of the FEPC's failure to abolish dis-

crimination against Mexican-American workers in the Upper Texas Gulf Coast oil industry.

24. NARASRFW, RCFEP, RG 228, CF 13-BR-34, Franklin Roosevelt as quoted in Lee Pressman to National War Labor Board, petition, February 14, 1945.

25. Ibid., W. Don Ellinger to Tom Mobley, July 12, 1944; "CIO Charged with Gross Race Bias: FEPC Held Hearing on Union Recently," *Houston Negro Labor News,* March 10, 1945, p. 1.

26. Davis, interviewed by author, April 13, 1999.

27. Ibid.

28. NARASRFW, RCFEP, RG 228, CF 13-BR-34, W. Don Ellinger to Will Maslow, November 11, 1944.

29. NARACP, RFMCS, RG 280, CF 302-1818, Tom Mobley to Ted Weiss, May 7, 1943, Martin Burns to Tom Mobley, January 14, 1944.

30. NARASRFW, RCFEP, RG 228, CF 13-BR-34, Will Maslow to W. Don Ellinger, December 27, 1944, Lee Pressman to National War Labor Board, petition, February 14, 1945, Leonard Brin to W. Don Ellinger, May 16, 1944.

31. Curtiss Papers, Burns interviewed by Hoffman November 9, 1976, 15–21, 27–30; "CIO Again Charged with Gross Race Bias; F.E.P.C. Held Hearing on Union Recently," *Houston Negro Labor News,* March 10, 1945, p. 1.

32. Alton, interviewed by author, December 1, 1993; Davis and Henry to Michael Botson, interview, May 3, 1994.

33. NARASRFW, RCFEP, RG 228, CF 13-BR-34, Ernest Martin to Will Maslow, May 29, 1944, W. Don Ellinger to Will Maslow, November 7, 1944; "Local CIO Hearing before NLRB Scheduled July 23," *Houston Informer,* July 17, 1943, p. 1; "CIO Union Asks End to Biased Contract," *Houston Informer,* March 3, 1945, p. 1.

34. NARACP, RPMG, RG 389, CF 3-38, Exhibit H.

35. NARACP, RNLRB, RG 25, CF 9630, "Official Report of Proceedings," pp. 65, 70–80, 41–44, 665, 663–69, Exhibit B-13.

36. Ibid., pp. 73–74.

37. Ibid., pp. 80, 316, 663–98, 757–62, 785–89, 869–80; "Friction at Hughes Increases over Directive from W.L.B.," *Houston Post,* June 24, 1944, p. 1; "Double Time to Cover Lost Time Offered by Hughes," *Houston Post,* June 25, 1944, p. 1; "Over 2,000 at Hughes Tool Stop Working," *Houston Chronicle,* June 24, 1944, p. 1.

38. "Union Asks Federal Steps in Situation at Hughes Tool Co.," *Houston Post,* June 26, 1944, P. 1; "Hughes Seeks Sunday Work After Delay," *Houston Chronicle,* June 25, 1944, p. 1.

39. "Hughes Tool Asks Review of Directive," *Houston Post,* June 28, 1944, p. 1.

40. "Hughes Unions to Hold Mass Meet Tonight," *Houston Chronicle,*

June 26, 1944, p. 1.; "Demand Made for Hughes to Comply with WLB Order," *Houston Post,* June 27, 1944, p. 1.

41. NARASRFW, RNWLB, RG 202, CF 111-2083-D, Leonard Berliner to Martin Burns, December 27, 1944; "Workers Return to Houston Plant," *Houston Informer,* July 1, 1944, p. 1.

42. "Demand Made for Hughes to Comply with WLB Order," *Houston Post,* June 27, 1944.

43. "Hughes Unions to Hold Mass Meet Tonight," *Houston Post,* June 26, 1944.

44. "F.D.R. May Be Asked to Take Hand in Hughes Tool Case," *Houston Post,* July 6, 1944, p. 1; NARACP, RNLRB, RG 25, CF 9630, "Official Report of Proceedings," pp. 810–14, Exhibits B-18, B-19, B-20.

45. "Hughes Seeks Sunday Work After Delay," *Houston Chronicle,* June 25, 1944.

46. "Hughes Unions to Hold Mass Meet Tonight," *Houston Post,* June 26, 1944.

47. NARACP, RPMG, RG 389, CF 3-38, Tab LL.

48. NARACP, RNLRB, RG 25, CF 9630, "Official Report of Proceedings," p. 965, Exhibit B-11.

49. NARACP, RPMG, RG 389, CF 3-38, Tabs E, F.

50. "President May Get Hughes Tool Case Thursday," *Houston Post,* August 10, 1944, 1944, p. 1, "War Labor Board Sends Hughes Tool Case to Vinson," *Houston Post,* August 13, 1944, p. 1; NARACP, RPMG, RG 389, CF 3-38, Tabs E, F.

51. NARACP, RPMG, RG 389, CF 3-38, General H. H. Arnold to Col. Frank Cawthon, memorandum, September 5, 1944, Col. Frank Cawthon to W. M. Streetman, notice, September 6, 1944, Col. Frank Cawthon to Matt Boehm, Order Appointing General Manager, September 6, 1944.

52. Ibid., Matt Boehm to Col. Frank Cawthon, September 6, 1944; Noah Dietrich to Col. Frank Cawthon, November 9, 1944.

53. Ibid., Tabs N, AA.

54. "Independent Union Head Calls Army Seizure of Hughes Plants Un-American," *Houston Post,* September 7, 1944, p. 1.

55. "Independents at Hughes Hit Army Orders," *Houston Post,* September 10, 1944, p. 5.

56. Quote from ibid.; "Hughes Officials and Workers Arrange Saturday Conference," *Houston Post,* September 8, 1944, p. 1; NARACP, RPMG, RG 389, CF 3-38, George Taylor to Franklin Roosevelt, August 29, 1944, Fred Vinson to Franklin Roosevelt, memorandum, August 29, 1944.

57. NARACP, RPMG, RG 389, CF 3-38, Hughes Tool Army Staff to War Department, memorandum, October 27, 1944.

58. Ibid., National War Labor Board Directive, November 30, 1944, Briga-

dier General Edward Greenbaum to Brigadier General A. E. Jones, memorandum, December 4, 1944, Brigadier General A. E. Jones to Col. Frank Cawthon, memorandum, December 5, 1944, Brigadier General Edward Greenbaum to Brigadier General A. E. Jones, memorandum, December 7, 1944, Brigadier General A. E. Jones to Col. Frank Cawthon, memorandum, December 7, 1944.

59. NARACP, RNLRB, RG 25, CF 9630, Exhibits R-37; NARACP, RPMG, RG 389, CF 3-38, Lee Pressman to Jack Ohly, November 1, 1944, Lt. Col. John Myers to Headquarters Army Service Forces, memorandum, December 9, 1944.

60. NARACP, RPMG, RG 389, CF 3-38, Exhibit H; "CIO Union Asks End to Biased Contract," *Houston Informer,* March 3, 1945, p. 1; "Support of FEPC Among Resolutions," Ibid., October 27, 1945, p. 1.

61. NARACP, RPMG, RG 389, CF 3-38, Exhibit H.

62. Ibid., Weekly Report, February 24, 1945.

63. Ibid., Exhibit H; John Morton Blum, *V Was for Victory,* 182–220.

64. NARACP, RPMG, RG 389, CF 3-38, Exhibit H, Weekly Report, August 11, 1945.

65. Ibid., Kelley and Streetman to Disputes Director, November 13, 1944.

66. NARASRFW, RCFEP, RG 228, CF 13-BR-34, Maslow to Ellinger, November 4, 1944.

67. NARACP, RPMG, RG 389, CF 3-38, Weekly Report, June 23, 1945.

68. NARACP, RPMG, RG 389, CF 3-38, Weekly Report, June 2, 1945, Weekly Reports, June 9, June 16, June 30, July 7, 1945.

69. Ibid., Weekly Report, August 18, 1945.

70. Zieger, *The CIO,* 212–27; Seidman, *American Labor,* 245–47. In order to maintain continuity I continue to refer to the USWA as the CIO.

71. Harry S. Truman, *Memoir,* 495; William T. Hogan, *Economic History of the Iron and Steel Industry in the United States,* 4:1612.

72. "Steel Strike Paralysis Spreads," *Steel Labor,* January 28, 1946, 85; Vincent Sweeney, *The United Steelworkers of America: Twenty Years Later, 1936–1956* (Pittsburgh: United Steelworkers of America, 1956), 61–65; Hogan, *Economic History of the Iron and Steel Industry,* 4:1614–16.

73. NARACP, RNLRB, RG 25, CF 402-46, "Official Report of Proceedings," Exhibits I-14A, I-14B, I-14C.

74. "Hughes Firm Offers New Work Scale," *Houston Chronicle,* January 5, 1946, p. 1; "Union Rejects Hughes Tool, Reed Offers," *Houston Chronicle,* January 7, 1946, p. 8; "Steelworkers at Hughes Seek Raise," *Houston Post,* October 21, 1946, p. 1.

75. NARACP, RNLRB, RG 25, CF 9630, Exhibit I-15A; *Houston Post,* December 22, 1945.

76. NARACP, RNLRB, RG 25, CF 402-46, "Result Disappointing to Local's Officials; Large Vote Indicates No Desire to Be Sucked in on Deal," *Indepen-*

dent Journal: Official Organ of Independent Metal Workers Union, December 17, 1945, p. 1 Exhibit I-16.

77. "Houston Steelworkers Ordered to Stay on Job," Houston Post, November 30, 1945, p. 1.

78. NARACP, RNLRB, RG 25, CF 402-46, T. B. Everitt, "Real Facts Regarding the Race Issue," Independent Journal: Official Organ of Independent Metal Workers Union, December 17, 1945, p. 1, Exhibit I-16.

79. "Goblin of Fear: Independent Union Head Raises Race Scare at Hughes," Houston Informer, September 8, 1945, p. 1.

80. NARACP, RNLRB, RG 25, CF 402-46, Everitt, "Real Facts Regarding the Race Issue."

81. "Independent Metalworkers at Hughes Tool Company Urged to Report for Work as Usual," Houston Chronicle, January 19, 1946, p. 1; "Independent Hughes Union not to Strike," Houston Chronicle, January 13, 1946, p. 14.

82. NARACP, RNLRB, RG 25, CF 402-46, Exhibit I-16, "Czar Murray Speaks" and "Bargaining Agent Meets Defeat in Strike Vote," both in Independent Journal: The Official Organ of Independent Metal Workers Union, December 17, 1945, p. 1.

83. Ibid., Richard Guess, "Independent Local No. 2 Speaks Out; Colored Representative Says CIO Circular Misleading," Independent Journal, December 17, 1945, p. 1.

84. Ibid.

CHAPTER 7

1. "Hughes to Be Open as Long as Possible," Houston Chronicle, January 22, 1946, p. 10.

2. "Unions Plea to Hughes Is Turned Down," Houston Chronicle, January 23, 1946, p. 1; "Hughes Tool Appeals Directly to CIO Head to End Walkout Here," Houston Chronicle, January 25, 1946, p. 1; "Hughes Union Sees End to Strike Soon," Houston Chronicle, January 29, 1946, p. 1.

3. "Other Major Steel Plants Here Closed," Houston Chronicle, January 21, 1946, p. 1; "Nine Plants Here Closed by Walkouts," Houston Chronicle, January 22, 1946, p. 1. The nine other plants struck by the CIO were: American Chain and Cable Company, American Can Company, Armco Steel, Continental Can Company, Dedman Foundry, Reed Roller Bit, Rheem Manufacturing Company, Tennessee Coal, Iron, and Railroad Company, Texas Electric Steel Casting.

4. "Union's Plea to Hughes Is Turned Down," Houston Chronicle, January 23, 1946, p. 1.

5. "Part of Workers Defy Pickets at Hughes," *Houston Chronicle*, January 21, 1946, p. 1; C. W. Rice, "Independent Union Defies Pickets; CIO Stands Pat for 18½ cents," *Houston Negro Labor News*, January 26, 1946, p. 1; "5,000 Negroes Quit Work with Whites," *Houston Informer*, January 22, 1946, p. 1; "CIO Leaders Get Strong Colored Support in Texas," *Houston Chronicle*, January 26, 1946, p. 1.

6. NARACP, RFMCS, RG 280, CF 465-240, Preliminary Report, March 4, 1946; "Nine Plants Here Closed by Walkouts," *Houston Chronicle*, January 22, 1946, p. 1.

7. "Threats at Hughes Are Investigated," *Houston Chronicle*, January 30, 1946, p. 1.

8. "Nonstrikers at Hughes Are Knocked Down," *Houston Chronicle*, January 26, 1946, p. 1; "Charge Filed in Attack on Hughes Boss," *Houston Chronicle*, February 7, 1946, p. 1.

9. "Attention, Hughes Tool Employees," *Houston Chronicle*, February 2, 1946, p. 3; NARACP, RNLRB, RG 25, CF 402-46, Ralph Neuhaus to All Employees of the Hughes Tool Company, January 25, 1946; "Hughes and Union Renew Negotiations," *Houston Chronicle*, January 26, 1946, p. 1.

10. Quote is in "Hughes Puts on Third Shift," *Houston Chronicle*, February 14, 1946, p. 1; see also "Hughes Returns to 3 Shifts as CIO Continues Demand," *Houston Post*, February 15, 1946, p. 1.

11. NARACP, RNLRB, RG 25, CF 402-46, T. D. Walker and R. L. Phelps to Ralph Neuhaus, January 8, 1946, D. Walker and R. L. Phelps to Ralph Neuhaus, December 28, 1945, Ralph Neuhaus to T. D. Walker and R. L. Phelps, January 4, 1946; "Dietrich, Murray Will Discuss Hughes Strike," *Houston Post*, March 15, 1946, p. 6.

12. NARACP, RNLRB, RG 25, CF 402-46, Ralph Neuhaus to Frank Hardesty, February 18, 1946, Howard Curtiss to Ralph Neuhaus, February 21, 1946.

13. "Returning Hughes Employees Vote of Confidence, Dietrich," *Houston Post*, February 5, 1946, p. 1; NARACP, RNLRB, RG 25, CF 402-46, Noah Dietrich to Frank Hardesty, January 23, 1946.

14. "Hughes and CIO Disagree on Wage Plan," *Houston Chronicle*, February 15, 1946, p. 1; "Wage, Price Hike Processing to Delay Hughes Settlement," *Houston Post*, February 19, 1946, p. 1; "Dietrich Sees No Basis for Continuing Hughes Strike," *Houston Post*, March 5, 1946, p. 1.

15. NARACP, RNLRB, RG 25, CF 402-46, Noah Dietrich to Philip Murray, n.d.; Alton, interviewed by author, December 1, 1993; Dearman, interviewed by author, August 1, 1994; Callender, interviewed by author, July 21, 1994.

16. Joel Seidman *American*, 228–32; Nelson Lichtenstein, *Labor's War at Home*, 228–30; B. Nelson, *Divided We Stand*, 186–206; Zieger, *The CIO*, 214–15, 217–27.

17. NARACP, RNLRB, RG 25, CF 402-46, Exhibit I-11.

18. NARACP, RNLRB, RG 25, CF 402-46, "Local Ex-President 2457, CIO, A Member," *Independent Journal,* December 17, 1945, p. 1, Exhibit I-16.

19. Curtiss Papers, "Let's Break It Up," IMW Handbill, n. d.; NARACP, RNLRB, RG 25, CF 402-46, *Independent Journal,* December 17, 1945, Exhibit I-16.

20. HTC, RG 1005, "All Hughes Tool Workers," photograph of Texas Communist party handbill, n. d.

21. NARACP, RNLRB, RG 25, CF 402-46, "Official Report of Proceedings," pp. 458–471, and David Butler and Richard Guess to Black Pastors, February 2, 1946.

22. "One Negro Crashes Steel Picket Line," *Houston Informer,* February 12, 1946, p. 1.

23. "Rev. Simpson Exhibits Stand by Steelworkers," *Houston Informer,* February 23, 1946, p. 4.

24. *Houston Negro Labor News,* March 2, 1946.

25. "Four Questioned in Slaying of Negro," *Houston Post,* February 19, 1946, p. 4; "$2,000 Reward for Killer," *Houston Informer,* February 19, 1946, p. 1.

26. "$2,000 Award for Arrest of Killer Posted," *Houston Chronicle,* February 18, 1946, p. 1.

27. "Flaw in Alibis of Two Held in Killing Found," *Houston Chronicle,* February 19, 1946, p. 1.

28. Ibid.; "Vance Muse Speaks; Police Working On Hot Tip, They Say," *Houston Informer,* February 23, 1946, p. 1.

29. Davis and Henry, interviewed by author, May 3, 1994; Henry, interviewed by author, August 5, 1944; "Men Deny Charges; Continue to Question Suspects in Murder," *Houston Informer,* February 26, 1946, p. 1; "Suspect in Guess Slaying Released," *Houston Informer,* March 2, 1946, p. 1.

30. "Over 3,000 Attend Labor Leader's Funeral," *Houston Negro Labor News,* March 2, 1946, p. 1.

31. Vance Muse, "A Tribute to the Memory and Principles of R. H. Guess," *Houston Informer,* March 9, 1946, p. 1; Victor Bernstein, "The Antilabor Front," 334.

32. Muse, "A Tribute," *Houston Informer,* March 9, 1946, p. 1

33. "Vance Muse Speaks at Guess's Funeral," *Houston Negro Labor News,* March 2, 1946, p. 8.

34. "Editorially Speaking: Chief Mourner," *Houston Informer,* February 26, 1946, p. 8.

35. *Houston Negro Labor News,* March 2, 1946.

36. Curtiss Papers, Howard Curtiss to Philip Murray, February 27, 1946.

37. NARACP, RFMCS, RG 280, CF 465-240, Progress Report, March 30, 1946; Curtiss Papers, Martin Burns interviewed by Alice Hoffman, November 9, 1976, pp. 21–23; "Hughes Returns to 3 Shifts as CIO Continues Demand," *Houston Post,* February 15, 1946, p. 1.

38. NARACP, RFMCS, RG 280, CF 465-240, Final Report, April 8, 1946; "Dietrich and Murray Will Discuss Hughes Strike," *Houston Post,* March 15, 1946, p. 6; "Dietrich Sees Hope of Strike End After Talk with Murray," *Houston Post,* March 22, 1946, p. 1; "Hughes, Union Leaders to Resume Talks Today," *Houston Post,* March 26, 1946.

39. Dearman, interviewed by author, August 1, 1944; Wilson, interviewed by author, November 30, 1993; Alton, interviewed by author, December 1, 1993; "77-Day Strike at Hughes Ends with Signing of Contract," *Houston Chronicle,* April 8, 1946, p. 1; "77-Day Strike of 3,000 Workers at Hughes Ends; Transit Walkout Is Over," *Houston Post,* April 8, 1946, p. 1; Joel Seidman, *The Yellow Dog Contract,* 30.

40. NARACP, RNLRB, RG 25, CF 402-46, "Contract between CIO Locals 1742 and 2457 and Hughes Tool," April 8, 1946.

41. "Union Discrimination against Race in Strike Settlement; Color Used," *Houston Negro Labor News,* April 13, 1946, p. 1.

42. "Dispute over Union Agreement at Hughes; CIO Blamed for Change in Work Rule; IMW Appeals Case," *Houston Negro Labor News,* April 20, 1946, p. 1; "Rice Off in Prediction of Steelworkers Settlement," *Houston Informer,* April 13, 1946, p. 1.

43. NLRB, *Decisions,* 69:294–98; NARACP, RNLRB, RG 25, CF 402-46, Tom Davis to Edwin Elliot, September 22, 1945, Petition for Certification of Representatives, September 13, 1945.

44. NARACP, RFMCS, RG 280, CF 465-240, Progress Report, March 14, 1946; NLRB, *Decisions,* 69:294–98

45. "IMW Winner at Hughes Plant," *Houston Chronicle,* August 2, 1946, p. 1; "CIO Loses Election at Hughes," *Houston Informer,* August 3, 1946, p. 1; NARACP, RFMCS, RG 280, CF 465-240, Preliminary Report, March 4, 1946; "Hughes, IMW Sign New Contract Covering 10 Points," *Houston Chronicle,* November 19, 1946, p. 1. At the time of the election Hughes Tool had trimmed its workforce down to approximately 4,000 from its wartime peak of nearly 6,800.

46. Carter Wesley, "The Rights of Others," *Houston Informer,* August 10, 1946.

47. Ibid.

48. Davis and Henry, interviewed by author, May 3, 1994.

49. Independent Metal Workers Collection, RG R-1, HMRC, John S. Gray III, "Social Inequality of Hughes Tool Company between 1928 and 1964," typescript, Rice University, 1981; Henry, interviewed by author, January 11, 1994; Dixie, interviewed by author, November 30, 1998; Davis and Henry, interviewed by author, May 3, 1994.

50. Independent Metal Workers Collection, RG R-1, HMRC, Gray, "Social Inequality"; Henry, interviewed by author, February 22, 1994.

51. NARACP, RNLRB, RG 25, CF 6768-62, "Official Report," p. 274; Botson, "Jim Crow," 102–103.

52. NARACP, RNLRB, RG 25, CF 6768-62, "Official Report," pp. 4–5, 274-275, Exhibit R-1.

53. Ibid., pp. 91–97, 472–77, 6–12; Davis and Henry, interviewed by author, May 3, 1994.

54. NLRB, *Decisions,* 147:1595.

55. Davis and Henry, interviewed by author, May 3, 1994; NARACP, RNLRB, RG 25, CF 6768-62, "Official Report," pp. 1020, Exhibit GC-2.

56. H. Hill, *Black Labor,* 109–21; Carter and Marcus, "Trade Union Practices and the Law," 385–86.

57. NLRB, *Decisions,* 104:329–31.

58. Ibid., 319–20, 329–30; NARACP, RNLRB, RG 25, CF 39-RC-133, L. M. Fagan to Ogden Fields, August 20, 1952, IAM Bulletin, August 21, 1952.

59. NARACP, RNLRB, RG 25, CF 39-RC-133, A. L. Curtis to Ogden Fields, n.d., George Leet to A. L. Curtis, August 25, 1952.

60. NLRB, *Decisions,* 104:320.

61. Ibid., 321, 329–30.

62. NARACP, RNLRB, RG 25, CF 39-CA-185, C. L. Stephens to Clifford Potter, Final Report, April 11, 1951, Clifford Potter, memorandum, December 21, 1950; Independent Metal Workers Union, Local 1 Collection, Texas Labor Archives, University of Texas at Arlington, RG 329 (hereafter cited as IMWU, Local 1), Hughes Bulletin No. 671, August 4, 1958, Bulletin (no number), February, 1959, Bulletin, No. 679, February 26, 1959.

63. NLRB, *Decisions,* 100:215; NLRB, *Decisions,* 147:1593; IMWU, Local 1, NLRB Vote Tally, July 28,1959.

64. Davis and Henry, interviewed by author, May 3, 1994.

CHAPTER 8

I thank George Ward, managing editor of the *Southwestern Historical Quarterly,* for allowing me to reproduce parts of this chapter that previously appeared as an article in that journal.

1. IMWU, Local 1, Hughes Tool Bulletin No. 671, August 4, 1958, Bulletin (no number) February 9, 1959, Bulletin No. 679. The drop in drilling activity is associated with the Suez Crisis of 1956 when Egyptian President Gamal Abdel Nassar ordered the scuttling of dozens of ships to block the Suez Canal before British and French troop seized the Canal Zone. The mass scuttling effectively blocked the passage of oil from the Middle East and Persian Gulf through the Red Sea, Suez Canal and into the Mediterranean Sea well in to 1957. The alternative route around the Cape of Good Hope to Europe would

take considerably longer for tankers. When the crisis subsided and the Suez Canal reopened the flow of cheap Middle Eastern and Persian Gulf Oil, it discouraged drilling in the Unites States and is one of the reasons why the demand for Hughes Tool's products dropped and the company cut its work force. A fascinating twist to the Suez Crisis is that the Texas Railroad Commission blocked any increases in Texas oil drilling and production that would have helped to alleviate shortages brought on by the Suez Crisis in order to drive up oil prices. See Yergin, *The Prize*, 493–95; Joe Pratt, interviewed by author, January 13, 2004.

2. NARACP, RNLRB, RG 25, CF 6768-62, "Official Report."

3. Ibid., Exhibit CP-3.

4. NAACP, Group III, Box 182, "The National Association for the Advancement of Colored People Appraises the First Year of the President's Committee On Equal Employment Opportunity," April 6, 1962; Marshall, *The Negro*, 226–31; Department of Labor, *Monthly Labor Review* 84 (May, 1961), 530; IMWU, Local 1, U.S. Department of Justice, *Amicus Curie in U.S. before the NLRB*, pp. 1–2.

5. NAACP, Group III, Box 182, "The National Association for the Advancement of Colored People Appraises the First Year"; Group III, Box 291, "Statement of Herbert Hill, Labor Secretary, National Association for the Advancement of Colored People before the Committee on Education and Labor of the U.S. House of Representatives, January 15, 1962, Washington, D.C."

6. NAACP, Group III, Box 182, "The National Association for the Advancement of Colored People Appraises the First Year"; NAACP, Group III, Box 291, "Statement of Herbert Hill,"

7. Henry, interviewed by author, May 9, 1997; NARACP, RNLRB, RG 25, CF 6768-62, "Official Report," pp. 54–63, 145–48, 178–84.

8. NARACP, RNLRB, RG 25, CF 6768-62, "Official Report," pp. 241–45.

9. Ibid., Exhibit GC-4.

10. The joint bargaining committees of Locals Nos. 1 and No.2 did meet on March 22, 1962 to reconsider the proposal. The white leadership offered a watered-down counter-proposal that merely asked the union to attempt to eliminate discrimination. Local No. 1's counterproposal stated that, "The parties agree that they will, within a period of two (2) years or sooner, attempt to provide a greater and more equitable opportunity for all employees." The black leadership rejected the counter-proposal because it found the language too weak and would leave job discrimination in place. See NARACP, RNLRB, RG 25, CF 6768-62, "Official Report," pp. 108–109, 209–19, 239–44, Exhibit R-3.

11. NAACP, Group V, Box 2309, L. A. Ashley to Robert Breaux, affidavit, June 14, 1962, and Ivory Davis to Field Examiner, 23rd Region, June 13, 1962.

12. NLRB, *Decisions,* 147:1596; NAACP, Group V, Box 2308, Ivory Davis and Columbus Henry to Hobart Taylor Jr., June 4, 1962, and Complaint Form,

Presidential Committee on Equal Employment Opportunity, June 22, 1962; Davis and Henry, interviewed by author, May 3, 1994.

13. NARACP, RNLRB, RG 25, CF 6768-62, Potter to Youngblood and Safos, December 19, 1961, Robert Breaux to Clifford Potter, Final Investigation Report, July 6, 1962.

14. Hobart Taylor Jr. to Ivory Davis, April 29, 1963, copy in author's possession; Ivory Davis to Hobart Taylor Jr., May 28, 1963, copy in author's possession; Hughes Tool Bulletin, October 30, 1964, copy in author's possession.

15. NARACP, RPMG, RG 389, CF 3-38, Will Maslow to W. Don Ellinger, November 4, 1944, Exhibit H.

16. NARACP, RNLRB, RG 25, CF 6768-62, "Official Report," Exhibits GC-3, GC-8.

17. NLRB, *Decisions,* 147:1596; NARACP, RNLRB, RG 25, CF 6768-62, "Official Report," pp. 138–42, Exhibits CP-2, CP-2A.

18. NLRB, *Decisions,* 147:1593.

19. NARACP, RNLRB, RG 25, CF 6768-62, "Official Report," Exhibits GC-3, GC-5, GC-6.

20. Ibid., pp. 65–72, 158–67, Exhibits GC-8, GC-9, GC-10, GC-11, GC-12. Officials of Hughes Tool responded that they were following the provisions of the 1959 contract and used that agreement to determine what employees were eligible for the bid.

21. Davis and Henry, interviewed by author, May 3, 1994; NARACP, RNLRB, RG 25, CF 6768-62, "Official Report," pp. 228–29.

22. NARACP, RNLRB, RG 25, CF 6768-62, "Official Report," Exhibit GC-7.

23. Ibid., pp. 292–94, Exhibits, GC-1A, GC-1B, GC-1C. Lorane Ashley filed the complaint as president of Local No. 2 and his name appeared on the form along with Ivory Davis.

24. NARACP, RNLRB, RG 25, CF 6768-62, "Official Report," Exhibit GC-1D.

25. Ibid., Exhibit GC-1F

26. NAACP, Group V, Box 2309, L. A. Ashley to Robert Carter, September 23, 1962, and Robert L. Carter to L. A. Ashley, September 27, 1962.

27. NAACP Records, Group III, Box 346, J. C. McGlon to Herbert Hill, October 14, 1957.

28. B. Nelson, "CIO Meant One Thing for the Whites," 135; Hill, interviewed by author, August 25, 1999.

29. L. A. Ashley to Robert Carter, September 23, 1962; L. A. Ashley to Robert Breaux, September 23, 1962; Robert Carter to L. A. Ashley, September 24, 1963, copies in author's possession; NARACP, RNLRB, RG 25, CF 6768-62, "Official Report," Exhibit GC-1G.

30. "Victorious Lawyer, Robert Lee Carter," *New York Times,* July 3, 1964.

31. Ibid.

32. Robert Carter to L. A. Ashley, October 24, 1962; Robert Carter to L. A. Ashley, October 25, 1962, copies in author's possession; "N.A.A.C.P. Takes Sides Here in Labor Hearing Dispute," *Houston Chronicle*, October 18, 1962; "N.A.A.C.P. Seeks to Oust Hughes Union," *Houston Chronicle*, October 26, 1962.

33. NARACP, RNLRB, RG 25, CF 6768-62, "Official Report," Exhibit GC-1K; Carter to Ashley, October 25, 1962. On October 2, 1962 Hughes Tool posted a notice throughout the plant announcing that it had secured federal subcontracting work for the NASA space program. One of the requirements in the contracts called for the posting and carrying out of a policy of nondiscrimination in employment practices. Signed by M.E. Montrose, Hughes Tool's president, and posted without consulting Local No. 1, the notice created furor in the plant because the company had publicly announced its intention to cease discriminatory practices in order to secure the government contract. In response to the commotion and in an effort to clarify Local No. 1's position T. B. Everitt issued an announcement declaring that Local No. 1 and Hughes Tool were bound by the collective bargaining agreement signed by them on December 18, 1961 and that the company's announcement did not alter the contract's segregationist provisions. Hughes Tool did not respond to Local No. 1's proclamation. See NARACP, RNLRB, RG 25, CF 6768-62, "Official Report," pp. 260–61, Exhibits CP-3, CP-4.

34. Tom Davis to Robert Carter, November 1, 1962; Robert Carter to Tom Davis, November 9, 1962, copies in author's possession.

35. NARACP, RNLRB, RG 25, CF 6768-62, "Official Report," Exhibits, GC-1I, GC-1L, GC-1M; Robert Carter to Ivory Davis, October 31, 1962; Robert Carter to Tom Davis, November 1, 1962, copies in author's possession; Bob Tutt, "Hughes Racial Labor Hassle Nears Accord," *Houston Chronicle*, November 1, 1962.

36. Robert Carter to Lorane Ashley, October 30, 1962; Lorane Ashley to T. B. Everitt, October 31, 1962, copies in author's possession.

37. NARACP, RNLRB, RG 25, CF 6768-62, "Official Report," Exhibits, R-11, R-12.

38. Robert Carter to Loran E. Ashley, November 28, 1962, copy in author's possession.

39. NARACP, RNLRB, RG 25, CF 6768-62, "Official Report," Exhibits, R-6, R-8.

40. Bill Stewart, interviewed by author, March 4, 1997; Davis and Henry, interviewed by author, May 4, 1994.

41. White unionists belonging to United Steelworkers of America Local 2708, which represented workers at Armco Steel Corporation's massive Houston works, successfully kept a segregated system of job promotions in place within an integrated local. Similar cases of racial discrimination in integrated

USWA locals occurred at the Atlantic Steel Company in Atlanta, Georgia, and Tennessee Coal and Iron Company in Birmingham, Alabama. The USWA and the steel companies instituted aptitude tests for blacks that effectively kept lines of promotion segregated. The federal courts upheld the legitimacy of the tests. See Marshall, *The Negro*, 185–88; *Race Relations Law Reporter*, "Whitefield v. United Steel Workers" 3 (February, 1958): 55–63; *Race Relations Law Reporter* "Whitefield v. United Steelworkers" 4 (Spring, 1959): 122–26; B. Nelson, "CIO Meant One thing for the Whites," 119–30.

42. Robert Carter to L. A. Ashley, November 8, 1962; Robert Carter to L. A. Ashley, November 9, 1962, copies in author's possession; NARACP, RNLRB, RG 25, CF 6768-62, "Official Report," pp. 38–43.

43. NARACP, RNLRB, RG 25, CF 6768-62, "Official Report," Exhibits R-11, R-12; Robert Carter to Lorane Ashley, November 28, 1962, copy in author's possession; Davis, interviewed by author, May 1, 1997.

44. NARACP, RNLRB, RG 25, CF 6768-62, "Official Report," pp. 94, 226, Exhibit R-13.

45. Ibid., p. 268, Exhibits R-2, R-6, R-7.

46. Davis and Henry, interviewed by author, May 3, 1994; Robert Carter to L. A. Ashley, December 3, 1962; Robert Carter to Tom Davis, December 3, 1962, copies in author's possession; "Hughes Tool White, Negro Unions Merge," *Houston Chronicle*, December 11, 1962; "Negro Local Cautious on Merger Move," *Houston Chronicle*, December 12, 1962.

47. NARACP, RNLRB, RG 25, CF 6768-62, Clifford Potter to George McInerny, November 28, 1962.

48. NARACP, RNLRB, RG 25, CF 6768-62, Clifford Potter to C. L. Stephens, April 5, 1963; NAACP, Group V, Box 2309, Columbus Henry to Ogden Fields, January 9, 1964; Davis and Henry, interviewed by author, May 3, 1994; Davis, interviewed by author, May 1, 1997; Henry, interviewed by author, January 23, 1996; NAACP, Group V, Box 2309, "Facts—Nothing but the Facts," handbill, Independent Metal Workers Union Local No. 2, November 29, 1963.

49. Davis, interviewed by author, February 2, 2002.

50. NARACP, RNLRB, RG 25, CF 6768-62, Potter to McInerny, November 28, 1962.

51. NAACP, Group V, Box 2309, L. A. Ashley to Robert Carter, telegram, November 29, 1962; NARACP, RNLRB, RG 25, CF 6768-62, "Official Report," pp. 193, 226–27, 264–69, 311–13.

52. Robert Carter to L. A. Ashley, November 28, 1962, copy in author's possession.

53. Ibid.

54. Henry, interviewed by author, January 23, 1996.

55. NAACP, Group V, Box 2309, Columbus Henry to Robert Carter, February 9, 1964.

56. NARACP, RNLRB, RG 25, CF 6768-62, "Official Report," pp. 98–99, 318–21.

57. Ibid., pp. 12–22, 37–41; Charles Culhane, "Negro Charges Hughes Withheld Training," *Houston Post,* December 12, 1962.

58. NARACP, RNLRB, RG 25, CF 6768-62, "Official Report," pp. 12–22, 37–41.

59. Charles Culhane, "Represents Whites, Hughes Union Chief Says NIRB [*sic*] Ends Hearing," *Houston Post,* December 13, 1962; Bob Tutt, "Hearing Ends: Hughes Ready to Halt Job Discrimination," *Houston Chronicle,* December 13, 1962; NARACP, RNLRB, RG 25, CF 6768-62, "Official Report," pp. 26–37, 293–96; NLRB, *Decisions,* 147:1602–1603.

60. NARACP, RNLRB, RG 25, CF 6768-62, Brief to Trial Examiner, February 8, 1963.

61. Ibid., "Official Report," pp. 26–37, 203–206; NLRB, *Decisions,* 147: 1602–1603.

62. NARACP, RNLRB, RG 25, CF 6768-62, Brief to Trial Examiner, February 8,1963.

63. NARACP, RNLRB, RG 25, CF 6768-62, "Official Report," pp. 20–24, 174–75, 313–17, 325–35; "Negro Seeks Equal Hughes Union Rights," *Houston Chronicle,* February 11, 1963.

64. NARACP, RNLRB, RG 25, CF 6768-62, "Official Report," p. 297.

65. Ibid., pp. 293–97, 324.

66. NLRB, *Decisions,* 147:1577, 1605–1607; Robert Carter to Columbus Henry and Ivory Davis, February 28,1963, copy in author's possession; Bob Tutt, "NLRB Asks Union Removal in Hughes Row," *Houston Chronicle,* February 28, 1963, morning edition; "NLRB Examiner Asks Removal of Union in Racial Row," *Houston Chronicle,* February 28, 1963, final edition; David Allred, "NLRB Is Asked to Oust All Hughes Tool Unions," *Houston Post,* March 1, 1963.

67. NAACP, Group III, Box A 182, Robert Carter to Messrs. Roy Wilkins, John Morsell, Gloster Current, Herbert Moon, and Herbert Hill, memorandum, February 28, 1963; Group V, Box 2309, Robert Carter to Columbus Henry and Ivory Davis, February 28, 1963.

68. NARACP, RNLRB, RG 25, CF 6768-62, Constitution of the Independent Metal Workers Union of the Hughes Tool Company, 1957, Exhibit R-1, Exhibit R-2; Stephens to Clifford Potter, May 8, 1963.

69. NARACP, RNLRB, RG 25, CF 6768-62, Robert Carter to Tom Davis, November 9, 1962; Stephens to Clifford Potter, May 8, 1963.

70. NAACP, Group V, Box 2309, Columbus Henry to Robert Carter, December 11, 1963; NARACP, RNLRB, RG 25, CF 6768-62, Clifford Potter to Arnold Ordman, December 17,1963.

71. NARACP, RNLRB, RG 25, CF 6768-62, Stephens to Potter, May 8, 1963,

Brief to the Trial Examiner, February 8, 1963, Affidavit of T. B. Everitt, January 18, 1963.

72. NAACP, Group V, Box 2309, Statement of Position of Local No. 2, Independent Metal Workers Union, February 8, 1963.

73. Ibid.

74. Hobart Taylor Jr. to Ivory Davis, April 29, 1963; Ivory Davis to Hobart Taylor Jr., May 28, 1963; Hughes Tool Bulletin (no number), October 30, 1964, copies in author's possession.

75. NAACP, Group V, Box 2309, letter to Will Maslow, February 29, 1964; Nelson, "CIO Meant One Thing for the Whites," 134–36.

76. NAACP, Group V, Box 2309, letter to Will Maslow, February 29, 1964.

77. NARACP, RNLRB, RG 25, CF 6768-62, Frank W. McCulloch to the Honorable Bob Casey, November 15, 1963, and Robert Carter to John H. Fanning, telegram, December 3, 1963.

78. NARACP, RNLRB, RG 25, CF 6768-62, McCulloch to Casey, November 15, 1963, Ogden Fields to the Honorable Adam Clayton Powell, December 3, 1963.

79. Ibid., Arnold Ordman to the Honorable John G. Tower, December 7, 1963, Carter to Fanning, telegram, December 3, 1963.

80. NAACP, Group V, Box 2309, Columbus Henry to T. B. Everitt, December 2, 1963; Columbus Henry to Ogden Fields, January 9, 1964.

81. NARACP, RNLRB, RG 25, CF 6768-62, Howard W. Kleeb to Frank W, McCulloch, August 30, 1963, C. L. Stephens to Clifford Potter, May 8, 1963; Hobart Taylor Jr. to Ivory Davis, April 29, 1963, copy in author's possession.

82. NARACP, RNLRB, RG 25, CF 6768-62, T. B. Everitt to the Honorable Bob Casey, October 22, 1963, T. B. Everitt to the Honorable Albert Thomas, October 22, 1963, The Honorable John G. Power, to Arnold Ordman, December 3, 1963; "Hughes Union Wants Probe of NLRB Here," *Houston Chronicle*, October 24, 1963.

83. NARACP, RNLRB, RG 25, CF 6768-62, Ogden W. Fields to the Honorable John G. Tower, December 11, 1963.

84. NLRB, *Decisions*, 147:1574; Doug Freelander, "NLRB Says Union Guilty of Race Discrimination," *Houston Post*, July 3, 1964; H. Hill, *Black Labor*, 133–40; Carter and Marcus, "Trade Union Practices and the Law," 385–97.

85. NAACP, Group V, Box 2309, Robert L. Carter and Maria L. Marcus, "Prevention of Racial Discrimination under the Title VII of the Civil Rights Act of 1964"; H. Hill, *Black Labor*, 47–50.

86. Doug Freelander, "NLRB Action against More Unions Is Hinted," *Houston Post*, July 4, 1964; "NAACP Takes Sides Here in Labor Hearing Dispute," *Houston Chronicle*, October 18, 1962.

87. Alvin DuVall, "Hughes Union Seeks New NLRB Election," *Houston*

Post, July 8, 1964; "Hughes Workers Vote Switch," *Houston Chronicle,* August 5, 1964; "USW Wins Election at Hughes," *Houston Post* August 6, 1964.

CONCLUSION

1. A sampling of the literature includes Cayton and Mitchell, *Black Workers and the New Unions;* Draper, *Conflict of Interests;* Dubovsky, *State and Labor in Modern America;* Philip S. Foner and Ronald L. Lewis, eds. *The Black Worker from the Founding of the CIO to the AFL-CIO Merger, 1936–1955;* H. Hill, *Black Labor;* Michael Honey, *Southern Labor and Black Civil Rights: Organizing Memphis Workers;* Julius Jacobson, ed. *The Negro and the American Labor Movement;* Marshall, *The Negro;* Marshall, *Labor in the South;* B. Nelson, *Divided We Stand;* Northrup, *Organized Labor and the Negro;* Reed, *Seedtime for the Modern Civil Rights Movement;* Harvard Sitkoff, *The Depression Decade;* Judith Stein, *Running Steel, Running America;* Zieger, ed., *Organized Labor in the Twentieth-Century South;* Zieger, ed., *Southern Labor in Transition.*

2. Marshall, "Some Reflections," 137–57. Marshall was Pres. Jimmy Carter's secretary of labor.

3. Beeth and Wintz, *Black Dixie;* Merline Pitre, *In Struggle against Jim Crow;* Obadele-Starks, *Black Unionism;* Howard Beeth, "Houston and History, Past and Present," 172–186; Robert A. Calvert, "The Civil Rights Movement in Texas;" Robert V. Haynes, "The Houston Mutiny and Riot of 1917," 418–439; Haynes, "Black Houstonians and the White Democratic Primary, 1920–45," 192–210; Sparks, "Heavenly Houston or Hellish Houston?" 335–66.

4. Haynes, "Black Houstonians," 192–210.

5. Amilcar Shabazz, *Advancing Democracy,* 5.

6. Thomas R. Cole, *No Color Is My Kind;* F. Kenneth Jensen, "The Houston Sit-In Movement of 1960–61," 211–22. My interpretation of the black elites' role in the desegregation of Houston's public accommodations is much more critical than Professor Cole's.

7. Davis, interviewed by author, May 1, 1997; Davis and Henry, interviewed by author, May 3, 1994.

8. NARACP, RNLRB, RG 25, CF 1661, p. 992.

MANUSCRIPT AND ARCHIVAL SOURCES

Cullinan, Joseph Stephen. Papers. Houston Metropolitan Research Center, Houston Public Library, Houston, Texas.

Curtiss, Howard. Papers. Historical Collection and Labor Archives, Pennsylvania State University, University Park, Pennsylvania.

Hughes Tool Collection. Houston Metropolitan Research Center, Houston Public Library, Houston, Texas.

Independent Metal Workers Union Collection. Houston Metropolitan Research Center, Houston Public Library, Houston, Texas.

Independent Metal Workers Union, Local 1 Collection. Texas Labor Archives, University of Texas at Arlington, RG 329.

McDonald, David. Papers. Historical Collections and Labor Archives, Pennsylvania State University, University Park, Pennsylvania.

National Archives and Records Administration. College Park, Md. Records of the Federal Mediation and Conciliation Service, RG 280.

———. College Park, Md. Records of the National Labor Relations Board, RG 25.

———. College Park, Md. Records of the Provost Marshall General, RG 389.

———. Southwest Region, Fort Worth. Records of the Committee on Fair Employment Practices, 1941–46, RG 228.

———. Southwest Region, Fort Worth. Records of the National War Labor Board, 1943–47, RG 202.

———. Washington, D.C. Records of the National War Labor Board (WW I), RG 2.

Oral History of the Texas Oil Industry. Center for American History, University of Texas at Austin.

National Association for the Advancement of Colored People. Records. Manuscript Division. Library of Congress.

Rice, C. W., and the *Negro Labor News* Collection. Houston Metropolitan Research Center, Houston Public Library, Houston, Texas.

Southern Conference for Human Welfare. Papers. Robert W. Woodruff Library, Atlanta University Center.

NEWSPAPERS AND PERIODICALS

Fortune.
Houston.
Houston Chronicle.
Houston Daily Post.
Houston Informer.
Houston Labor Journal.
Houston Labor Messenger.
Houston Negro Labor News.
Houston Post.
Houston Post-Dispatch.
Houston Press.
Hughes News.
Iron Age.
Race Relations Law Reporter.
Steel.
Steel Labor.
Tan Month.

GOVERNMENT DOCUMENTS

Bureau of Labor Statistics. *Strikes in the Unites States, 1880–1936.* Bulletin no. 651. Washington, D.C.

Cox, A. B. *Studies of Employment Problems in Texas, Preliminary Report, Part 1, Causes of Unemployment in Texas and Ways of Increasing Employment, Bureau of Business Research.* Austin: University of Texas, November, 1935.

Department of Labor. *Monthly Labor Review.*

National Labor Relations Board. *Court Decisions Relating to the National Labor Relations Act.* Vol. 4. Washington, D.C.: Government Printing Office, 1944.

———. *Decisions and Orders of the National Labor Relations Board.* Vols. 27, 33, 36, 45, 53, 56, 69, 88, 100, 104, 147. Washington, D.C.: Government Printing Office, 1940–64.

National War Labor Board. *War Labor Report: Reports of Decisions and Orders.* Vols. 11, 14, 16. Washington, D.C.: Bureau of National Affairs, 1944.

INTERVIEWS BY AUTHOR

Alton, Allison. October 13, December 1, 1993.

Callender, Harry. July 21, 1994.

Davis, Ivory. Various interviews between May 3, 1994, and May 2003.

Dearman, Wayne. August 1, 1994.

Dixie, Chris. November 30, 1998.

Easterwood, Maurice. October 13, November 29, 1993.

Gray, John. November 19, 1998.

Henry, Columbus. Various interviews between October 13, 1993, and April 5, 1998.

Hensley, Arthur. July 27, 1994.

Hill, Herbert. August 25, 1999.

Kuldell, Robert. July 27, 1999.

Mabry, Halbert. October 13, 26, 1993.

McMahon, George. April 17, 1997.

Rhone, Lonnie. November 5, 1998.

Stewart, Bill. March 25, 1997.

Wilson, C. D. October 13, November 30, 1993.

BOOKS AND ARTICLES

Allen, Ruth. *Chapters in the History of Organized Labor in Texas.* Austin: University of Texas, 1941.

American Iron and Steel Institute. *Collective Bargaining in the Steel Industry: Why Steel Favors Employee Representation Plans to Professional Unions.* American Iron and Steel Institute, 1934.

American Petroleum Institute. *Petroleum Facts and Figures.* 9th ed. New York: American Petroleum Institute, 1950.

Arnesen, Eric. "Up from Exclusion: Black and White Workers, Race, and the State of Labor History." *Reviews in American History* 26 (March, 1998): 146–74.

Badger, Anthony J. *The New Deal: The Depression Years, 1933–1940.* New York: Hill and Wang, 1989.

Beauboeuf, Bruce Andre. "World War I and Houston's Emergence as an Industrial City." In *Major Problems in Texas History,* ed. Sam W. Haynes and Cary D. Wintz, 352–60. Boston: Houghton Mifflin, 2002.

Beeth, Howard. "Houston and History, Past and Present: A Look at Black Houston in the 1920s." *Southern Studies* 25 (Summer, 1986): 172–86.

Beeth, Howard, and Cary D. Wintz, eds. *Black Dixie: Afro-Texan History and Culture in Houston.* College Station: Texas A&M University Press, 1992.

Bernstein, Irving. *The Lean Years, 1920–1933.* Vol. 1 of *A History of the American Worker.* Boston: Houghton Mifflin, 1970.

———. *The Turbulent Years, 1933–1941.* Vol. 2 of *A History of the American Worker.* Boston: Houghton Mifflin, 1970.

Bernstein, Victor H. "The Antilabor Front." *Antioch Review* 3 (September, 1943): 328–40.

Berryman, Marsha Gaunt. "Houston in the Early Depression, 1929–1932." Master's thesis, University of Houston, 1965.

Best, Gary Dean. *Pride, Prejudice, and Politics: Roosevelt versus Recovery, 1933–1938.* New York: Praeger, 1991.

Biles, Roger. *A New Deal for the American People.* Dekalb: Northern Illinois University Press, 1991.

Blum, John Morton. *V Was for Victory: Politics and American Culture during World War II.* New York: Harcourt, Brace and Jovanovich, 1976.

Bodnar, John. *The Transplanted: A History of Immigrants in Urban America.* Bloomington: Indiana University Press, 1985.

Botson, Michael R., Jr. "Jim Crow Wearing Steel-Toed Shoes and Safety Glasses: Dual Unionism at the Hughes Tool Company, 1918–1942." *Houston Review* 16 (1994): 101–16.

———. "The Labor History of Houston's Hughes Tool Company, 1901–1964: From Autocracy and Jim Crow to Industrial Democracy and Civil Rights." Ph.D. diss., University of Houston, 1999.

———. "Organized Labor at the Hughes Tool Company, 1918–1942: From Welfare to the Steel Workers Organizing Committee." Master's thesis, University of Houston, 1994.

———. "No Gold Watch for Jim Crow's Retirement: The Abolition of Segregated Unionism at Houston's Hughes Tool Company." *Southwestern Historical Quarterly* 101 (April, 1998): 497–521.

Brewer, Thomas B. "State Anti-Labor Legislation in Texas—A Case Study." *Labor History* 11 (Winter, 1970): 58–76.

Brody, David. "The CIO after 50 Years: A Historical Reckoning." *Dissent* (Fall, 1985): 457–72.

———. "Hill Discounts Larger Context." *New Politics* 3 (Summer, 1987): 38–41.

———. *In Labor's Cause: Main Themes on the History of the American Worker.* New York: Oxford University Press, 1993.

———. "The Old Labor History and the New: In Search of an American Working Class." *Labor History* 20 (Winter): 111–26.

———. "Reconciling the Old Labor History and the New Labor History." *Pacific Historical Review* 32 (February, 1993): 1–18.

———. "The Rise and Decline of Welfare Capitalism." In *Change and Continuity in Twentieth-Century America: The 1920s,* ed. John Braeman, Robert H. Bremner, and David Brody, 147–78. Columbus: Ohio State University Press, 1968.

———. *Steelworkers in America: The Nonunion Era.* New York: Harper and Row, 1962.

Brown, Peter Harry, and Pat H. Broeske. *Howard Hughes: The Untold Story.* New York: Dutton, 1996.

Burran, James Albert, III. "Racial Violence in the South during World War II." Ph.D. diss., University of Tennessee, Knoxville, 1977.

Calvert, Robert A. "The Civil Rights Movement in Texas." In *The Texas Heritage,* ed. Ben Proctor and Archie P. McDonald. 4th ed. Wheeling, Ill.: Harlan Davidson, 2003.

Calvert, Robert A., Arnoldo De León, and Gregg Cantrell. *The History of Texas.* 3rd ed. Wheeling, Ill.: Harlan Davidson, 2002.

Campbell, Randolph A. *Gone to Texas: A History of the Lone Star State.* New York: Oxford University Press, 2003.

Carleton, Don E. *Red Scare: Right-Wing Hysteria, Fifties Fanaticism, and Their Legacy in Texas.* Austin: Texas Monthly Press, 1985.

Carleton, Don E., and Thomas Kreneck. *Houston: Back Where We Started.* Houston: DeMenil, 1979.

Carroll, B. H. *Standard History of Houston, Texas: From a Study of Original Sources.* Knoxville: H. W. Crew, 1912.

Carter, Robert L,. and Maria L. Marcus. "Trade Union Practices and the Law." In *The Negro and American Labor Movement,* ed. Julius Jacobson, 380–400. Garden City, N.Y.: Anchor Books, 1968.

Casebeer, Kenneth M. "Clashing Views of the Wagner Act: Leon Keyserling's Files." *Labor's Heritage* 2 (April, 1990): 44–55.

Cayton, Horace R., and George S. Mitchell. *Black Workers and the New Unions.* Chapel Hill: University of North Carolina Press, 1939.

Clark, James A., and Michel T. Halbouty. *Spindletop.* New York: Random House, 1952.

Cohen, Lizbeth. "The Legacy of Brody's *Steelworkers.*" *Labor History* 34 (Fall, 1993): 469–73.

Cohnay, Harry P., and James Neary. "Unaffiliated Local and Single-Employer Unions in the United States, 1961." *Monthly Labor Review* 85 (September, 1962): 975–82.

Cole, Thomas R. *No Color Is My Kind: The Life of Eldrewey Stearns and the Integration of Houston.* Austin: University of Texas Press, 1997.

Commons, John R., et al. *History of Labour in the United States, 1896–1932.* Vols. 3, 4. New York: Augustus M. Kelley, 1966.

Connor, Valerie Jean. *The National War Labor Board: Stability, Social Justice, and the Voluntary State in World War I.* Chapel Hill: University of North Carolina Press, 1983.

Dawley, Alan, and Joe William Trotter Jr. "Race and Class." *Labor History* 35 (Fall, 1994): 486–94.

De León, Arnoldo. *Ethnicity in the Sunbelt: A History of Mexican Americans in Houston.* Houston: University of Houston, Mexican-American Studies Program, 1989.

———. *They Called Them Greasers: Anglo Attitudes toward Mexicans in Texas, 1821–1900.* Austin: University of Texas Press, 1983.

Derber, Milton, and Edwin Young. *Labor and the New Deal.* Madison: University of Wisconsin Press, 1957.

Directory of City of Houston, 1910–1911. Houston: Morrison and Fourmey, 1911.

Directory of City of Houston, 1913. Houston: Morrison and Fourmey, 1913.

Draper, Alan. *Conflict of Interests: Organized Labor and the Civil Rights Movement in the South, 1954–1968.* Ithaca: ILR Press, 1994.

Dubovsky, Melvyn. *Industrialism and the American Worker, 1865–1920.* 3rd ed. Arlington Heights: Harlan Davidson, 1996.

———. "Lost in a Fog: Labor Historians' Unrequited Search for a Synthesis." *Labor History* 32 (Spring, 1991): 295–300.

———. *The State and Labor in Modern America.* Chapel Hill: University of North Carolina Press, 1994.

Dubovsky, Melvyn, and Warren Van Tyne, eds. *Labor Leaders in America.* Urbana: University of Illinois Press, 1987.

Dulles, Foster Rhea, and Melvyn Dubovsky. *Labor in America: A History.* 5th ed. Arlington Heights: Harlan Davidson, 1993.

Ernst, Daniel. "The Yellow Dog Contract and Liberal Reform, 1917–1932." *Labor History* 30 (Spring, 1989): 251–74.

Feagin, Joseph R. *Free Enterprise City: Houston in Political and Economic Perspective.* New Brunswick: Rutgers University Press, 1988.

Fink, Leon. "Intellectuals versus Workers: Academic Requirements and the Creation of Labor History." *Journal of American History* 96 (April, 1991): 395–421.

———. "A Memoir of Selig Perlman and His Life at the University of Wisconsin: Based on an Interview of Mark Perlman." *Labor History* 32 (Fall, 1991): 503–25.

———. *Workingmen's Democracy: The Knights of Labor and American Politics.* Urbana: University of Illinois Press, 1985.

Fisher, Robert. "Organizing in the Private City: The Case of Houston, Texas." In *Black Dixie: Afro-Texan History and Culture in Houston,* ed. Howard Beeth and Cary Wintz, 253–77. College Station: Texas A&M University Press, 1992.

———. "Where Seldom Is Heard a Discouraging Word: The Political Economy of Houston, Texas." *Amerikastudien* 33 (1988): 73–91.

Foner, Philip S., and Ronald L. Lewis, eds. *The Black Worker during the Era of the American Federation of Labor and the Railroad Brotherhoods*. Vol. 4 of *The Black Worker: A Documentary History from Colonial Times to Present*. Philadelphia: Temple University Press, 1979.

———. *The Black Worker from 1900–1919*. Vol. 5 of *The Black Worker: A Documentary History from Colonial Times to Present*. Philadelphia: Temple University Press, 1980.

———. *The Black Worker from the Founding of the CIO to the AFL-CIO Merger, 1936–1955*. Vol. 7 of *The Black Worker: A Documentary History from Colonial Times to Present*. Philadelphia: Temple University Press, 1983.

Galenson, Walter. *The CIO Challenge to the AFL: A History of the American Labor Movement, 1935–1941*. Cambridge: Harvard University Press, 1960.

Gitelman, H. M. "Welfare Capitalism Reconsidered." *Labor History* 33 (Winter, 1992): 1–31.

Goldfield, Michael. "Race and the CIO: The Possibilities for Racial Egalitarianism during the 1930s and 1940s." *International Labor and Working-Class History* 44 (Fall, 1993): 1–32.

Greater Houston (Texas) City Directory. Vol. 45. Houston: Morrison and Fourmey, 1941.

Green, George Norris. "Discord in Dallas: Auto Workers, City Fathers, and the Ford Motor Company, 1937–1941." *Labor's Heritage* 4 (July, 1989): 20–33.

———. *The Establishment in Texas Politics: The Primitive Years, 1938–1957*. Westport, Conn.: Greenwood Press, 1979.

———. "ILGWU in Texas." *Journal of Mexican American History* 1 (Spring, 1971): 144–63.

———. "Texas State Industrial Union Council." In vol. 6 of *The Handbook of Texas*. Austin: Texas State Historical Association, 1996. Accessible online at http://www.tsha.utexas.edu/handbook/online/articles/view/TT/octbg.html.

Green, James. "Democracy Comes to Little Siberia: Steel Workers Organize in Aliquippa, Pennsylvania, 1933–1937." *Labor's Heritage* 5 (Summer, 1993): 4–27.

Greer, William Lee. "The Texas Gulf Coast Oil Strike of 1917." Master's thesis, University of Houston, 1964.

Griffith, Barbara S. *The Crisis of American Labor: Operation Dixie and the Defeat of the CIO*. Philadelphia: Temple University Press, 1988.

Hack, Richard. *Hughes: The Private Diaries, Memos, and Letters*. Beverly Hills: New Millennium Press, 2001.

Halpern, Rick. "Interracial Unionism in the Southwest: Fort Worth's Packinghouse Workers, 1937–1954." In *Organized Labor in the Twentieth-Century South*, ed. Robert Zieger, 158–82. Knoxville: University of Tennessee Press, 1991.

Hamilton, Charles R. "Images of an Industry: The Hughes Tool Company Collection." *Houston Review* 15 (1993): 45–54.

Harris, William H. *The Harder We Run: Black Workers since the Civil War.* New York: Oxford University Press, 1982.

Haynes, Robert V. "Black Houstonians and the White Democratic Primary, 1920–45." In *Black Dixie: Afro-Texan History and Culture in Houston,* ed. Howard Beeth and Cary Wintz, 192–210. College Station: Texas A&M University Press, 1992.

———. "The Houston Mutiny and Riot of 1917." *Southwestern Historical Quarterly* 76 (April, 1973): 418–39.

———. *A Night of Violence: The Houston Riot of 1917.* Baton Rouge: Louisiana State University Press, 1976.

Heppenheimer, T. A. "Howard Hughes the Inventor." *American Heritage of Invention and Technology* 14 (Winter, 1999): 36–46.

Hill, Herbert. "The AFL-CIO and the Black Workers: Twenty-Five Years after the Merger." *Journal of Intergroup Relations* 10 (Spring, 1982): 1–80.

———. *Black Labor and the American Legal System: Race, Work, and the Law.* Madison: University of Wisconsin Press, 1985.

———. "Lichtenstein's Fictions: Meany, Reuther, and the 1964 Civil Rights Act." *New Politics* 7 (Summer, 1998): 82–107.

———. "Lichtenstein's Fictions Revisited: Race and the New Labor History." *New Politics* 8 (Winter, 1999): 148–63.

———. "Myth-Making as Labor History: Herbert Gutman and the United Mine Workers of America." *International Journal of Politics, Culture, and Society* 2 (Winter, 1988): 132–95.

———. "The Problem of Race in American Labor History." *Reviews in American History* 24 (June, 1996): 189–208.

———. "Race and Ethnicity in Organized Labor: The Historical Sources of Resistance to Affirmative Action." *Journal of Intergroup Relations.* 4 (Winter, 1984): 5–50.

———. "Race and the Steelworkers Union: White Privilege and Black Struggles, Review Essay of Judith Stein's *Running Steel, Running America.*" *New Politics* 9 (Winter 2000)..

———. "Racial Practices of Organized Labor." In *The Negro and the American Labor Movement,* ed. Julius Jacobson, 286–357. New York: Anchor Books, 1968.

———. "Racism within Organized Labor: A Report of Five Years of the AFL-CIO, 1955–1960." *Journal of Negro Education* 30 (Spring, 1961): 109–18.

Hill, Patricia Evridge. *Dallas: The Making of a Modern City.* Austin: University of Texas Press, 1996.

Hogan, William T. *Economic History of the Iron and Steel Industry in the United States.* 5 Vols. Lexington: D. C. Heath, 1971.

Holt, Wythe. "The New American Labor Law History." *Labor History* 30 (Spring, 1989): 275–93.

Honey, Michael K. "Industrial Unionism and Racial Justice in Memphis." In

Organized Labor in the Twentieth-Century South, ed. Robert H. Zieger, 135–57. Knoxville: University of Tennessee Press, 1991.

———. *Southern Labor and Black Civil Rights: Organizing Memphis Workers.* Urbana: University of Illinois Press, 1993.

Huberman, Leo. *The Labor Spy Racket.* New York: Modern Age Books, 1937.

Jacobson, Julius, ed. *The Negro and the American Labor Movement.* Garden City, N.Y.: Anchor Books, 1968.

Jacoby, Sanford M. *Employing Bureaucracy: Managers, Unions, and the Transformation of Work in American Industry, 1900–1945.* New York: Columbia University Press, 1985.

———. *Modern Manors: Welfare Capitalism since the New Deal.* Princeton: Princeton University Press, 1997.

Jensen, F. Kenneth. "The Houston Sit-In Movement of 1960–61." In *Black Dixie: Afro-Texan History and Culture in Houston,* ed. Howard Beeth and Cary Wintz, 211–222. College Station: Texas A&M University Press, 1992.

Keats, John. *Howard Hughes.* New York: Random House, 1966.

Kelley, Robin D. G. *Hammer and Hoe: Alabama Communists during the Great Depression.* Chapel Hill: University of North Carolina Press, 1990.

———. "We Are Not What We Seem: Rethinking Black Working-Class Opposition in the Jim Crow South." *Journal of American History* 80 (June, 1993): 75–112.

Kelly, Brian. *Race, Class, and Power in the Alabama Coalfields, 1908–1921.* Chapel Hill: University of North Carolina Press, 2001.

Kennedy, Stetson. *Southern Exposure.* New York: Doubleday, 1946.

Kessler-Harris, Alice. "The Limits of Union-Centered History: Responses to Kimeldorf." *Labor History* 32 (Winter, 1991): 107–10.

Kimeldorf, Howard. "Bringing Unions Back In (Or Why We Need a New Old Labor History)." *Labor History* 32 (Winter, 1991): 91–103.

King, John O. *Joseph Stephen Cullinan: A Study in the Texas Petroleum Industry, 1897–1937.* Nashville: Vanderbilt University Press for the Texas Gulf Coast Historical Association, 1970.

Klarman, Michael J. "How *Brown* Changed Race Relations: The Backlash Thesis." *Journal of American History* 81 (June, 1994): 81–118.

Korstad, Robert, and Nelson Lichtenstein. "Opportunities Found and Lost: Labor Radicals and the Early Civil Rights Movement." *Journal of American History* 75 (December, 1988).

Krenek, Harry L. "Jake Wolters: An Iron Fist in a Velvet Glove." *Houston Review* 7 (1985): 101–10.

Larson, Henrietta, and Kenneth Wiggins Porter. *History of the Humble Oil and Refining Company.* New York: Harper and Brothers, 1959.

Lawson, Steve F. "Freedom Then, Freedom Now: The Historiography of the Civil Rights Movement." *American Historical Review* 96 (July, 1991): 456–71.

Letwin, Daniel. *The Challenge of Interracial Unionism: Alabama Coal Miners, 1878–1921.* Chapel Hill: University of North Carolina Press, 1998.

Leuchtenberg, William E. *Franklin D. Roosevelt and the New Deal, 1932–1940.* New York: Harper and Row, 1963.

———. *The Perils of Prosperity, 1914–1932.* Chicago; University of Chicago Press, 1958.

Lichtenstein, Nelson. *Labor's War at Home: The CIO in World War II.* Cambridge: Cambridge University Press, 1982.

———. *The Most Dangerous Man in Detroit: Walter Reuther and the Fate of American Labor.* New York: Basic Books, 1995.

———. "Walter Reuther in Black and White: A Rejoinder to Herbert Hill." *New Politics* 3 (Winter, 1999): 133–47.

Lichtenstein, Nelson, and Howell John Harris, eds. *Industrial Democracy in America: The Ambiguous Promise.* Cambridge: Cambridge University Press, 1993.

Lovell, E. Thomas. "Houston's Reaction to the New Deal, 1932–1936." Master's thesis, University of Houston, 1964.

Maroney, James C. "Labor's Struggle for Acceptance: The Houston Worker in a Changing Society, 1900–1929." *Houston Review* 6 (1984): 5–24

———. "Organized Labor in Texas, 1900–1929." Ph.D. diss., University of Houston, 1975.

Marshall, F. Ray. *Labor in the South.* Cambridge: Harvard University Press, 1967.

———. *The Negro and Organized Labor.* New York: John Wiley and Sons, 1965.

———. "Some Reflections on Labor History." *Southwestern Historical Quarterly* 75 (October, 1971): 137–57.

———. "Union Racial Problems in the South." *Industrial Relations: A Journal of Economy and Society* 1 (May, 1962): 117–28.

———. "Unions and the Negro Community." *Industrial and Labor Relations Review* 17 (January, 1964): 179–202.

Marshall, F. Ray, and Vernon M. Briggs Jr. *The Negro and Apprenticeship.* Baltimore: Johns Hopkins University Press.

Maverick, Maury. *A Maverick America.* New York: J. J. Little and Ives, 1937.

Maxwell, Robert. "Texas Economic Growth, 1890 to World War II: From Frontier to Industrial Giant." In *Readings in Texas History*, ed. Cary Wintz, 183–224. Boston: American Press, 1983.

McCartin, Joseph. "An American Feeling: Workers, Managers, and the Struggle over Industrial Democracy in the World War I Era." In *Industrial Democracy in America: The Ambiguous Promise,* ed. Nelson Lichtenstein and Howell John Thomas, 67–86. Cambridge: Cambridge University Press, 1993.

———. *Labor's Great War: The Struggle for Industrial Democracy and the Ori-*

gins of Modern American Labor Relations. Chapel Hill: University of North Carolina Press, 1997.

McComb, David G. *Houston: The Bayou City.* Austin: University of Texas Press, 1969.

McDonald, David. *Union Man.* New York: Dutton, 1969.

McElvaine, Robert S. *Down and Out in the Great Depression: Letters from the Forgotten Man.* Chapel Hill: University of North Carolina Press, 1983.

Metzgar, Jack. *Striking Steel: Solidarity Remembered.* Philadelphia: Temple University Press, 2000.

Montgomery, David. *Beyond Equality: Labor and the Radical Republicans, 1862–1872.* Urbana: University of Illinois Press, 1981.

———. "The Limits of Union-Centered Labor History: Responses to Kimeldorf." *Labor History* 32 (Winter, 1991): 110–16.

Montgomery, William Edward. "The Depression in Houston during the Hoover Era, 1929–1932." Master's thesis, University of Texas at Austin, 1966.

Morgan, George T., Jr. "The Gospel of Wealth Goes South: John Henry Kirby and Labor's Struggle for Self-Determination, 1901–1916." *Southwestern Historical Quarterly* 75 (October, 1971): 186–97.

———. "No Compromise—No Recognition: John Henry Kirby, the Southern Lumber Operators' Association, and Unionism in the Piney Woods." *Labor History* 10 (Spring, 1969): 193–204.

Mullennix, Grady Lee. "A History of the Texas State Federation of Labor." Ph.D. diss., University of Texas at Austin, 1955.

National Industrial Conference Board. *Collective Bargaining through Employee Representation.* New York: National Industrial Conference Board, 1933.

Nelson, Bruce. "CIO Meant One Thing for the Whites and Another Thing for Us: Steelworkers and Civil Rights, 1936–1974." In *Southern Labor in Transition, 1940–1995,* ed. Robert Zieger, 113–45.

———. "Class, Race, and Democracy in the CIO: The 'New' Labor History Meets the 'Wages of Whiteness.'" *International Review of Social History* 41 (December, 1996): 365–80.

———. *Divided We Stand: American Workers and the Struggle for Black Equality.* Princeton: University of Princeton Press, 2001.

———. "Organized Labor and the Struggle for Black Equality during World War II." *Journal of American History* 80 (December, 1993): 952–88.

Nelson, Daniel. "The Company Union Movement, 1900–1937: A Reexamination." *Business History Review* 56 (Autumn 1982): 335–57.

———. *Managers and Workers: Origins of the New Factory System in the United States, 1880-1920.* Madison: University of Wisconsin Press, 1975.

Nicholson, Patrick. *Mr. Jim: The Biography of James Smither Abercrombie.* Houston: Gulf Publishing, 1983.

Norrell, Robert J. "Caste in Steel: Jim Crow Careers in Birmingham, Alabama." *Journal of American History* 73 (December, 1986): 669–94.

Northrup, Herbert R. *Organized Labor and the Negro*. New York: Harper and Brothers, 1944.

Norwood, Stephen H. *Strikebreaking and Intimidation: Mercenaries and Masculinity in Twentieth-Century America*. Chapel Hill: University of North Carolina Press, 2002.

Obadele-Starks, Ernest. "Black Labor, the Black Middle Class, and Organized Protest along the Upper Texas Gulf Coast, 1883–1945." *Southwestern Historical Quarterly* 103 (July, 1999): 52–65.

———. "Black Texans and Theater Craft Unionism: The Struggle for Racial Equality." *Southwestern Historical Quarterly,* 106 (April 2003).

———. *Black Unionism in the Industrial South*. College Station: Texas A&M University Press, 2000.

O'Connor, Harvey. *History of Oil Workers International Union (CIO)*. Denver: Oil Workers International Union (CIO), 1950.

Olson, Bruce A. "The Houston Light Guards: A Study of Houston's Post-Reconstruction Militia and Its Membership, 1873–1903." *Houston Review* 7 (1985): 111–42.

Olson, Bruce A., and Jack L. Howard. "Armed Elites Confront Labor: The Texas Militia and the Houston Strikes of 1880 and 1898." *Labor's Heritage* 7 (Summer, 1995): 52–61.

Page, H. Weber. *Houston and Harris County Facts*. Houston: Facts Publishing, 1939.

Pitre, Merline. *In Struggle against Jim Crow: Lulu White and the NAACP, 1900–1957*. College Station: Texas A&M University Press, 1999.

Platt, Harold L. "Houston at the Crossroads: The Emergence of the Urban Center of the Southwest." *Journal of the West* (Spring, 1979): 51–61.

Polakoff, Murray E. "The Development of the Texas State Congress of Industrial Organizations Council." Ph.D. diss., Columbia University, 1955.

Pratt, Joseph A. *The Growth of a Refining Region*. Greenwich, Conn.: JAI Press, 1980.

———. "The Oil Workers International Unions' Organization of the Upper Texas Gulf Coast, 1935–1945." Senior thesis, Rice University, 1970.

President's Committee on Civil Rights. *To Secure These Rights*. New York: Simon and Schuster, 1947.

Reed, Merl E. *Seedtime for the Modern Civil Rights Movement: The President's Committee on Fair Employment Practice, 1941–1946*. Baton Rouge: Louisiana State University Press, 1991.

Rees, Jonathan. "Giving with One Hand and Taking Away with the Other: The Failure of Welfare Capitalism at United States Steel." *Labor's Heritage* 9 (Fall, 1997): 20–31.

Reese, James V. "The Evolution of an Early Texas Union: The Screwmen's Benevolent Association of Galveston, 1866–1891." *Southwestern Historical Quarterly* 75 (October, 1971): 158–57.

———. "The Early History of Labor Organizations in Texas, 1838–1876." *Southwestern Historical Quarterly* 72 (July, 1968): 1–20.

———. "The Worker in Texas, 1821–1876." Ph.D. diss., University of Texas at Austin, 1964.

Rhinehart, Marilyn. "A Lesson in Unity: The Houston Municipal Workers Strike of 1946." *Houston Review* 4 (Fall, 1982): 137–53.

Rose, James D. *Duquesne and the Rise of Steel Unionism.* Urbana: University of Illinois Press, 2001.

Rosenthal, Rob. "Everything Moved but the Tide: The Seattle General Strike of 1919." *Labor's Heritage* 4 (Fall, 1992): 34–51.

Rundell, Walter, Jr. *Early Texas Oil: A Photographic History, 1866–1936.* College Station: Texas A&M University Press, 1977.

Schacht, John. "Labor History in Academy: A Layman's Guide to a Century of Scholarship." *Labor's Heritage* 5 (Winter, 1994): 4–21.

Schlesinger, Arthur M. *The Coming of the New Deal.* Boston: Houghton Mifflin, 1958.

Seidman, Joel. *American Labor from Defense to Reconversion.* Chicago: University of Chicago Press, 1953.

———. *The Yellow Dog Contract.* Baltimore: Johns Hopkins University Press, 1932.

Shabazz, Amilcar. *Advancing Democracy: African Americans and the Struggle for Access and Equity in Higher Education in Texas.* Chapel Hill: University of North Carolina Press, 2003.

Shostak, Arthur B. *America's Forgotten Labor Organization: A Survey of the Role of the Single-Firm Independent Union in American Industry.* Westport, Conn.: Greenwood Press, 1962.

Sitkoff, Harvard. *The Depression Decade.* Vol. 1 of *A New Deal for Blacks: The Emergence of Civil Rights as a National Issue.* New York: Oxford University Press, 1978.

Slichter, Sumner H. *Union Policies and Industrial Management.* Washington, D.C.: Brookings Institution, 1941.

Smith, C. Calvin. "The Houston Race Riot of 1917 Revisited." *Houston Review* 13 (1991): 85–102.

SoRelle, James M. "An De Po Cullud Man Is in the Wus Fix uv Awl: Black Occupational Status in Houston, Texas, 1920–1940." *Houston Review* (Spring, 1979): 15–26.

———. "The Darker Side of Heaven: The Black Community in Houston, Texas, 1917–1945." Ph.D. diss., Kent State University, 1980.

Sparks, Randy. "Heavenly Houston or Hellish Houston? Black Unemployment and Relief Efforts, 1929–1936." *Southern Studies* 25 (Winter, 1986): 335–66.

Steel Workers Organizing Committee. *First Wage and Policy Convention of the Steel Workers Organizing Committee: Pittsburgh Pennsylvania, December 14, 15, and 16, 1937.* Indianapolis: Allied Printing, 1937.

Stein, Judith. "Responses: The Ins and Outs of the CIO." *International Labor and Working-Class History* 44 (Fall, 1993): 53–63.

———. *Running Steel, Running America: Race, Economic Policy, and the Decline of Liberalism.* Chapel Hill: University of North Carolina Press, 1998.

———. "Southern Workers in National Unions: Birmingham Steelworkers, 1936–1951." In *Organized Labor in the Twentieth-Century South,* ed. Robert H. Zieger, 183–222. Knoxville: University of Tennessee Press, 1991.

Stricker, Frank. "Affluence for Whom? Another Look at Prosperity and Working Classes in the 1920s." *Labor History* 24 (Winter, 1983): 5–33.

Sweeney, Vincent D. *The United Steelworkers of America: Twenty Years Later, 1936–1956.* Pittsburgh: United Steelworkers of America, 1956.

Taft, Philip. *Organizing Dixie: Alabama Workers in the Industrial Era.* Westport: Greenwood Press, 1981.

Taylor, Hobart T. "C. W. Rice, Labor Leader." Senior thesis, Prairie View State Normal and Industrial College, 1939.

Teel, Robert Eli. "Discrimination against Negro Workers in Texas." Master's thesis, University of Texas, 1947.

Texas State Federation of Labor. *Convention Proceedings* (1905).

Todes, Jay Littman. "Organized Employer Opposition to Unionism in Texas, 1900–1930." Master's thesis, University of Texas at Austin, 1949.

Trotter, Joe William, Jr. "African-American Workers: New Directions in U.S. Labor Historiography." *Labor History* 35 (Fall, 1994): 495–523.

———. *Coal, Class, and Color: Blacks in Southern West Virginia, 1915–1932.* Urbana: University of Illinois Press, 1990.

Truman, Harry S. *Memoir: Year of Decisions.* Garden City, N.Y.: Doubleday, 1955.

Wakestein, Allen M. "The Origins of the Open-Shop Movement, 1919–1920." *Journal of American History* 51 (December, 1964): 460–75.

Wheeler, Kenneth W. *To Wear a City's Crown: The Beginnings of Urban Growth in Texas, 1836–1865.* Cambridge: Harvard University Press, 1968.

Williamson, Harold F., Ralph L. Andreano, Arnold R. Daum, Gilbert C. Klose. *The American Petroleum Industry.* Vol 2, *The Age of Energy, 1899–1959.* Evanston: Northwestern University Press, 1963.

Wolfskill, George. *The Revolt of the Conservatives: A History of the American Liberty League, 1933–1940.* Westport, Conn.: Greenwood Press, 1962.

Writers' Program of the Works Progress Administration in the State of Texas. *Houston: A History and Guide.* Houston: 1942.

Yergin, Daniel. *The Prize: The Epic Quest for Oil, Money, and Power.* New York: Simon and Schuster, 1991.

Zamora, Emilio. "The Failed Promise of Wartime Opportunity for Mexicans in the Texas Oil Industry." *Southwestern Historical Quarterly* 95 (January, 1992): 323–50.

————. *The World of the Mexican American Worker in Texas*. College Station: Texas A&M University Press, 1993.

Zieger, Robert H. *American Workers, American Unions*. 2nd ed. Baltimore: Johns Hopkins University Press, 1994.

————. *The CIO, 1935–1955*. Chapel Hill: University of North Carolina Press, 1995.

————, ed. *Organized Labor in the Twentieth-Century South*. Knoxville: University of Tennessee Press, 1991.

————, ed. *Southern Labor in Transition, 1940–1995*. Knoxville: University of Tennessee Press, 1997.

Ziegler, Robert E. "The Limits of Power: The Amalgamated Association of Street Railway Employees in Houston, Texas, 1897–1905." *Labor History* 18 (Winter, 1977): 71–90.

————. "The Workingman in Houston, Texas, 1865–1914." Ph.D. diss., Texas Tech University, 1972.

Photos and tables are indicated with *italic* type.

National Labor Relations Board
  (*continued*)
  159–61, 191; Wagner Act empower-
  ment, 82–83
National Labor Union, 16–17
National Recovery Administration
  (NRA), 62, 66
National War Labor Board (NWLB):
  and army takeover, 139–42; limi-
  tations, 200–201*n*23; maintenance
  of membership dispute, 126–37,
  221–22*n*83; strikes, 50, 138–39;
  wage guidelines, 42–43
Neel, R. G., 176, 177
Neely, William, *168*
"The Negro and the United Mine
  Workers" (Gutman), 5–6
Nehi, 91
Nelson, Bruce, 6–7
Neuhasu, Ralph, 142–43, 146, 148
New Orleans Regional Labor Board,
  79
NIRA (National Industrial Recovery
  Act), 62–68, 71, 78–80
NLB (National Labor Board), 62–63,
  67–68, 72, 73–74, 78–79
NLRB. *See* National Labor Relations
  Board (NLRB)
NRA (National Recovery Adminis-
  tration), 62, 66
NWLB. *See* National War Labor
  Board (NWLB)

Obadele-Starks, Ernest, 9
O'Daniel, W. Lee, 91, 139–40
Office of Price Administration
  (OPA), 142–43, 148
oil industry, generally, 12–13, 60–61,
  66, 132–33, 163, 231–32*m*
OPA (Office of Price Administration), 142–43, 148
open shop policy, origins, 50–51

Page, Philip, 40, 114
Painter, Theophilus, 188
PCEEO (President's Committee of
  Equal Employment Opportunity),
  164–65
Petroleum Administration for War
  (PAW), 132–33
Pinkerton Detective Agency, 87
Plans for Progress, 164–65
Polk, Joe, 53
population statistics, 13, 15, 20, 24–
  25, 38
Potter, Clifford, 121, 173, 175, 179, 183
Prather, Ed, 199*m*1
Prescott, C., 85
President's Committee of Equal Em-
  ployment Opportunity (PCEEO),
  164–65
Pressman, Lee, 140
pricing regulation, 62, 142–43, 148
printers unions, 13, 14
production process, *39*, 57–58, *64*,
  65, *110*, *134*
Pruett, Jackson, 218*n*21

racial discrimination (generally):
  AFL practices, 63–64, 89, 213*n*32;
  and decertification ruling, 184–85,
  187, 190–91; education, 4, 181, 188–
  89; and government contract
  changes, 163–65, 166–67, 234*n*33;
  Houston's tradition, 14–16, 22; and
  integrated unions, 234–35*n*41; labor movement beginnings, 16–19,
  21–22; as strikebreaking tool, 24,
  29; voting, 188; Wagner Act, 83. *See
  also* company unions; Congress of
  Industrial Organization (CIO); Independent Metal Workers (IMW);
  job classification system
railroad/streetcar strikes, 24, 25–26,
  27–33, 50–51

ISBN 1-58544-438-3